SCHOOLBOOKS AND KRAGS

THE UNITED STATES ARMY IN THE PHILIPPINES, 1898-1902

John Morgan Gates

CONTRIBUTIONS IN MILITARY HISTORY
NUMBER 3

GREENWOOD PRESS INC.

Westport, Connecticut • London, England

Library of Congress Cataloging in Publication Data

Gates, John Morgan, 1937-
Schoolbooks and Krags.

(Contribution[s] in military history, no. 3)
Bibliography: p.
1. Philippine Islands—History—Insurrection,
1899-1901. 2. United States. Army—History.
I. Title. II. Series.
DS679.G38   959.9′031   77-140917
ISBN 0-8371-5818-4

Library of Congress Catalog Card Number: 77-140917

ISBN: 0-8371-5818-4

First published in 1973

Greenwood Press, Inc., Publishing Division
51 Riverside Avenue, Westport, Connecticut 06880

Manufactured in the United States of America

To Linda and Nancy

WITHDRAWN

CONTENTS

PREFACE

For most Americans, the typical image of the United States Army's efforts to pacify the Philippine Islands is undoubtedly one of brutally repressive measures and unspeakable atrocities. "Civilize 'em with a Krag," the line from an old army song quoted often in history textbooks, seemed to confirm that American soldiers had only one solution to the problems presented by Emilio Aguinaldo's Filipino revolutionaries: the brute force symbolized by the army's newly issued Krag-Jörgensen rifles. As is the case with most stereotypes, this one has its basis in fact; Americans did commit atrocities in the Philippines. But, as is also true of most stereotypes, the simplistic image that it provides often obscures the historical reality to which it applies and prevents the observer from seeing other more accurate or significant points.

This book did not begin as an attempt to rehabilitate the army from the Philippine stereotype, and I sincerely hope that it will be seen as something more than that. It was originally motivated by a long-standing interest in guerrilla and counterguerrilla warfare. The decision to embark upon a Ph.D. program forced me to reorient my general interest in why groups succeed or fail in revolutionary guerrilla wars to a more specific question. How had the United States Army, an alien intruder, small in number and confused as to its mission when it came to the Philippines in 1898, gained supremacy over the forces of indigenous revolutionaries, skilled in guerrilla warfare and operating in a favorable environment? The answer presented here leads one far from the stereotype of brutal repression into a seldom-told story of enlightened military government, understanding and reform-oriented army officers and an excellent example of well-conceived counterguerrilla operations stressing political, economic, and social, as well as traditional military activity.

The usual emphasis on brutality and atrocity has turned attention away from a host of benevolent and humane efforts undertaken by individual American soldiers and the military government between 1898 and 1902. To focus on incidents of severity in the Philippines obscures the important relationship between the work of the army and the civilian colonial government established by William Howard Taft and the Philippine Commission, a regime that is often praised by the same authors who readily condemn the military. Furthermore, the stereotype of American campaigning in the Philippines makes almost inexplicable the tremendous success of the pacification program and the willingness of numerous Filipinos, including many who had fought in the revolution, to work with the colonial government as the Filipino-American War drew to its close. This book, by concentrating on activities far removed from the already well-publicized and exaggerated atrocities of the Philippine campaign, seeks to provide a more comprehensive and accurate explanation of American success.

ACKNOWLEDGMENTS

I am indebted to many more people than I can mention by name for their help in bringing this work to completion. A few individuals, however, merit special acknowledgment, and I would particularly like to thank Professors Theodore Ropp and Irving B. Holley, Jr., of Duke University for their help and encouragement; David P. Sturtevant of Muskingum College for the many suggestions he made for the improvement of my manuscript; Ernest S. Osgood, a colleague, who also read the manuscript with care; and David Wehrle and Julie Wood, students at The College of Wooster who aided me in numerous small but essential tasks. A research trip to the Philippines was made possible in part by a Great Lakes Colleges Association Humanities Award using funds provided by the Carnegie Corporation. My travel and research have also been supported by grants from The College of Wooster Faculty Development Fund. I cannot end without a special thanks to my wife Priscilla, who gave me encouragement and substantial help in all stages of my work. I alone am responsible for any errors that may be present.

JOHN M. GATES
Wooster, Ohio

SCHOOLBOOKS
AND KRAGS

1

UNFORESEEN PROBLEMS OF VICTORY

The first sketchy accounts of the American naval victory at Manila Bay reached the United States on May 2, 1898. The reports of the May 1 action were fragmentary, having come from Madrid by way of London, but few Americans doubted that Commodore George Dewey's triumph over the Spanish squadron had been complete. America's war with Spain was only in its second week, but already it seemed that press predictions of a short and glorious war would come true.

President William McKinley conferred with his Secretaries of War and the Navy immediately after receipt of the first news from Manila. Although the country awaited further word of Dewey's accomplishment in high spirits, the President had cause for uneasiness. Sufficient time had not elapsed for an official report of Dewey's action to reach Washington, and the President did not know how much damage the American fleet had sustained or what capability it retained for carrying out other operations in the Philippines. The President feared that it might be lying helpless and vulnerable to Spanish reprisal. The situation facing the President called for swift action, and the President made his decision at once. Within a day after receiving the first rumors of Dewey's success, he issued orders for the immediate organization of a military force to be dispatched to the Philippines.[1]

Though the President had made the decision to send a

3

military force to the Philippines hurriedly, he was soon aware
of the numerous problems that came as a consequence of that
decision. Dewey's official report of the battle at Manila arrived
in Washington on May 7, and several messages that followed
shed even more light on the situation developing there. Dewey,
appointed Admiral immediately after the President's receipt of
his official report, stated that he could take the city of Manila
at any moment but that he would require a force of 5,000 men
to retain possession and "control [the] Philippine islands."[2]
He estimated the size of the Spanish force at 10,000 men, and
he mentioned the presence of approximately 30,000 Philippine revolutionaries whom he thought would act in cooperation
with the Americans. Messages received in the Department of
State from American consular representatives in the Far East
also mentioned the development of a revolt against Spain, and
at least one consul, E. Spencer Pratt, had had contact with
Emilio Aguinaldo, the revolution's leader. The Americans,
however, did not know the extent of the revolutionary movement, and President McKinley was too busy with the more important task at hand, the war with Spain, to give the Philippine
nationalists much thought.[3] In the future he would regret this
oversight.

The Chief Executive had not formulated a Philippine
policy at the time of his decision to dispatch a military force
there. From the beginning of the war with Spain, Cuba had
been the focal point in the American war plans, but the unex-
pected magnitude of Dewey's victory altered things greatly.
McKinley and the nation were faced with an opportunity for
imperialistic expansion that could not be ignored, but the President did not know what course to follow. He opened the way
for a wave of speculation and debate over his plans for the
islands when he chose to send an expeditionary force there. He
was content for the moment, however, to allow the problem of
an American Philippine policy to remain undecided.[4] This
question of policy would haunt him in the weeks to come.

The President's failure to develop a Philippine policy at an
early date and his refusal to consider seriously the problems
that might arise from the presence of a revolution in the islands
made the already difficult task of organizing an expeditionary

force even more complicated. The President gave command of the force to Major General Wesley Merritt, and Merritt spent the month of May collecting the necessary troops in San Francisco. Upon receipt of information from Admiral Dewey regarding the number of the Spanish and Filipino forces in the islands, the President authorized an increase in the size of the expedition from 5,000 to over 15,000. The change resulted from suggestions made by both General Merritt and Major General Nelson A. Miles, Commanding General of the Army. A controversy ensued between the two generals, however, over the composition of the force, and it was apparent that the army was not certain of its exact mission in the Philippines.[5]

General Merritt conferred with President McKinley on May 12, but the President did not make clear at that time what the precise goal of the Philippine force would be. The General did not know, for example, whether his task was to subdue and hold all of the Spanish territory in the Philippine archipelago or merely seize Manila, the capital. In his ignorance, he preferred to take a large view of his mission in the islands, and he no doubt had dreams of gaining fame and glory at the head of a victorious army composed almost entirely of regular troops. He even contemplated eventual hostilities with the Philippine revolutionaries when he wrote the President that "it seems more than probable that we will have the so-called insurgents to fight as well as the Spaniards." They would, he was sure, regard the presence of the Americans in the islands "with the intense hatred born of race and religion."[6] Merritt's superior, General Miles, thought that a force made up of volunteers would be sufficient, for he assumed that the President's goal in the islands was of a more limited nature. Miles thought that the expeditionary force was being sent not to conquer the islands, but to gain command quickly of the harbor of Manila.[7] The President did little to clarify this matter, and if any policy for the Philippines existed in his mind as of mid-May, 1898, he did not communicate it to either General Miles or General Merritt.

The President's options for a Philippine policy were too numerous for the leaders of the army to be expected to arrive at a concept of their mission by themselves. Assuming that they would be successful in their attempt to take Manila and garrison

Manila Bay, what was to be their next move? Did the President expect them to retain the city in their control or to occupy it in conjunction with the revolutionaries? Were they to mount other military operations in the Philippines, and, if so, were these to be confined to the main island of Luzon or to extend to the major port cities in the Visayan Islands to the south? Even had the President made clear the immediate task of the army in the Philippines, other questions remained in the minds of the men preparing to leave for Manila. What was their ultimate goal? What would they do when peace came? Were the islands to be returned to Spain in exchange for concessions in the Caribbean? Would the Filipino nationalists be recognized and given the islands under the protection of the United States? Or, would the decision be made in Washington to keep all or a part of the Philippines for a short time or for some indefinite period? In short, was the army going to the Philippines to conquer a colony, to seize a naval base, to fight for Cuban freedom, or to aid the Filipino revolutionaries? No one seemed to have the answers to these questions, but the questions were, nevertheless, of great importance. Sooner or later they would have to be answered, and the army would be faced with the continuing problem of defining its mission until they were.

The letter of instructions that President McKinley sent to General Merritt did little to dispel the confusion that had developed. The mission of the expeditionary force was vaguely outlined as that of "completing the reduction of the Spanish power" in the islands and maintaining order and security there while they were in the possession of the United States.[8] The President made no mention of whether such possession, if achieved, would be permanent or temporary. Of particular importance, there was no mention of the revolutionaries and no statement on the type of relationship, if any, the army was expected to have with them. The President said nothing concerning the future disposition of the Philippines should they fall to the Americans. He refused to commit himself on that question at such an early date, and, in terms of the difficult diplomatic problems that would face the army in its dealings with Aguinaldo and his followers, the instructions were completely useless. The American commanders on the scene would have to deal with those problems as they arose.

The President's instructions, silent on so many important issues, did provide excellent guidelines for the conduct of the provisional military government that he envisioned would soon be functioning in the Philippines. McKinley's directive impressed upon General Merritt the beneficent purpose of the United States in the islands, and it provided him with a framework within which to conduct his dealings with whatever native inhabitants might fall under his control. The General was instructed to publish a proclamation immediately upon his arrival in the islands to the effect that the American troops did not come to make war upon the Philippine people but to protect them. Local customs, laws, and governmental routines were to be respected as far as possible, and the directive included instructions for the disposition of public property and revenues. Since the President did not indicate the length of time the military government might be expected to function, Merritt knew that it might be the first step in the formation of a permanent American colonial government.[9]

The first units of the American expeditionary force arrived in the Philippines on June 30, 1898. Despite the President's well-drawn orders for the formation of a provisional government, they were poorly prepared for the work ahead of them. They were over 7,000 miles from their homeland and some 10,000 miles from their nation's capital. Before them lay an archipelago of more than 7,000 islands inhabited by some 7 million people, many of them hostile. The population of the area was culturally diverse and included many different ethnic groups speaking a variety of languages and living in a state of civilization that ranged from the Hispanized residents of Manila to the primitive pagan tribes in the mountains of Luzon.

An immediate problem facing the army was that of the Filipino revolutionaries. In the months ahead, the army would be required to deal with Aguinaldo on a day-to-day basis, relying in whole or in part on the ability of the expedition's commander to prevent serious incidents. The conquest of Manila would prove an easy task, but the administration of the military government would require enormous energy and ingenuity on the part of the Americans. Continued indecision on the part of officials in Washington about future American policy would make the army's work more difficult. Within this maze of frustration and confusion, the problems created by Aguinaldo seemed to defy solution. It was the Filipino nationalists, rather than the Spaniards, who soon became the major American difficulty in the islands.

The revolution that eventually presented the American army with so many problems had its roots in a number of economic and social changes taking place in the Philippines in the century and a half that preceded it. During that time, the islands underwent a transition in which numerous local subsistence economies were brought into some semblance of integration through the development of export crops such as sugar, hemp, indigo, and tobacco.[10]

During most of the eighteenth century and before, three economies existed side by side in the Philippines: the native economy based on subsistence agriculture; the small Spanish bureaucratic, religious, and trading community centered in Manila; and a relatively small but extremely important Chinese community of merchants and artisans catering to the needs of the Spaniards. Because of their commercial activities, the Chinese stood as the link between the two economies of the Spaniard and the Filipino. In cultural affairs, members of the Spanish religious orders in the islands served a similar function. The friars were often the sole link between the Spanish bureaucracy in Manila and the Filipinos in the provinces.

Starting in the middle of the eighteenth century, the colony began an economic transformation. A few traders in Manila had succeeded in monopolizing the galleon trade, and many Spaniards sought other economic opportunities as a result. At the same time, in an attempt to increase the revenue derived from economic activities in the colony, Spanish administrators tried to stimulate the development of commercial agriculture, industry, and trade. Although the Chinese had monopolized many of these activities, Spaniards had long viewed the presence of the Chinese in large numbers as a danger. Attempts to restrict their activities or to expel them had proved futile in the past, but the Spanish authorities renewed their efforts in this direction with increased effectiveness in the mid-eighteenth century. The important series of economic and social changes that preceded the Philippine Revolution dates roughly from the relatively efficient expulsion of Chinese that took place in 1755.

Although between 5,000 and 10,000 Chinese remained in the Philippines after 1755, the expulsion of perhaps twice that number had opened numerous opportunities in trade and commerce for Spaniards, mestizos of mixed Chinese and Filipino ancestry, and Filipinos or indios, as they were called by their Spanish rulers. Since a large share of the Spanish community was already employed in the government or clerical bureaucracy, the major share of the new economic opportunities fell to the mestizos and indios. This was particularly true in the production and marketing of export crops where, in the initial period of crop development, the major share of the produce came from relatively small holdings worked by them. The profits from these activities as well as the new commercial opportunities resulting from the expulsion of the Chinese gave many mestizos and indios the capital required to acquire more land or to engage in further commercial activity. By making loans to poor indios to cover the expenses incurred in fiestas, marriages, baptisms, funerals, and litigation, mestizos and wealthy indios accumulated even greater amounts of capital and larger tracts of land. As might be expected, social change followed these economic developments.

Although mestizos made up only about 5 percent of the population in the Philippines, they soon became more important than their numerical strength warranted. Residing predominantly in Central Luzon, although they could be found in other regions in smaller numbers, mestizos achieved positions of power and wealth as wholesalers, retailers, artisans, and landholders. Significantly, while mestizos had little difficulty achieving success in the occupations traditionally associated with their Chinese ancestors, they usually adopted the language and culture of their Filipino mothers or, as was true in most cases, a blend of Filipino and Hispanic customs. Mestizos often set the trend in style and manner for those indios who were similarly successful in commerce and agriculture. The result was the development of a class of newly rich who were culturally distinct from the great mass of the non-Spanish population.

The mestizos and indios who acquired wealth during the century following the explusion of the Chinese in 1755 formed an elite that soon displaced the hereditary indio leaders who had ruled over the subsistence economy of the earlier period. Land ownership and money replaced birth and the number of unfree dependents one held as symbols of status. Among the new elite, traditional cultural norms and patterns gave way to what can only be described as a Filipino variety of Hispanic culture. As the sons of the newly rich acquired experience and education in Manila or, for a few, in Spain, the Hispanization of the elite proceeded even more rapidly. Through their travels to and from Manila, members of this wealthy class in the provinces kept abreast of the latest cultural developments in the urban center and transferred them back to the provincial towns. Culturally as well as economically, the pluralistic society in the colony was being destroyed.

During the last half of the nineteenth century, several developments worked to accelerate the changes that had begun in the previous century. The Spanish government opened several Philippine ports to world trade in the 1850s. Direct communication with Spain through the newly opened Suez Canal and a more liberal tariff came to the islands in the following decade. These developments, particularly the regular steamship service between Spain and Manila, increased the influx of European immigrants and ideas as well as goods. All of these changes coincided with the resurgence of liberalism in Spain, and the "generation of '68" in the mother country set an example for Filipino and Spanish students alike. The short, but liberal, rule of Governor-General Carlos Maria de la Torre (1869-1871) brought the new liberalism of Spain directly to the Philippines.

Sons of the mestizo and indio elite who attended the improving educational institutions of Manila and the universities of Europe formed a small intellectual and professional community in Manila which transcended ethnic barriers. This group was an important element in the development of national consciousness and liberal thought in the Philippines. These *ilustrados,* or enlightened ones, as they were called, became the major brokers of the developing Filipino-Hispanic culture and the self-appointed spokesmen for their less educated and less acculturated countrymen. They spurred the development of such outward manifestations of the new culture as newspapers, periodicals, theaters, and European dress. These things, like previous cultural changes, soon spread to the provinces.

The changes taking place in the nineteenth century significantly altered traditional patterns and created great stress for several elements in Philippine society. For example, the new class of educated Filipinos resented the discrimination practiced by the Spaniards in appointments to positions in the ecclesiastical, military, and civil bureaucracy. The *ilustrados* longed for equality both between themselves and the Spaniards in the Philippines and between the colony and the mother country. The nationalism that developed represented a positive rather than a negative response to European penetration into the Philippines, but the results were no less disturbing. The more the mestizo and indio elite became urbanized and Hispanized, the more their intellectual spokesmen demanded liberal reforms similar to those being instituted in Europe.

The nationalism and liberalism spreading among the *ilustrado* class provided a direct threat to the Spaniards in the colony who benefited from the discrimination that had been practiced, but the new developments were particularly threatening for members of the religious orders who had held sway over the colony for more than three centuries. Many friars had been in a position to dominate the political and economic life of the towns and villages outside of Manila. The orders also held considerable property, much of it valuable agricultural land, coveted by the emerging Filipino elite, and it was no coincidence that opposition to the friars was greatest in areas such as Cavite Province where a large share of the arable land was under religious control. Nationalistic and liberal *ilustrados* made no secret of the fact that they resented the power wielded by the friars, and they accused them of all manner of injustice, cruelty, and oppression. The friars reacted by working to quash the growing spirit of nationalism and liberalism evident in the Philippines.

A resurgence of Chinese influence in many areas of the Philippine economy in the last half of the nineteenth century

made the need for reform seem even more urgent in the eyes of
many Filipinos and added to the stress of social and economic
change. As the number of Spaniards and Hispanized Filipinos
grew, the threat of the alien Chinese community lessened. In
an attempt to stimulate the economic growth of the colony further, Spanish officials lessened restrictions on Chinese
economic activity and immigration. By the 1890s the Chinese
had not only regained their preeminent position as merchants
and artisans, but they had surpassed their previous level of success. These developments undoubtedly provided a source of insecurity and worry for many Filipinos, particularly those who
had been the beneficiaries of the restrictive policy. Furthermore, the importation of Chinese laborers came at a time
when the urban proletariat in Manila was increasing, thus
restricting the opportunities available to Filipino laborers. The
success of the Chinese in the export economy, primarily as
shippers and wholesalers, and their dominance in the retail
trade caused mestizos and wealthy indios to turn almost exclusively to landholding and the professions as the means of
maintaining their newly won status and wealth.

One can only guess at the effects that social and economic
change had on the Philippine peasantry. The Hispanization of
the elite probably made the gulf between the lower classes and
their leaders greater than it had ever been in the past.[11] The
accumulation of land by rich mestizos and indios at the expense
of their less fortunate neighbors certainly could have created a
feeling of insecurity and some degree of alienation among
tenants and the rural proletariat of the export economy. The
stress of the change from a subsistence, rice-growing economy
to one based on the cultivation of crops for export must have
been tremendous. All of these strains were compounded by
population growth in the last half of the century.

The revolution that started in 1896 represented the reaction of the Hispanized Filipino elite and their more urbanized
or Hispanized countrymen to the changes taking place. Their
initial protest against Spanish rule was relatively conservative,
begun in the 1870s by emigré *ilustrados* in Spain and other
areas outside of the Philippines. These early propagandists
deplored conditions in their homeland and demanded reforms

in the Spanish colonial system. In particular, they agitated for limitations on the power of the Governor-General, an end to the deportation of Filipinos for political dissent, an extension of civil government into areas under military control, the recognition in the islands of the civil liberties guaranteed by the Spanish constitution, improved educational facilities for Filipinos, competitive civil service appointments, and the reform of the local police organization, the Guardia Civil. Their most important demand was for either the expulsion of the friars representing religious orders in the Philippines or, at the very least, the secularization of the parishes and the end of the friars' domination of the political and economic life of the towns.[12]

The center of reform agitation shifted from Filipino propagandists abroad to activists in the islands when, by 1892, some Filipinos became convinced that the Spanish government was not willing to undertake reform on the scale that they desired. The dissidents added independence as a goal and founded a secret society, the Katipunan, to prepare for eventual rebellion. The Filipino masses provided the base of support for the Katipunan, whereas the propaganda movement had been supported primarily by the educated native elite. When Spaniards in Manila discovered that a revolutionary plot was well advanced in August, 1896, they took repressive measures immediately.[13]

The Philippine Revolt began prematurely when members of the Katipunan sought to prevent the total destruction of their movement by the Spanish police. The Katipunan was most active among the Tagalog-speaking inhabitants of central Luzon, and the center of the rebellion was in Cavite Province, south of Manila. Emilio Aguinaldo soon rose to leadership in the Cavite Katipunan, and he was finally recognized as the head of the revolution. When a Spanish offensive nullified initial Filipino success in Cavite, a year of guerrilla warfare followed. By August, 1897, the Spaniards succeeded in surrounding a large group of revolutionaries in the mountains of central Luzon. A bloody and possibly inconclusive campaign was avoided when Pedro A. Paterno, a neutral Filipino, convinced both the Spaniards and the revolutionaries to seek a solution through negotiation. As a result, both parties signed three documents in December that made up the Pact of Biac-na-Bató. Under the terms of the agreement, Aguinaldo and twenty-seven of his associates went into voluntary exile in Hong Kong in exchange for a monetary payment to be made in three installments. They were to receive 400,000 pesos immediately, another 200,000 pesos after the revolutionaries had surrendered at least 700 firearms, and a final 200,000 pesos after the Te Deum was sung to signify the end of the insurrection. The Spanish Governor-General promised to issue a general amnesty and to use an additional sum of 900,000 pesos to indemnify those Filipinos who had suffered as a consequence of the revolt. Although Aguinaldo demanded and expected reforms, they were not part of the written agreement.[14]

Spaniards in the Philippines hailed the Pact of Biac-na-Bató as the end of the revolution; but, although the islands were relatively quiet in the next few months, the idea of independence and the spirit of revolt were not dead. Aguinaldo and the other insurgents in Hong Kong guarded the 400,000 pesos they had received from the Spaniards and planned to use the money to provoke rebellion at some future date.[15] The first payment of 200,000 pesos never reached them in Hong Kong, for it was divided among revolutionaries remaining in the Philippines. The last payment was never made. The 900,000 pesos to be used to indemnify those who had suffered in the islands was never distributed, and those Filipinos who expected that reforms would accompany the end of the hostilities were disappointed. When the Spanish regime continued its adminstration relatively unchanged, a noticeable number of minor disturbances and police raids occurred.

The revolutionary activity that began slowly in March 1898 differed in some important aspects from that of 1896. For the first time in the Philippine Revolt, uprisings were not confined to Luzon, but took place in the Visayan Islands to the south as well. The revolt was losing its localized character. Many educated Filipinos who had previously refused to support the Katipunan were becoming more favorably disposed toward the idea of independence.[16] The revolutionaries seemed to be meeting with greater success than they had before, and the Spaniards seemed powerless to prevent the wave of uprisings that increased during March and April. Although the tension preceding the outbreak of war between Spain and the United States seemed to have paralyzed the Spaniards in the Philippines, it had just the opposite effect on the Filipino revolutionaries. War that might bring the downfall of Spanish rule seemed their salvation, and they were encouraged by the possibility that it was imminent.[17]

The heightened tensions and aspirations in the islands resulting from the Spanish-American War had resuscitated the revolt. On April 24, Aguinaldo met with E. Spencer Pratt, the American consular representative in Singapore. That same day, Pratt cabled Dewey at Hong Kong that the rebel chief was willing to meet the Commodore and arrange for cooperation between the Americans and the revolutionary forces mustering themselves in the Philippines. Dewey, not knowing what awaited him in the islands, replied: "Tell Aguinaldo come soon as possible." But the Commodore did not wait for Aguinaldo's arrival in Hong Kong before departing for Manila. After his naval victory and successful seizure of the Spanish navy base at Cavite, Dewey found that the revolution in the islands was not sufficiently developed to be advantageous to the Americans in their war against Spain. He decided that Aguinaldo's presence might be useful and gave orders for the transportation of Aguinaldo and some of his exiled staff to the islands. The Filipinos arrived in Cavite on May 19.[18]

Upon his arrival in the Philippines, Aguinaldo organized a revolutionary army, set up a government, and began to extend his control over the region adjacent to Manila. In haste the Spanish authorities had raised local militia regiments to meet the threat posed by the Americans. Many of the militiamen had participated in the revolutionary committees existing in 1896, and when Aguinaldo issued his call to arms from Cavite most of the local units, approximately 10,000 men, deserted to the revolutionaries. By June 15, all but one of the militia commanders had joined the revolution, and by the end of the month the Spanish forces around Manila had been forced to withdraw into the walled city. In other parts of Luzon their situation was even worse.[19]

Rebels living in the hills, remnants of bands organized in

1896, descended into the valleys, and Spanish units all over Luzon were surprised and overwhelmed. By the end of June, central Luzon was in Filipino hands, and uprisings had begun on many of the islands to the south. The stories of what befell the various Spanish units in the islands were similar. Cut off from communication with Manila, they were left without supplies or hope of reinforcement. Civil Guards and local troops deserted, leaving the Spanish forces and the civilians who had taken refuge with them to face the rebels alone. Aid from neighboring military posts was impossible because all units were either similarly engaged or threatened, and Spanish commanders in the provinces consolidated their troops by abandoning vast areas and numerous towns to the revolutionaries without a fight.[20]

The Spanish collapse was paralleled by the formation of Aguinaldo's revolutionary government. He extended its control in the islands to keep pace with Filipino military successes and, in a series of proclamations, developed the organic framework for both his government and his revolutionary movement. On May 24, he proclaimed himself dictator, promising to deliver his power to a president and cabinet as soon as the islands passed into his control. He promised he would also convene a constitutional assembly at that time and accompanied his proclamation with a general call to arms directed to the Philippine people. On June 18 and 20, he issued proclamations providing for municipal elections and setting forth the regulations for the provinces and municipalities. On the twenty-third, he proclaimed the revolutionary government, the sole duty of which was to continue the struggle for Philippine independence, and appointed himself the president of the revolutionary organization. Other organic acts were issued during the month from both Aguinaldo's headquarters in Cavite and revolutionary leaders in the field.[21]

Since Aguinaldo had been brought to the Philippines by the Americans, he expected that they would look favorably upon his work of organizing a government there. After his conferences with American consuls in Singapore and Hong Kong, he thought that the United States would help him establish an independent Philippine state. Admiral Dewey's actions in May had confirmed his belief, and he was convinced that American military intervention in the islands would further the goals of the Philippine Revolt.[22]

The rapidity with which Aguinaldo organized his army and revolutionary government and his failure to place himself under Admiral Dewey's command surprised the Americans. Messages arriving in Washington from American consular representatives in the Far East had been completely mistaken about the goals of Aguinaldo and his associates. Consul Pratt assured the Department of State in April that the Filipino leader hoped the United States would assume protection of the Philippines and that he desired American advice and assistance in establishing a government there.[23] The consul in Hong Kong, Rounseville Wildman, notified Washington in May that several Filipinos, "all very wealthy landholders, bankers, and advocates of Manila," desired to give their allegiance and that of their families to the United States.[24] That same month Oscar F. Williams, consul in Manila, assured the government that the natives of the Philippines "would swear allegiance to and cheerfully follow our flag," and in one of his moments of imperialistic zeal he indicated that in his estimation "few United States troops will be needed for conquest and fewer still for occupancy." He concluded his assessment of the situation in the islands with the statement that American civil government would "be easy of organization and gratefully received." In June, he informed Washington that Aguinaldo had said "his friends all hoped that the Philippines would be held as a colony of [the] United States."[25]

The rapid development of Aguinaldo's revolutionary movement and the discussions that had taken place between him and the American consuls caused alarm in Washington. Although President McKinley had made no formal decision on American policy in the islands, he did want to maintain a free hand for a decision at a later date. The growth of the Philippine revolutionary government loomed as a major stumbling block in his plans, and a lively correspondence took place between Washington and its representatives in the Far East concerning the latters' relationship with Aguinaldo. The Secretary of Navy wired Dewey on May 26 that he was not to have political alliances with the revolutionaries or any faction in the Philippines that would incur liability to maintain their cause in the future.[26] The Secretary of State cabled Consul Pratt on June 16 to "avoid unauthorized negotiations with Philippine insurgents." In a letter sent the same day, he warned Pratt that the "insurgents" had neither asked nor received American recognition and the Secretary cautioned that:

> If, in the course of your conferences with General Aguinaldo, you acted upon the assumption that this government would cooperate with him for the furtherance of any plan of his own, or that, in accepting his cooperation, it would consider itself pledged to recognize any political claims which he may put forward, your action was unauthorized and can not be approved.[27]

The message was clear. The President had decided not to support the cause of the Philippine revolutionaries at this time.

Although no formal Philippine policy had been developed, the President was proceeding in the direction that the American imperialists hoped he would from the beginning. The ardent expansionist Senator Henry Cabot Lodge wrote to Theodore Roosevelt on May 24 that, "in confidence but in absolute certainty," he thought, "that the administration is grasping the whole policy at last." Lodge was convinced by June 15 that it had become not a question of whether the United States should take a part of the Philippines, but one of "how much." The Secretary of State dined with the Senator and Alfred Thayer Mahan, the naval theorist, and Lodge wrote Roosevelt afterward that the Secretary "thought we could not escape our destiny" in the islands.[28] Although undecided on many of the major questions concerning policy in the Philippines and remaining silent in public on the question of the islands, the President seemed inclined to keep at least part of the territory placed in the offering by Dewey's success.[29]

The advance detachment of the American expeditionary force landed at Cavite on June 30, and the relations between the American troops and the Filipinos were amicable during the first few days. Still, Brigadier General Thomas M. Anderson, the unit commander, reported that Aguinaldo "seemed very suspicious and not at all friendly," although he seemed willing to cooperate.[30] The General was keenly aware of the possibility of conflict with the revolutionaries, but he was also aware of Washington's intention to make no commitments to them. Observing all of the official military courtesies in his dealings with the Filipinos, he avoided diplomatic or political discussion. Although he acknowledged Aguinaldo's position as a military leader, the General ignored his assumption of civil authority. Arrangements were made with the rebel leader to allow the American troops to move into position on the sea side of the siege lines facing Manila, and Aguinaldo obligingly arranged for the Americans to obtain supplies, food, and transport from the local inhabitants. The Filipinos, suspicious of American intentions in the islands, soon interrupted this flow of supplies, and General Anderson was only able to restore it by threatening to levy the countryside for what his men needed. Aguinaldo refused to place himself under the authority of either the American army or Admiral Dewey, and he made known his desire to take Manila without the aid of the Americans.[31]

General Anderson understood the conditions in the islands as shown by his reports to Washington, but he was in a difficult situation. He recognized that any attempt to establish an American government there would bring about a conflict with the Filipino nationalists, but he was powerless to solve the problems facing him. He only commanded the advance detachment of the expeditionary force, and his command would soon fall to General Merritt when the latter arrived in the islands. Furthermore, Washington expected General Anderson to act in concert with Admiral Dewey. Instructions from the United States had not been framed with the problems of dealing with a revolutionary government in mind, and, aside from a general knowledge that he was to make no commitments, General Anderson had little but his own resourcefulness to guide him in his conduct. The policy he followed was by necessity a cautious one. He had come to an agreement with the Filipinos regarding the placement of American troops before Manila, and he let Aguinaldo know verbally that recognition of his government was impossible.[32] The General conducted himself as well as could have been expected in his tenuous position as a temporary commander, poorly instructed, with an ill-defined mission.

The revolutionaries were as uneasy about the presence of the Americans as General Anderson was about Aguinaldo. In particular, the continued arrival of American troops during the month of July made Aguinaldo suspicious. As he watched the American force grow from its initial contingent of approximately 2,500 men to over 10,000, he was prompted to write to Consul Williams for an explanation. "Why do not the American generals operate in conjunction with the Filipino generals?" he asked. "Is it intended, indeed, to carry out annexation against the wish of these people?"[33] Williams found these questions impossible to answer. It was doubtful that, as of the beginning of August, 1898, even President McKinley could have given Aguinaldo a satisfactory reply.

General Merritt arrived in the Philippines on August 1, and his subsequent actions did nothing to allay Aguinaldo's already growing suspicions. Merritt noted, as had Anderson, that the Filipino revolutionaries posed a serious problem, and he decided immediately that the assault on Manila should be made without their cooperation.[34] The General made plans during the first week in August for the forthcoming operation against the city. Although he had decided that Aguinaldo's men should not be allowed to penetrate the city, he warned his officers to avoid "forcible encounters" in carrying out the orders to prohibit their entrance. He added, however, that "pillage, rapine, or violence by the native inhabitants or disorderly insurgents must be prevented at any cost."[35] The attack began on August 13, and the American advance met with little resistance. By the afternoon the city had surrendered. For the most part, the Americans were successful in their attempt to prevent Aguinaldo's army from entering the city, although many armed Filipinos forced themselves into the suburban districts of Paco and Malate.[36]

As might have been expected, the American attack on Manila precipitated a crisis with the revolutionaries. Merritt's fear that they might loot the city led him to demand that

Aguinaldo keep his troops from participating in the attack. Upon its commencement, however, this proved impossible, and a number of incidents occurred between the advancing Filipino and American troops. The Americans forcibly prevented the revolutionary army from crossing the Spanish lines and entering the city, but the Americans suspected that some of the street firing upon their troops came from Filipino troops establishing themselves in the suburbs. By the end of the day General Merritt ordered General Anderson to evict the revolutionaries from the suburbs, but this was impossible. Anderson did succeed in segregating the Filipino units and establishing an American defensive perimeter close to the old Spanish lines. Relations with the revolutionaries were strained to the breaking point.[37]

General Merritt, in conjunction with Admiral Dewey, cabled Washington on August 13 seeking instructions to help them deal with the situation that had developed. The General stated that the revolutionaries were outside of Manila pressing their demand "for joint occupation of the city." "Situation difficult," he continued. "Inform me at once how far I shall proceed in forcing obedience in this matter and others that may arise." So that there would be no question as to the type of instructions he desired, he concluded with a direct query—"Is Government willing to use all means to make the natives submit to the authority of the United States?"[38] His message was not received in Washington until August 17, but the Adjutant General dispatched the following reply that same day.

> The President directs that there must be no joint occupation with the insurgents. The United States in the possession of Manila city, Manila Bay, and harbor must preserve the peace and protect persons and property within the territory occupied by their military and naval forces. The insurgents and all others must recognize the military occupation and authority of the United States and the cessation of hostilities proclaimed by the President. Use whatever means in your judgement are necessary to this end. All law-abiding people must be treated alike.[39]

The cessation of hostilities mentioned in the message referred

to the peace protocol signed by Spanish and American rep-
presentatives on August 12. News of this had not reached the
Philippines until the sixteenth. As of that date, all thoughts of
further military operations against the Spaniards were abandoned, no doubt with some relief, for the problems facing the
expeditionary force in Manila were immense.

According to the protocol signed on the twelfth, the city,
bay, and harbor of Manila were to be occupied by the
American army pending the conclusion of a peace treaty with
Spain. The treaty, to be drafted at a later date, would determine
the "control, disposition, and government of the Philippines."[40] As a consequence, the problems inherent in governing a city and its environs totaling over 400,000 in population
that had just undergone a three-month siege fell to the United
States Army. Fortunately, the President had supplied a set of
instructions relating to the military occupation of Manila.

The army lacked specific instructions for dealing with its
second problem, the Philippine revolutionaries. However, the
messages received on August 16 and 17 did provide some insight into what was expected. The Filipino government remained unrecognized by the United States although the protocol seemed to allow for this at a later date. American
authority in Manila was to be supreme, and there was to be no
joint occupation of the city with Aguinaldo's forces. Although
the military commanders in the islands still did not know what
the Philippine policy of the government would be, the peace
protocol had obviously left a great deal open for discussion in
the future. The army would have to wait and see what might
develop from the peace conference in Paris.

The Filipino revolutionaries, like the Americans in the
islands, were not completely sure of what policy to follow, and
the events accompanying the seizure of Manila by the United
States only confused them more. Some Filipino leaders, after talking with General Anderson, believed that the Americans were not trying to possess the islands as a colony.[41]
Since the Philippines were not under firm Filipino control, the
threat of a Spanish reconquest was still present, and some Filipinos saw a need for the American presence. Others sought a protectorate status under the United States.[42] Aguinaldo and many

of the members of his government, however, were seeking foreign recognition, and he ordered that the attacks against the Spaniards be continued to gain a seat for the Filipinos at the peace table.[43] He had written before the American attack on Manila that "protection or annexation will be acceptable only when it can be clearly seen that the recognition of our Independence, either by force of arms or diplomacy, is impossible."[44] Felipe Agoncillo, a member of the revolutionary junta in Hong Kong, wrote Aguinaldo on August 15 that they must prepare to fight if they did not gain independence in the forthcoming peace treaty.[45] Because of their incomplete knowledge of American intentions and the statements made to them by American consuls and military men before the attack on Manila, the revolutionaries were inclined to refrain from any rash acts until they saw how they fared in the forthcoming peace discussions.

In Washington, President McKinley still lacked a clearly formulated Philippine policy when the protocol ending the war with Spain was signed in August. He was closer, however, than he had been in May when he had dispatched the expeditionary force. When Great Britain approached the United States about peace terms, McKinley issued a reply early in June that required only the cession by Spain of a port in the Philippines, the rest of the islands to remain a Spanish colony. By the middle of the month the President had added, as a condition, just consideration for the Philippine revolutionaries in any terms of settlement. By the time for the signing of the protocol, the President had changed his mind on both points. Senator Lodge was convinced that McKinley wanted to hold the islands but was "a little timid about it."[46] The President told his cabinet in July, shortly after receiving the Spanish request for peace terms, that he was certain the American people would not be willing to see the islands returned to Spain. On the question of the revolutionaries, he had definitely instructed all American agents dealing with them to make no commitments that might in any way prevent American freedom of action at the peace table. The presence of American troops in Manila made the key question not whether or not the United States should take a part of the islands but whether or not it should leave. McKinley made his final decision when he instructed his commissioners in Paris on September 16 that "the United States cannot accept less than the cession in full right and sovereignty of the island of Luzon."[47]

By October 26, the President made a second, even more sweeping decision in the slow development of his ideas concerning the Philippines. On that date he had the Secretary of State send a message to the peace commissioners in Paris that "the acceptance of the cession of Luzon alone, leaving the rest of the islands subject to Spanish rule, or to be the subject of future contention, can not be justified on political, commercial, or humanitarian grounds."[48] The cession of the whole of the Philippines was to be required.

In arriving at his decision, the President had been influenced by many factors. A growing wave of opinion in the United States favored the retention of the islands. A poll of newspaper views on the Philippine question printed by the *Literary Digest* in mid-September reported a sweeping majority in favor of either the possession of the entire archipelago or the retention of a naval base. Extracts from the religious and commercial press showed similar sentiment.[49] Prominent expansionists, such as Theodore Roosevelt, Alfred Thayer Mahan, and Senator Henry Cabot Lodge, also brought pressure to bear on the President for the retention of the islands.[50] The concerns of foreign policy likewise entered into the President's thinking. The government of Great Britain urged the United States to keep the islands, and there was always the threat that they might fall into the hands of a rival power such as Germany or Japan. When the President undertook a trip through the Midwest to help him assess popular thought on the subject of the Philippines, the hearty reception he received for vague generalities concerning the occupation of the islands further influenced him.[51]

In arriving at his decision, the President carefully appraised the alternatives open to him. In a speech delivered in 1899, he summed up the situation as he had seen it the previous year. There was, he thought, universal agreement among Americans that the islands should not be returned to Spain. A protectorate would have given the United States responsibility without an assurance of adequate authority over the people, "even for their own good." To abandon the islands altogether, tossing them "into the arena of contention for the strife of nations," or leaving them "to the anarchy and chaos of no protectorate at all" was, for the President, "too shameful to be considered." He thus made what in his eyes seemed the only decision possible. The United States was to keep the islands to insure the "welfare and happiness and the rights of the inhabitants."[52] There seemed no other choice.

Unfortunately, the President lacked a keen appreciation of the situation that had developed in the Philippines since the fall of Manila. Misleading and conflicting reports from the Far East misrepresented conditions in the islands, and the President arrived at his decision with little or no insight into the actual state of affairs there. General Anderson and General Merritt both warned him of the possibility of conflict with Filipino nationalists, but these reports were more than offset by communications from other Americans in the area. Consul Williams wrote on September 5 that representatives of 4,000 Visayan soldiers, businessmen, and some revolutionary leaders in those southern islands had pledged loyalty to the United States.[53] Consul Wildman at Hong Kong wrote regarding the revolution's participants that, "in spite of all statements to the contrary, I know that they are fighting for annexation to the United States first, and for independence secondly."[54] Testimony given before the peace commissioners in Paris and statements taken from American military men in Manila seemed to confirm the reports of the consuls.

General Merritt was relieved by Major General Elwell S. Otis on August 29 so that the he could appear in Paris, bringing with him depositions on the Philippine situation by American officers in the islands. Merritt, showing a change of mind, stated that he thought there was no danger of conflict as long as the United States and not Spain retained the islands. He assured the peace commissioners that the islands other than Luzon were not a part of Aguinaldo's revolt. Eduard André, the Belgian consul in Manila, wrote that he was convinced the rebellion represented only one-half of one percent of the archipelago's inhabitants. Other depositions included statements to the effect that many of the Filipinos were perfectly willing to accept an American government and were anxious for the United States to take possession of the islands. One report stated that Aguinaldo was experiencing considerable difficulty in maintaining control over his loosely organized forces, and most of the reports stated that his government was a government in name only. The opinions presented in Paris on the subject of the Filipino capacity for self-government were similar to that of Major J. Franklin Bell—"they are unfit."[55] Optimistic communiqués from Merritt's successor, General Otis, also helped to keep the President in the dark as to the true situation in the Philippines.[56]

Conditions in the islands differed markedly from those portrayed in the communications the President received, and, as a result, the evolution of his policy failed to keep pace with events. While the President was hammering out his Philippine policy in Washington, friction between the Americans and the Filipinos developed rapidly. General Otis inherited from his predecessor the serious problem of the Filipino troops lodged in the suburbs of Manila. An accidental clash took place between American and Filipino troops on August 14, and Aguinaldo refused to withdraw his men, stating that he desired an advance position should the United States return the city to the Spaniards as a result of the peace settlement. General Merritt had demanded that the Filipino units be withdrawn, and he had promised that if the United States withdrew from the islands Aguinaldo would be left "in as good condition as he was found."[57] When General Merritt's emissary was unwilling or unable to clarify the meaning of the General's promise, Aguinaldo became apprehensive and suspicious.[58] The revolutionary leaders, however, remained cautious, desiring to see what took place at the peace conference, and they took pains to avoid further conflict between their troops and the Americans.[59] They refused to leave the suburbs of the city, although Aguinaldo did concede the American right to occupy Manila proper and turned over the waterworks to Major Bell.[60]

To effect the withdrawal of the Filipino troops close to the American lines, General Otis told Aguinaldo on September 8 that he would "be obliged to resort to forcible action" if they

were not removed by the fifteenth.[61] When a three-man commission sent by the revolutionaries asked Otis to withdraw his
demands, the General refused, but he did give the commission a
less forcefully worded request on September 13. Three days
later, Aguinaldo replied that he had issued the appropriate orders, although one unit failed to withdraw because its commander refused to follow Aguinaldo's order. Filipino troops also remained in the suburbs of Paco and Pandacan, and
Aguinaldo maintained that these two areas were not officially a
part of the city. General Otis, no doubt complying with a
message received from Washington, took "a conciliatory
course toward all," and he did not push for further withdrawal
of Aguinaldo's troops at that time.[62]

For the next month, General Otis and his command
busied themselves with the administrative problems of organizing
a military government in Manila, but on October 14 he precipitated another crisis by demanding that the revolutionaries
withdraw their troops from Paco and Pandacan by the twentieth. He had, at that time, completed a survey of the city, and
he voiced the opinion that the areas were an integral part of
Manila. The Filipino soldiers there had proved a great annoyance, extorting contributions from Manila citizens, kidnapping some, and preventing American troops from passing their
lines or going up the Pasig River. The territory held by
Aguinaldo's troops was both a salient into the American lines
and a strategic bend in the river. Aguinaldo again retreated in
the face of pressure from General Otis after first protesting
both in writing and through emissaries. For the second time
since the capture of Manila, conflict between the Americans
and the Filipinos had been barely avoided. Aguinaldo had
stepped back from the brink, and the Americans were again encouraged in their belief that war could be prevented. By the end
of October, General Otis was convinced that his relations with
the revolutionaries were improving, and once again he concentrated on the task of developing the military government in
Manila.[63]

While acceding to the American wishes in regard to
Manila, Aguinaldo continued to extend his control over the rest
of the archipelago and increased his efforts to consolidate the

position of the revolutionary government as the ruling body of
the Philippines. The situation that resulted from the signing of
the peace protocol aided him. The Americans were forbidden
to operate outside of the city and harbor of Manila, and the
Spanish forces still in the islands could not rely on Manila for
reinforcements, supplies, or direction. The main body of the
Spanish army was interned in the walled city of Manila. It was
an easy task for bands of Filipinos to rise up and drive out the
Spaniards, and what had taken place on Luzon in the days
following Dewey's victory was repeated in the islands to the
south.[64]

Aguinaldo formed a governmental organization that exercised all of the normal functions of a national state. As his officers spread throughout the islands, they selected electors and
established municipal governments. Suffrage was limited to
men "marked out by their good conduct, their wealth, and their
social position," and in many instances the electors only rep-
presented a fraction of the population of their municipality.[65]
The revolutionary congress was largely appointed, although
some of its members were elected.

In administrative matters Aguinaldo's government differed little from that of the Spaniards. Natives took the place
of the friars in local administration, but agencies like the postal
and telegraph services were the same as they had been under
Spain. They even used the same personnel. The church, under
the local native clergy, was placed in almost the same relationship to the government that it had held previously. Parish
priests were required to recognize the authority of Aguinaldo,
to preach patriotic sermons, and to collect the fees that had
been prescribed by the Spanish regulations.[66]

The new financial system was a modification of the
Spanish one. The revolutionaries confiscated Spanish and
church property, and they drew up property lists for the more
well-to-do citizenry. Contributions, forced in some cases, were
collected by local committees. The sale of hemp, primarily in
southern Luzon and the Visayan Islands, was either undertaken directly by the revolutionary government or heavily
taxed. The revenue-collecting system organized by the revolutionaries in 1898 was both complex and comprehensive.[67]

At the end of August, Aguinaldo appealed to foreign powers for recognition of his government. Filipino correspondents and representatives were in several cities including London, Paris, Washington, and Yokohama.[68] The revolutionary junta in Hong Kong acted as a coordinating committee for these foreign operations. The most extensive relations between the Filipino government and a foreign power were those with Japan. Mariano Ponce, the Philippine representative there, was aided by the Chinese revolutionary Sun Yat-sen. Sun placed Ponce in contact with Japanese political and military leaders interested in Japanese expansion and Asian unity. The Japanese were cautious, however, for they wanted neither a break with the United States nor the possible occupation of the Philippines by an even less favorable nation such as Germany.[69] The Filipinos had a government in the Philippines, but, even in the country most favorable to their aims, they were unable to gain recognition.

Despite his failure to gain foreign recognition, Aguinaldo was in effective control of the Philippines. His decrees were obeyed throughout the Christian portions of the archipelago, his representatives usually possessed the only firearms, and his government was centered in Luzon, the seat of Spanish power. He headed a military dictatorship that exercised all of the normal powers of a government. His influence even extended inside the area of Manila controlled by the Americans. Aguinaldo's tax collectors operated covertly there, and other revolutionaries gained positions of confidence in the American military government. One, Teodoro Sandico, was employed by the Provost-Marshal-General's office, and he secured the release of several revolutionaries from the city's prisons. Given such power, Aguinaldo was unwilling to recognize American sovereignty in the islands voluntarily.[70]

General Otis viewed the situation that was developing with alarm, but he hoped that he would be able to solve the problem presented by the Filipino nationalists without resorting to the use of force. He asked Washington for 5,000 additional troops in September "to supply losses and give greater confidence,"[71] although he did not contemplate using them against the Filipinos. Instead, he hoped that Aguinaldo's government would fall victim to its own internal dissensions. Otis thought that the vast majority of Filipinos would peacefully accept any American decision concerning the future of the islands, and he believed that the educated and wealthy members of the Philippine community, some of whom had conferred with him in Manila, preferred rule by the United States to that of Aguinaldo. He was certain this was the case with the local people other than the Tagalog and particularly with the inhabitants of the Visayan Islands.[72]

Aguinaldo's troubles were real, but they were certainly not insurmountable. It was true that the leaders of the Philippine Revolt were divided. The traditional elite group, primarily Filipino and mestizo landowners, businessmen, and professional men—all relatively well educated—were against a break with the United States. They recognized the futility of war and were willing, if necessary, to recognize American sovereignty in the islands. They were suspicious of the ability of their countrymen to establish a government capable of providing the security and stability they valued. The other major group in the leadership of the independence movement consisted of the newly appointed military officers, civil servants, and native clergy who owed their status and position to the revolution itself. For them, to acknowledge American sovereignty in the islands would be to voluntarily surrender the prestige and advantage they had obtained through their fight with Spain. From a personal standpoint, they would be placing themselves again in a subservient position to both a colonial power and their wealthier countrymen. Since this group was more numerous than the established elite, the defection of conservative upper-class Filipinos from the revolutionary movement would not bring about the downfall of Aguinaldo's government.[73]

One serious problem for Aguinaldo was the friction caused by differences between the revolutionary leaders and many of those they sought to lead. Also, abuses committed in the name of the revolution often alienated the people. A great tendency toward regionalism existed in the Philippines, and the islands were split not only geographically, but also ethnically. Many people, in particular those in the Visayas, were reluctant to give allegiance to Aguinaldo's Tagalog followers from

Luzon. Many members of the Filipino elite were more committed to property than they were to patriotism. The revolutionary government in the provinces required close supervision, and some Filipino leaders feared that discontent in non-Tagalog areas might develop into open rebellion. Revolutionary troops had taken to pillaging alien groups, such as the Chinese, and had committed crimes of extortion, looting, and assault on their own people. Sentiment among the Filipino masses was not overwhelmingly in favor of the revolution. Some of the people were still loyal to the friars, and, although most of the Spanish clergy had been imprisoned from the beginning of the revolution, in the province of Pangasinan and the surrounding area religious fraternities organized before the revolution refused to recognize Aguinaldo's government. In the province of Pampanga, inhabitants of the pueblo of Macabebe, led by their chief, Eugenio Blanco, had stood by Spain during the first stage of the revolution, and they refused to recognize Aguinaldo's government. The revolutionaries, however, had almost a monopoly on the possession of firearms, and theirs was the only organized governmental body functioning throughout the islands. The resistance that developed was, as a consequence, relatively ineffectual.[74]

The cohesive force holding the Filipinos together was a fear of the Americans. This was, at least in part, a consequence of anti-American propaganda begun by the Spaniards and continued by the Filipinos. It pictured the Americans as barbarians who had destroyed the American natives and would do the same in the Philippines. The Americans were portrayed as a threat to the Philippine religion, and their primary motive in coming to the islands was said to be that of enslaving the people. Figuring prominently in the propaganda were stories of the treatment accorded the American Negro and lynchings in the American South. The Filipino revolutionaries also publicized statements made in the United States by members of the Anti-Imperialist League and others who argued for an end to American involvement in the islands.[75] The relatively high literacy rate among the natives aided the revolution's leaders in their propaganda efforts. Although few Filipinos could write, nearly 40 percent could read at least in their local dialect.[76]

Aguinaldo's proclamations, decrees, and other revolutionary material could find an audience in any part of the islands.

The actions of some unthinking American soldiers in Manila lent credence to propaganda about the danger of a United States occupation of the islands. General Anderson observed that soldiers, "to get what they considered trophies, did a good deal of what the Filipinos considered looting," and they often treated the local inhabitants "with a good-natured condescension which exasperated the natives all the more because they feared to resent it."[77] Some soldiers incurred debts with local merchants and then refused to pay. Others over-indulged in the cheap native vino, and, according to the official history of one volunteer regiment, "it was not rare to see some burly soldier pass through the streets of Cavite hurling off a pack of Filipino citizens and soldiers who were trying to apprehend him."[78] The American soldiers called the Filipinos "niggers," and it did not take the Filipinos long to tell from the tone of the voice or the context that it was used as a term of disrespect.[79]

General Otis, hoping that the problem presented by the revolution would solve itself, suffered from bad advice and poor knowledge of the real conditions in the islands. His contact with Filipinos in Manila was primarily with those men of education and property who had the most to gain from the presence of the United States. He both underestimated the extent and power of Aguinaldo's government and the resentment that was being directed against the Americans. The revolutionary leadership had led the Philippine people to expect independence. When collapse of Aguinaldo's government failed to materialize, General Otis finally saw that it would soon have control of the entire archipelago with the exception of the Cavite naval base and Manila.[80]

Reports reaching the Philippines from Paris told of the American intention of acquiring all of the islands, and the situation facing General Otis worsened. The issue of independence was one that Aguinaldo could use to unite disaffected groups in the islands and present a united front against the Americans. Otis, recognizing the seriousness of the American predicament, cabled Washington in November that, in the event of hostilities, he would need 25,000 troops at his disposal. He also stated that he would retain volunteer units until they could be replaced by regular troops sent from the United States. He recommended that an attempt be made to forestall Aguinaldo's bid to gain control of the Visayas. The port of Iloilo, second only to Manila in importance, was the only city of any size remaining under Spanish control, and the General thought that it was possible for American troops to relieve the Spanish garrison there before it surrendered to the Filipinos. Time, of course, was running out, for the signing of a treaty ending Spanish rule in the Philippines would give the Spanish troops little reason to hold the city.[81]

The Americans made the decision to send troops to Iloilo in December. On December 10, the Treaty of Paris was signed, giving the Philippines to the United States, but the agreement was not binding until ratified. In the Philippines, General Otis could not wait for the Senate to put its final seal of approval on the treaty. Three days after the signing, a group of bankers, merchants, and business firms in Iloilo petitioned the General asking for American protection. The Spanish garrison was still there, and swift American action could prevent the city from falling to the rebels. On December 14, General Otis asked Washington if he should take any action in light of the situation at Iloilo; but, because of President McKinley's absence from the capital, Otis did not received his answer until December 23. He was told at that time to send troops to the city, but the message he received also contained this warning. "It is most important that there should be no conflict with the insurgents. Be conciliatory, but firm."[82] The General dispatched a force commanded by Brigadier General Marcus P. Miller on December 26, and three days later he received a message from the Secretary of War advising him to occupy all strategic points in the islands before the revolutionaries could get possession of them.[83] Such tardy advice was unnecessary. With the exception of Iloilo, no strategic points existed that were not already occupied or under siege by the Filipinos. The situation in the islands had progressed far beyond the plans and ideas of the administration in Washington. Even General Otis was reacting too late to the conditions that had developed.

By the end of December 1898, relations between the Americans and the revolutionaries were strained to the breaking point. The signing of the Treaty of Paris left no room for doubt in the minds of the Filipino nationalists that the American troops would not be departing from the islands and that independence, if gained at all, would probably have to be won. On the other hand, almost the entire archipelago was under at least the nominal control of Aguinaldo, and to occupy the islands the Americans would first have to displace Aguinaldo's government. Even at Iloilo General Miller's force was too late to prevent the city from falling into the hands of the rebels. The Spaniards had already departed for Manila when the Americans arrived, and General Miller's troops remained in their ships riding at anchor off the port. An impasse had been reached in which, to prevent war, one or the other of the participants would have to give ground. Philippine independence and American sovereignty in the islands were incompatible.[84]

Americans in both Washington and the Philippines continued to believe that the problem could be solved without recourse to violence. They hoped that the Filipinos might accept American sovereignty once they recognized the benevolent intentions of the United States. The formation of an acceptable colonial government was thus uppermost in the minds of both General Otis and President McKinley. The President impressed upon the General that he was to give the Filipinos "as kind and beneficent a government as possible . . . that they may be encouraged in their industries, and made secure in life and property."[85] This had been an important element in the President's original instructions to the expeditionary force, and at the very moment of the crisis with the revolutionaries, General Otis was implementing McKinley's ideas of benevolent government in the administration of Manila. The General also attempted to prevent news from the United States from making the situation in the islands any worse. He resorted to censorship of American press releases that might agitate the Filipinos or give them cause to think that the Treaty of Paris might not be ratified by the Senate. Cables such as that stating the hope of Boston anti-imperialists that Aguinaldo might become the "Washington" of a new nation "absolutely free" from European or American influence were censored upon receipt in Manila.[86]

In his conduct of the Iloilo expedition, General Otis exhibited extreme caution. He instructed General Miller to make known to the inhabitants the intentions and purposes of the United States, and, as a gesture of goodwill, Miller transported to Iloilo several local soldiers, inhabitants of the Visayas, whom the Spaniards had discharged in Manila. Otis cautioned Miller not to force a landing in the city. The merchants who had originally petitioned the Americans for protection also asked Miller not to land in Iloilo because the revolutionary force threatened to burn the city. In Manila, General Otis received reliable information that, at the Filipino capital of Malolos, Aguinaldo had appointed a new cabinet of men hostile to America. They were closely watching the conduct of Miller's expedition in the hope of being provided with an incident that they could use to their advantage in further stirring up the people against the United States.[87] The revolutionaries, although increasingly unfavorable in their attitude toward the Americans, still acted with caution. They were waiting and hoping to gain foreign recognition and to increase their political and military position in the islands before chancing a conflict with the Americans.[88]

President McKinley continued to hope that the policy he had evolved for the islands, based on his ideas concerning the development of a benevolent government there, would succeed. He summed up his position in a letter sent to the Secretary of War on December 21. In that document, McKinley outlined the policy that he intended to follow, and it resembled in content and in wording the letter of instruction that he had given to General Merritt in May. The commanding officer in the Philippines was to announce to the inhabitants that the Americans came "not as invaders or conquerors, but as friends, to protect the natives in their homes, in their employments, and in their personal and religious rights." The President noted that all persons cooperating with the government of the United States would receive "the reward of its support and protection," but others would be brought, "with firmness if need be," within the lawful rule assumed by it. The laws administered by the military government in the islands were to be as similar as possible to those already in existence there. The letter of instruction ended with a clear-cut statement of what the President expected from the army in Manila.

> It should be the earnest and paramount aim of the military administration to win the confidence, respect and affection of the inhabitants of the Philippines by assuring them in every possible way that full measure of individual rights and liberties which is the heritage of free peoples, and by proving to them that the mission of the United States is one of benevolent assimilation, substituting the mild sway of justice and right for arbitrary rule.[89]

The President was certain that in a situation such as that faced by General Miller at Iloilo an immediate accord could be reached with the revolutionaries, if they could only be made aware of American purposes in the islands.[90]

President McKinley was completely out of touch with the realities of the Philippine situation. His formal act of instructing General Otis that the occupation of the entire archipelago had become "immediately necessary" and that the military government was to be "extended with all possible dispatch to the whole of the ceded territory" did not make those things possible. The President ignored entirely the problems presented by an insurgent government controlling almost all of the Philippines. He overlooked the fact that the American army was confined to the limits of Manila and Cavite, completely surrounded by Filipino troops. Most important of all, the President ignored, or failed to see, that many Filipinos did not want to be "benevolently assimilated" and that under the leadership of Aguinaldo or the pressure of his government they would be willing to fight before seeing themselves "under the free flag of the United States."[91]

In formulating his Philippine policy, President McKinley did not keep in step with the rapid development of events in the islands. Had he decided to retain them earlier than October, American consuls in the Far East, Admiral Dewey, and the officers of the expeditionary force might have acted differently in their relations with the Filipino revolutionaries. Certainly, many Americans were responsible for making the Filipinos expect independence. Without doubt, some efforts could have been made to relieve Spanish garrisons in strategic parts of the islands while they still held such positions had the orders from Washington to take such action come in August or September rather than at the end of December. Even the acceptance of an American government might have been gained had the men charged with that task at the end of 1898 known that it would be their mission from the first moment of arrival in the islands in June. McKinley's decisions on all of these points, however, had been bypassed by the course of events in the Philippines, before there was even a remote possibility of carrying out the instructions he issued.

No matter how indecisive the President's actions had been, he was not completely responsible for the conditions existing in the island at the end of 1898. General Otis misled his Commander in Chief as much as the Amerian consuls had misled the President at an earlier date. Otis was constantly optimistic in his appraisal of the problems facing him and was always quick to assure Washington that the situation could be handled without the use of force. In October he stated that Filipinos of education and property, men favorable to American annexation, were gaining ascendancy in the revolutionary government. At that time he reported that he did not anticipate trouble and that the revolutionaries in the Visayas were not allied with Aguinaldo and would "welcome" rule by the United States. Again in November he cabled that there was "no serious difficulty anticipated."[92] On December 8, he wrote that conditions were improving and that he could see "signs of revolutionary disintegration," and on January 2 he wired that the Filipino government was weakening "and unable to hold representative men." He noted that Aguinaldo's troops had been driven out from the province of Tarlac by the inhabitants. He ended his message by stating his belief "that it is possible to avoid conflict."[93] Given the consistent tenor of Otis' dispatches, the President could naturally assume, as he did, that the vast majority of Filipinos would peacefully accept a benevolent American government.

Despite his reports to Washington, however, General Otis

seemed to recognize the predicament facing him. Not only was he extremely cautious in his instructions to Miller, lying off Iloilo, but he declined to publish President McKinley's letter of December 21 outlining the policy to be followed by the United States in the islands. General Otis knew that the statements contained in the instructions that referred to American sovereignty could be used by Apolinario Mabini, the new leader of Aguinaldo's cabinet and the foremost propagandist of the revulution, to excite the people even further against the Americans. Instead, on January 4, 1899, General Otis published his own expertly edited version of the proclamation in which he stressed the benevolent intentions of the Americans but declined to mention the question of the establishment of an American colonial government or the title to the Philippines given the Americans in the Treaty of Paris. Unfortunately, General Miller sent the President's letter in its entirety to the citizens of Iloilo on January 3, and General Otis's attempt to decrease tensions in the islands backfired.[94]

As Otis feared, the unedited publication of McKinley's letter created new tensions between the Americans and the Filipinos. The revolutionaries made much propaganda of the use of terms such as "right of cession" and "sovereignty," which they equated with despotism. Aguinaldo also noticed and pointed out that Otis signed his proclamation "Military Governor of the Philippines," rather than the title he had used previously, that of Military Governor in the Philippines. Aguinaldo answered Otis's proclamation with a fiery one of his own on January 5. In concluding his lengthy statement, he wrote that his government could not remain indifferent to the "violent and aggressive seizure of a portion of its territory." He ended by saying that his government was "disposed to open hostilities if the American troops attempt to take forcible possession of the Visaya islands." The line had been drawn, and Aguinaldo's policy had become that of his advisor Mabini, "inflexible in opposition to the efforts of the party of older and more conservative Filipinos to establish a *modus vivendi* with the Americans."[95]

General Otis reported the increasing friction in his dispatches to Washington in the early days of 1899, though he was still optimistic about the possibility of a peaceful solution to the problem. Manila was filled with rumors of an impending attack by the revolutionary army, and disaffected Spaniards in the city continued, as they had for some time, to circulate stories of America's evil intentions in the islands. Some of the Spanish soldiers even enlisted in the Filipino ranks. The situation at Iloilo was stalemated, and Otis knew that any attempt to take that city or any other port in the Visayas would mean war. Conservative Filipinos in the revolutionary camp, including those of property and those who thought that resistance to the Americans would be futile, sought to withdraw from Aguinaldo's government. Many fled to Manila and the safety of American protection. The Filipinos around Manila became increasingly hostile to the Americans, and the troops surrounding the city seemed to delight in trying to provoke the American units there. At any moment war could begin.[96]

President McKinley wanted to avoid the conflict that seemed imminent, and he refused to relinquish his hope that war could be averted if only the Filipinos could be made to understand that the Americans had come to the islands in the people's best interests. He was convinced of America's benevolent purposes there, and he sought to impress this on the revolutionaries before it was too late. On January 8, in a last minute effort to maintain peace, the President made another bid to obtain recognition of American sovereignty from the Filipino leaders. He cabled Otis that "time given the insurgents can not hurt us and must weaken and discourage them. They will come to see our benevolent purpose and recognize that before we can give their people good government our sovereignty must be complete and unquestioned." He expected Otis to avoid bringing the crisis to any conclusion and to prevent a conflict through the use of "tact and kindness." He commended Otis for his frequent conferences on an unofficial basis with the more conservative Filipino leaders, and he offered to send civil commissioners to aid the General in the delicate task of obtaining recognition of American rule through the use of diplomacy rather than force. To impress it again upon Otis and perhaps reassure himself, he noted that American presence in the islands was to "improve the condition of the inhabitants, securing them peace, liberty, and the pursuit of their highest good." Two days later General Otis replied to the President's message saying that both he and Admiral Dewey thought that commissioners could do excellent work in the islands.[97] Commissioners, however, could not reach the Philippines in less than two months, and time was in short supply.

The President and the policy that he developed to guide American actions in the Philippines placed General Otis in a virtually impossible position. The question of American sovereignty or American presence in the islands had been decided. It was not a matter of discussion but a fact that the General was expected to communicate to the Filipinos without provoking a conflict. The promise of benevolence was thought sufficient to gain their acquiescence in an American occupation. There was no alternative road to peace from the American viewpoint. The General was without instructions for dealing with a government or a people that refused to accept the American colonial regime. He could only hope that Aguinaldo and his followers would see the futility of resisting a nation as large and powerful as the United States. General Otis, however, did not lose his optimism. He still thought that a peaceful solution to the problem might be found, but even he recognized that the month of January was crucial.[98]

Among the Filipinos there was great activity. Aguinaldo's troops ringed Manila, and what artillery he had in his possession was emplaced with them. Although Aguinaldo personally favored guerrilla warfare as a means of resisting the invader, he decided to use a more conventional form of resistance under the urgings of Antonio Luna, one of his more powerful generals. The Filipinos wanted to keep a regular force in the field to gain foreign recognition. The revolutionary army had been organized on a local basis, but by January 1899 it was slowly becoming a national force. It was supported by a militia, some of whom were organized within the city of Manila. The preparations taking place in the Filipino camp were sufficient evidence that they expected war. In towns throughout Luzon people were storing arms, digging trenches, and preparing for a fight. The revolutionaries desired to avoid conflict, if possible, to gain time to obtain equipment and foreign aid, hopefully from Japan; but for them too, time was running short.[99]

Americans and Filipinos made a final effort to solve their problems at the conference table in mid-January. Influenced by the urgings of moderate Filipinos and their mutual desire to preserve peace, both General Otis and Aguinaldo appointed commissioners to meet and discuss the sources of friction between the Americans and Filipinos in the hope of lessening tensions. The first meeting took place on January 11, but it ended without any fruitful discussion. The Filipinos stated their desire for "absolute independence," and the Americans answered that it was impossible to recognize any sovereignty in the islands other than that of the United States. In a reply to the American commissioners' query about the thoughts of the Filipinos regarding a protectorate, Aguinaldo's representatives answered that that subject was not covered by their instructions. The Filipinos sought to gain recognition of their status as a government and failed. The second conference accomplished no more. At the third and fourth meetings the Filipino representatives begged the Americans to recognize their independence for the sake of peace. The Americans replied that war would only be brought on by acts of the revolutionaries. The fifth meeting was also a failure. Neither side could or would compromise. The Filipino nationalists wanted independence and were convinced that they constituted a legitimate government. The Americans, military men only able to operate within the instructions sent from Washington, could do little more than assure the Filipinos that American intentions in the Philippines were benevolent. They could not alter their demand that the Filipinos recognize American sovereignty.[100]

The attempt to stave off hostilities through discussion ended in an impasse. The final meeting of the American and Filipino representatives ended on January 29 with the statement that there was no further business to be transacted. Six days before, at its capital in Malolos, the revolutionary government had promulgated the constitution of the Philippine Republic, and Aguinaldo continued his preparations for war. In Manila, tensions multiplied; Filipinos fled in droves from the city; and the friction between the Americans and the inhabitants increased when a Filipino child and a woman were accidentally shot by American soldiers. General Otis's troops, like Aguinaldo's, were preparing for the difficulties ahead, and contingency plans were already drawn to deal with the expected attack. Both Aguinaldo and General Otis hoped for peace, but they must have known that peace was impossible. War seemed an inevitable consequence of the irreconcilable positions taken by the two parties to the controversy. On February 3, General Otis wrote Admiral Dewey concerning the troubled situation outside of Manila. "There has been a great deal of friction along the lines the past two days, and we will be unable to tamely submit to the insulting conduct and threatening demonstrations of these insurgents much longer."[101] The fire was laid, it would take only the smallest spark to ignite it.

The members of the Philippine expeditionary force had been given a difficult, if not impossible, task. Over 7,000 miles from their home base, dealing with a people different in race and culture, their role as a military, governing, and diplomatic force had proven too much. There was no official colonial agency to aid them; no experience in the immediate past of the army to set precedents for action. Their knowledge of the situation in the Philippines and of the inhabitants was inadequate. Instructions from Washington were always too scanty, too late, or too rigid to help them deal with the rapid growth of the Filipino government. When President McKinley finally made his decision to keep the islands the problem had already developed beyond the point where a diplomatic solution was possible. Negotiations, if the abortive attempt at military diplomacy in January 1899 might be called that, came only after the course of events had made negotiation impossible. American goals in the islands, no matter how humanitarian they might have been, were set forth in complete ignorance of actual conditions there. The result was a situation neither the Filipinos nor the Americans had foreseen or desired.

NOTES

1. Nelson A. Miles to Secretary of War, May 3, 1898, McKinley-to Secretary of War, May 4, 1898, The Adjutant General's Office, *Correspondence Relating to the War with Spain, April 15, 1898-July 30, 1902* (Washington, 1902), II, 635. Cited hereafter as *Correspondence*. For a general survey of events in Washington following receipt of the news of Dewey's victory, see H. Wayne Morgan, *William McKinley and His America* (Syracuse, 1963), 386-87.

2. Dewey to Secretary of the Navy, May 13, 1898, U.S., Congress, House, *Annual Reports of the Navy Department for the Year 1898: Appendix to the Report of the Chief of the Bureau of Navigation*, HD 3, 55th Cong., 3d sess., 1898, 97. The abbreviations HD for United States House of Representatives Document and SD for United States Senate Document will be used in the notes throughout this work.

3. For Dewey's messages, see ibid., 68-69, 97-130. For messages from American consuls in the Far East, see U.S., Congress, Senate *A Treaty of Peace Between the United States and Spain*, SD 62, 55th Cong., 3d sess., 1898, 319-61.

4. For material on the President's indecision and the

development of the debate over imperialism, see Paolo E. Coletta, "McKinley, the Peace Negotiations, and the Acquisition of the Philippines," *Pacific Historical Review* 30 (1961): 341-50; Morgan, *McKinley*, 387-88; Ernest R. May, *Imperial Democracy: The Emergence of America as a Great Power* (New York, 1961), 244-49; Foster Rhea Dulles, *The Imperial Years* (New York, 1956), 148-55.

5. For correspondence of the army staff bureaus dealing with the collection and organization of the expeditionary force up to the embarkation of the first units on May 25, 1898, see *Correspondence*, II, 635-72. Opinions of Miles and Merritt on the composition and size of the force are in Merritt to McKinley, May 13, 1898, Miles to Secretary of War, May 16, 1898, II, 643-44, 647-48. For an overview of the work done by the War Department and the staff bureaus at this time and throughout the war see Graham A. Cosmas, *An Army for Empire: The United States Army in the Spanish-American War* (Columbia, Mo., 1971).

6. Merritt to McKinley, May 15 and 17, 1898, ibid., 646, 648. General Merritt was probably encouraged in his plans for the Philippine expedition by a cable that he received on May 16 from the Adjutant General's Office stating that his command would include *only* the Philippine Islands, although it was designated the Department of the Pacific. He was told that this fact would not be mentioned in the official orders, but would be communicated to him in a confidential letter of instructions. See Theodore Schwan to Merritt, May 16, 1898, ibid., 649.

7. Miles to Secretary of War, May 18, 1898, ibid., 648-49.

8. McKinley to Merritt, May 19, 1898, ibid., 676-78. Although sent to the Secretary of War on May 19, the President's instructions were not forwarded to General Merritt until May 28, three days after the first contingent of troops had already departed for the Philippines.

9. Ibid.

10. The summary of social and economic developments in the Philippines during the nineteenth century is based primarily on Edgar Wickberg, *The Chinese in Philippine Life, 1850-1898* (New Haven, 1965), 29-41 and chap. 5 in particular. See also Edgar Wickberg, "The Chinese Mestizo in Philippine History," *Journal of Southeast Asian History* 5 (1964): 62-100; Cesar Adib Majul, *Apolinario Mabini, Revolutionary* (Manila, 1964),

chaps. 2-4; and Bonifacio S. Salamanca, *The Filipino Reaction to American Rule, 1901-1913* (n.p., 1968), 6-25.

11. Wickberg, *The Chinese in Philippine Life*, 134.

12. On the propaganda movement and the demands of the propagandists, see Teodoro A. Agoncillo, *The Revolt of the Masses: The Story of Bonifacio and the Katipunan* (Quezon City, 1956), 18-31: James A. LeRoy, *The Americans in the Philippines*, 2 vols. (Boston, 1914), I, 63-73; Apolinario Mabini, *La Revolucion Filipina (con otros documentos de la época)*, comp. Teodoro M. Kalaw (Manila, 1931), 289-90. On the extensive power exercised by the friars, see *Lands Held for Ecclesiastical or Religious Uses in the Philippine Islands*, SD 190, 56th Cong., 2d sess., 1901, 47-91; Cesar Adib Majul, "The Political and Constitutional Ideas of the Philippine Revolution" printed in *Philippine Social Sciences and Humanities Review* 21 (1956): 92-136.

13. The most detailed work on the early stages of the Philippine Revolt is Agoncillo's *Revolt of the Masses*. The story is told from the Spanish viewpoint in Manuel Sastrón, *La insurreción en Filipinas y guerra hispano-americana en el archipiélago* (Madrid, 1901). The best American account is LeRoy, *Americans in the Philippines,* I, 42-147.

14. The Pact of Bia-an-Bató became the center of a continuing controversy over the question of whether or not reforms were promised. Two things are certain, however. The Spanish Governor-General refused to consider Aguinaldo's original demands, and no written agreement was signed promising any reforms. See Fernando Primo de Rivera, *Memoria dirigida al senado por el capitán general D. Fernando Primo de Rivera y Sobremonte acerca de su gestión en filipinas, Agosto de 1898* (Madrid, 1898), 130-142; Emilo Aguinaldo, "True Review of the Philippine Revolution," *Congressional Record: Appendix,* 57th Cong., 1st sess., XXXV (1902), 440. Aguinaldo maintained that promises of reform had been made on the Governor-General's honor as a gentleman and a soldier, but his claim is not substantiated by other revolutionary sources. See letters of Mariano Ponce in *Mariano Ponce: cartas sobre la revolución, 1897-1900,* comp. Teodoro M. Kalaw (Manila, 1932), 89-116 *passim*; Mabini, *La Revolución,* 305-306. Recent Philippine scholarship has freed the Spanish Governor-General from any charges of deceit. See Teodoro A. Agoncillo,

"Malolos: The Crisis of the Republic," *Philippine Social Sciences and Humanities Review* 25 (1960): 70-75.

15. Leonardo H. Fernandez, *The Philippine Republic* (New York, 1926), 48-50.

16. Ibid., 63.

17. Enrique Altamirano, *Filipinas, relato histórico de actos y hechos realizados en los últimos dias de nuestra dominación* (Madrid, 1902), 23-24; John Foreman, *The Philippine Islands* (2d ed., New York, 1899), 550-57.

18. Pratt to William R. Day, Apr. 28, 1898, *A Treaty of Peace*, SD 62, 55th Cong., 3d sess., 342 and Dewey to Secretary of Navy, June 27, 1898, *Navy Department, 1898, Appendix*, HD 3, 55th Cong., 3d sess., 103.

19. John R. M. Taylor, "The Philippine Insurrection Against the United States—A Compilation of Documents with Notes and Introduction," 5 vols. (1906), 10-14AJ; Pió del Pilar to Aguinaldo, May 31,1898, ibid., 10MG. Cited hereafter as Taylor, "Compilation." This work was completed while the author, an army officer, was working in the Bureau of Insular Affairs. It was never published. Copies of the work in galley proof are available on microfilm from the United States National Archives. It consists of a two volume commentary and three volumes of exhibits taken from the Philippine Insurgent Records (PIR) captured by the Americans. The PIR have subsequently been returned to the Philippine government, but microfilm copies of the records were retained by the National Archives. An interesting history of Taylor's work and the reasons it was never published is John Thomas Farrell, "An Abandoned Approach to Philippine History: John R. M. Taylor and the Philippine Insurrection Records," *Catholic Historical Review* 39 (1954): 385-407.

An excellent summary of the rapid spread of Filipino control through the islands after the landing of Aguinaldo is contained in U.S., Congress, House, "The Philippine Insurrection, 1896-1898: An Account, from Spanish Sources Principally, Prepared by Direction of Maj. Gen. George W. Davis, U. S. Army, Commanding the Division of the Philippines, by Maj. John S. Mallory, First U. S. Infantry," *Annual Reports of the War Department for the Fiscal Year Ended June 30, 1903*, HD 2, 58th Cong., 2d sess., 1903, III, 399-433.

20. On the Spanish collapse, in addition to *War Depart-*

ment, 1903, HD 2, 58th Cong., 2d sess., III, 399-433, see Altamirano, *Filipinas;* Sastrón, *La insurrección,* 429-45; Antonio del Rio, *Sitio y rendición de Santa Cruz de la Laguna: suerte de la colonia* (Manila, 1899).

21. John R. M. Taylor, *Report on the Organization for the Administration of Civil Government Instituted by Emilio Aguinaldo and His Followers in the Philippine Archipelago* (Washington, 1903), 19-34. Aguinaldo's call to arms can be found in U.S., Congress, Senate, *Communications Between the Executive Department of the Government and Aguinaldo,* SD 208, 56th Cong., 1st sess., 1900, 88-89. See also unsigned circular, June 3, 1898, and Mariano Triás to Local Presidents of Dasmariñas and Imus, June 4, 1898, in Taylor, "Compilation," 11-12MG.

22. See *A Treaty of Peace,* SD 62, 55th Cong., 3d sess., 319-61 for consular reports. An excellent summary of the early relations between the Americans and the revolutionaries is Philippine Information Society, "Were Promises Made to Aguinaldo," *Facts about the Filipinos* I (No. 2, 1901). Comments such as Dewey's "Don't give it up, Don Emilio" were bound to make Aguinaldo think that the Americans supported his enterprise. See testimony of Dewey in U.S., Congress, Senate, *Affairs in the Philippine Islands: Hearings before the Committee on the Philippines of the United States Senate,* SD 331, 57th Cong., 1st sess., 1902, 3 pts., pt. 3, 2928.

23. Pratt to Day, Apr. 30, 1898, *A Treaty of Peace,* SD 62, 55th Cong., 3d sess., 342-43.

24. Wildman to Day, May 6 and 14, 1898, ibid., 334-35.

25. Williams to Day, May 12, 1898, *Correspondence,* II, 718-19 and Williams to Day, June 16, 1898, *A Treaty of Peace,* SD 62, 55th Cong., 3d sess., 329.

26. *Navy Department, 1898, Appendix,* HD 3, 55th Cong., 3d sess., 101.

27. Day to Pratt, June 16, 1898, *A Treaty of Peace,* SD 62, 55th Cong., 3d sess., 353, 354.

28. Lodge to Roosevelt, May 24, and June 15 and 24, 1898, in Henry Cabot Lodge, *Selections from the Correspondence of Theodore Roosevelt and Henry Cabot Lodge, 1884-1918,* 2 vols. (New York, 1925), I, 299, 311, 313.

29. Coletta, "McKinley," 343; Morgan, *McKinley,* 387-88.

30. Anderson to the Adjutant General [AG], July 9, 1898, *Correspondence,* II, 778.

31. Anderson to AG, July 9, 18, and 21, 1898, ibid., 778, 781, 809; Dewey to Secretary of Navy, June 27, 1898, U.S., Congress, House, *Navy Department, 1898,* Appendix, HD 3, 55th Cong., 3d sess., 103. The correspondence between the American military representatives and Aguinaldo is in *Communications* SD 208, 56th Cong., 1st sess., 4-17.

32. Ibid.

33. Aguinaldo to Williams, Aug. 1, 1898, *A Treaty of Peace,* SD 62, 55th Cong., 3d sess., 398.

34. Merritt to AG, Aug. 1, 1898, *Correspondence,* II, 743.

35. *Annual Reports of the War Department for the Fiscal Year Ended June 30, 1898,* HD 2, 55th Cong., 3d sess., 1898, III, 83.

36. Ibid., 39-46, 678.

37. Ibid.

38. Merritt and Dewey to AG, Aug. 13, 1898, *Correspondence,* II, 754.

39. AG to Merritt, Aug. 17, 1898, ibid. A similar message to Dewey is in *Navy Department, 1898, Appendix,* HD 3, 55th Cong., 3d sess., 124.

40. *A Treaty of Peace,* SD 62, 55th Cong., 3d sess., 277.

41. Felipe Buencamino to Aguinaldo, July 25, 1898, Taylor, "Compilation," 68 MG.

42. Antonio Regidor to José Basa, July 30, 1898, Philippine Insurgent Records, 1896-1901 with Associated Records of the U. S. War Department, 1900-1906, 450.2, cited hereafter as PIR; Felipe Agoncillo to Aguinaldo, Aug. 1, 1898, PIR 471.4; Galicano Apacible to Apolinario Mabini, Aug. 2, 1898, PIR 453.3. Captain John R. M. Taylor collected what he thought were the most important documents in the Philippine Insurgent Records into folders prior to preparing his compilation. The contents of the folders, along with the remainder of the records are contained on microfilm in the United States National Archives. PIR citations such as 450.2 refer to enclosure number two of folder 450.

43. Aguinaldo, "To Foreign Governments," Aug. 6, 1898, *Communications,* SD 208, 56th Cong., 1st sess., 99; Agoncillo to McKinley, Aug. 15, 1898, PIR 102.5. Aguinaldo, memorandum, Aug. 13, 1898, PIR 427.5.

44. Aguinaldo to Teodoro Sandico, Aug. 10, 1898, PIR 5.7.

45. Agoncillo to Aguinaldo, Aug. 15, 1898, PIR 471.7.

46. Lodge to Roosevelt, July 12, 1898, Lodge, *Selections*, I, 323,

47. U.S., Congress, Senate, *Papers Relating to the Treaty with Spain*, SD 148, 56th Cong., 2d sess., 1901, 7. See also Garel A. Grunder and William E. Livezey, *The Philippines and the United States* (Norman, 1951), 25-26; Coletta, "McKinley," 343.

48. *Papers*, SD 148, 56th Cong., 2d sess., 35.

49. Harry Richmond Lynn, "The Genesis of America's Philippine Policy" (Ph.D. diss., University of Kentucky, 1936), 65-68.

50. Julius W. Pratt, *Expansionists of 1898* (Baltimore, 1936), 326-28.

51. Morgan, *McKinley*, chap. 18; May, *Imperial Democracy*, chap. 17; Grunder and Livezey, *Philippines*, chap. 2.

52. Speech at a dinner of the Home Market Club of Boston, Feb. 16, 1899, *Speeches and Addresses of William McKinley from March 1, 1897 to May 30, 1900* (New York, 1900), 187-89.

53. Williams to Day, Sept., 5, 1898, *A Treaty of Peace*, SD 62, 55th Cong., 3d sess., 333.

54. Wildman to John Bassett Moore, July 18, 1898, ibid., 336.

55. Ibid., 380. See also the testimony and/or depositions of Merritt, 362-70; André, 386-89; F. V. Greene, 374-75, 404-29; Frank S. Bourns, 375-78; Dewey, 383-84; Charles L. Jewett, 385-86; John Foreman, 441-71.

56. Otis to AG, Sept. 15 and 16, Oct. 19, 1898, *Correspondence*, II, 790, 791, 827.

57. Ibid., 818. Italics in original omitted.

58. Ibid.

59. See unsigned circular, Aug. 29, 1898, PIR 21.4.

60. *Annual Reports of the War Department for the Fiscal Year ended June 30, 1899*, HD 2, 56th Cong., 1st sess., 1899, V, 344-47.

61. Otis to Aguinaldo, Sept. 8, 1898, ibid., 9.

62. Henry C. Corbin [AG] to Otis, Sept. 7, 1898, *Correspondence*, II, 788. The details of this incident are found in *War Department, 1899*, HD 2, 56th Cong., 1st sess., V, 6-10.

63. *War Department, 1899*, HD 2, 56th Cong., 1st sess., V, 16-21; Otis to AG, Oct. 19, 25 & 30, 1898, *Correspondence*, II, 804-805, 831, 843.

64. Taylor, "Compilation," 32AJ.

65. Ibid., and Majul, *Mabini*, 75-77. In Lipa, Batangas Province, there were 25 votes out of a population of about 40,000; at Vigan in Ilocos Sur, 116 out of 19,000; other election returns were comparable, according to Taylor.

66. Francisco Macabulos to Local President of Tarlac, Aug. 9, 1898, PIR 897.5. On the operation of the entire government see Taylor, "Compilation," 49-53AJ.

67. Secretary of Treasury to Governor of Manila and Other Provinces, Aug. 10, 1898, PIR 312.7; Taylor "Compilation," 92-100HS.

68. Aguinaldo, decree, Aug. 10, 1898, PIR 432.2.

69. The relations between the insurgents and the Japanese are covered in Enrique J. Corpus, "Japan and the Philippine Revolution," *The Philippine Social Science Review* 6 (1934): 249-98; Marius B. Jansen, *The Japanese and Sun Yat-sen* (Cambridge, Mass., 1954), 64-74; James K. Eyre, Jr., "Japanese Imperialism and the Aguinaldo Insurrection," *United States Naval Institute Proceedings* 75 (1949): 901-907. Eyre also deals with the Japanese interest in the Philippines in his "Japan and the American Annexation of the Philippines," *Pacific Historical Review* 11 (1942): 55-71 and his "Early Japanese Imperialism and the Philippines," *United States Naval Institute Proceedings* 75 (1949): 1267-75.

70. Taylor, *Report*, 15-19; Taylor, "Compilation," 62-64AJ; Aguinaldo, decree, Aug. 22, 1898, PIR 82.7.

71. *War Department, 1899* HD 2, 56th Cong., 1st sess., V, 41.

72. Otis to AG, Oct. 19, Nov. 13, Nov. 27, 1898, Otis to Secretary of War, Dec. 8, 1898, *Correspondence*, II, 827, 836, 840, 851-52.

73. The difference in outlook between the established native elite and others in the revolutionary movement is set forth in Agoncillo, *Malolos*, in particular 397, 563-64; Majul, *Political and Constitutional Ideas*, 61, 162-64, 182-83; and Majul, *Mabini*, 77. See also Taylor, "Compilation," 56AJ.

74. On these Filipino problems see Sandico to Aguinaldo,

Sept. 28, 1898, PIR 416.7; unsigned telegram to Aguinaldo, Sept. 4, 1898, PIR 26.4; Taylor, "Compilation," 43-48AJ. On the religious movement in Pangasinan, see David R. Sturtevant, "Guardia de Honor: Revitalization within the Revolution," *Asian Studies* 4 (1966): 342-52.

75. On the Spanish and insurgent propaganda, see Taylor, "Compilation," 7AJ; John Barrett, "Some Phases of the Philippine Situation," *Review of Reviews* 22 (1899): 68-70; U.S., Congress, Senate, *Trip Through the Island of Luzon*, SD 196, 56th Cong., 1st sess., 1900, 20 (this document is the November 23, 1898 report of Paymaster W. B. Wilcox and Cadet L. R. Sargent).

76. Bureau of the Census, *Census of the Philippine Islands, 1903*, 4 vols. (Washington, 1905), II, 78; *Luzon*, SD 196, 56th Cong., 1st sess., 19.

77. Thomas M. Anderson, "Our Rule in the Philippines," *North American Review* 170 (1900): 282.

78. State of Oregon, *The Official Records of the Oregon Volunteers in the Spanish War and the Philippine Insurrection* (Salem, 1903), 38.

79. Bradley A. Fiske, *War Time in Manila* (Boston, 1913), 89, 105; Albert G. Robinson, *The Philippines: the War and the People, a Record of Personal Observations and Experiences* (New York, 1901), 58; *Affairs in the Philippine Islands*, SD 331, 57th Cong., 1st sess., pt. 2. 985.

80. *War Department, 1899*, HD 2, 56th Cong., 1st sess., V, 53-56.

81. Otis to AG, Nov. 27, 1898, Otis to Secretary of War, Dec. 8, 1898, *Correspondence*, II, 840, 851-52.

82. *War Department, 1899*, HD 2, 56th Cong., 1st sess., V, 55.

83. Russell A. Alger to Otis, Dec. 29, 1898, *Correspondence*, II, 863.

84. On the development of the situation at Iloilo, see *War Department, 1899*, HD 2, 56th Cong., 1st sess., V, 55-67.

85. Corbin to Otis, Dec. 4, 1898, *Correspondence*, II, 850.

86. See the Dec. 9, 1898 telegram from London to *The American*, a Manila newspaper, Aguinaldo Collection, Minnesota State Historical Society.

87. The Dec. 24, 1898 instructions from Otis to Miller are in *War Department, 1899,* HD 2, 56th Cong., 1st sess., V, 57-59 and 60-65.

88. LeRoy, *Americans in the Philippines,* I, 378-424.

89. The Dec. 21, 1898 letter of the President is contained in Corbin to Otis, Dec. 21, 1898, *Correspondence,* II, 858-59.

90. Corbin to Otis, Jan. 1, 1899, ibid., 866.

91. Corbin to Otis, Dec. 21, 1898, ibid., 858 and 859.

92. Otis to AG, Oct. 19, Nov. 13, 1898, ibid., 827, 836.

93. Otis to Secretary of War, Dec. 8, 1898, ibid., 851; Otis to AG, Jan. 2, 1899, ibid., 866-67.

94. See testimony of Otis, *Affairs in the Philippine Islands,* SD 331, 57th Cong., 1st sess., pt. 1, 773-75. His version of McKinley's letter is in *War Department, 1899,* HD 2, 56th Cong., 1st sess., V, 68-69. See also 65-67.

95. *War Department, 1899,* HD 2, 56th Cong., 1st sess., V, 76-78; and James A. LeRoy, "Mabini on the Failure of the Filipino Revolution," *American Historical Review* 11 (1906): 845.

96. Otis to AG, Jan. 4 and 8, 1899, *Correspondence,* II, 867-68, 872.

97. McKinley to Otis, Jan. 8, 1899, *Correspondence,* II, 873, Otis to AG, Jan. 10, 1898, ibid., 876.

98. Otis to AG, Jan. 10 and 11, 1899, ibid., 876-77.

99. Taylor, "Compilation," 76-81AJ; Quirino Eleazar to Local Chiefs from Lucban to Guinayangan, Jan. 7, 1899, PIR 1261.6; Aguinaldo to Sandatahan of Manila, Jan. 9, 1899, PIR 206.4; Secretary of Interior to Provincial Chiefs of Tarlac, Pangasinan, Ilocos, and Nueva Ecija, Jan. 11, 1899, PIR 174.4; Mariano Noriel to Aguinaldo, Jan. 14, 1899, PIR 1090.2; Aguinaldo to Ponce, Dec. 7, 1898, PIR 390.1.

100. *Affairs in the Philippine Islands,* SD 331, 57th Cong., 1st sess., pt. 3, 2709-37; Otis to AG, Jan. 12, 1899, *Correspondence,* II, 908-909; *War Department, 1899,* HD 2, 56th Cong., 1st sess., V, 80-83 contain the American reports of the conferences. See also copies of the Jan. 4 and 11, 1899 instructions to the revolutionary commissioners, Taylor, "Compilation," 71-72 KU.

101. War Department, 1899, HD 2, 56th Cong., 1st sess., V, 90; Otis to AG, Jan. 10, 14 and 22, 1899, *Correspondence*, II, 876, 878, 886; Richard Brinsley Sheridan, *The Filipino Martyrs: a Story of the Crime of February 4, 1899* (London, 1900), 139, 152; Aguinaldo, "True Review," 444.

2

PROGRESSIVES IN UNIFORM:
THE MILITARY GOVERNMENT OF MANILA

The American army in the Philippines failed in its role as a diplomatic agent of the McKinley administration, but in its capacity as governor of the city and harbor of Manila it manifestly succeeded. From the moment of occupation in August 1898, the army set about developing an efficient and capable government. This was a job that the members of the force understood.

The work ahead of the army in Manila after the fall of the city was staggering. Filipino troops had surrounded the city since the first of June; by the time of the American occupation the effects of the siege were apparent. Inside the walled city, some 70,000 people were crowded into an area that usually housed about 10,000. Food was scarce, and the revolutionaries had cut off the water supply, leaving the city dependent on its cisterns. The machinery of government that functioned for both the city and the colony was thoroughly disorganized. Government officers had been moved into temporary quarters within the walls, and many important record collections had been lost or thrown into disorder. The Spanish civil officials abandoned most of their offices before the transfer of authority, records, and property to the American army; without exception, they refused to continue in the service of the new government. The higher courts had not been in session since May; and civil court justices had made no effort to protect their court records when they abandoned their posts. The city's schools were closed, and its churches were filled to capacity with the sick and refugees from the suburbs and adjoining provinces. The port was closed, commerce was at a standstill, and the whole of the colony's economy was disrupted. The 13,000 disaffected Spanish prisoners within the city walls and the Filipino army on its outskirts were both potential sources of disorder. Rubbish and garbage, accumulated during the siege, lay strewn about the city. This refuse, the privation of the siege, and the abnormally large population combined to make a public health hazard of immense proportions. The normal daily routine of the archipelago's foremost city had ceased completely. If the army did not respond immediately to the problems facing it, the situation would certainly degenerate into anarchy.[1]

In establishing a government to deal with the problems of Manila, the army had some guidelines for its actions, but the length of time the military government was expected to function was unknown. Except for the decision that occupation of the city was not to be shared with the revolutionaries, the future of the Spanish colony was, as far as the army knew, still undecided. The expeditionary force was operating under the instructions issued by the President on May 19, and the army proceeded to put them into effect in governing the 400,000 residents in its charge.

The instructions that President McKinley had given General Merritt in May were clear on the question of how the army should conduct its government of occupation. It was to insure the security of the inhabitants in their persons and property and to make them understand that the American troops had not come to make war upon the people of the Philippines but to protect them. According to the President's instructions, the occupation was to be as free from severity as possible. Spanish laws were to continue in force so far as practicable, and the administration of justice was to remain in the hands of those officials already delegated that task, providing they were willing to accept the authority of the United States. Public revenues and real property such as telegraph lines, cables, schools, and other public facilities were to be at the disposal of the occupying army, but private property was to be strictly respected.

Taxes and customs duties were to remain in force and to be collected by the forces of occupation. In short, the President
wanted General Merritt to set up as benevolent and liberal a
military government as was possible given the wartime conditions that he expected would prevail. His instructions established a basis for the complete development of military government in the Philippines.[2]

To insure that his own troops understood the President's
instructions, General Merritt issued an order to the American
forces before the attack on Manila in which he outlined the idea
of benevolent government envisioned by the President. The
General told them that they came "not as despoilers and op-
pressors, but simply as the instruments of a strong, free government whose purposes are beneficent." Appealing directly to the
pride of his troops, he stated that he had faith in them "as representatives of a high civilization," and he assured them of his
conviction that they would conduct themselves in their relations with the Filipinos so "as to convince them of the lofty
nature of the mission which you have come to execute." He
ended the instructions to his men with the admonition that, although he did not expect that any acts contrary to the spirit of
his order would be committed, any soldier proving unworthy of
his confidence would be punished "on the spot with the max-
imum penalties known to military law."[3]

Acting in accordance with the President's instructions,
General Merritt issued a public proclamation on August 14 in
which he outlined the policy to be followed in administering the
city. He first spoke of the beneficent purpose of the Americans
and their intention to protect the inhabitants of the Philippines
"in their homes, in their employments, and in their personal
and religious rights."[4] Although the duty of policing the city
was to be in the hands of the Provost-Marshal-General,
municipal laws were to continue in force as long as they proved
compatible with the purposes of the military government. The
General immediately opened the port to the commerce of all
nations, and he gave his assurance that churches, educational
institutions, libraries, and other cultural facilities would be protected. He ended his proclamation by advising the Filipinos
that as long as they cooperated with the army they would not be
disturbed.

President McKinley's instructions to the expeditionary force regarding the establishment of military government in the Philippines and General Merritt's proclamation to the inhabitants of Manila bore a striking resemblance to instructions and proclamations issued much earlier during similar American experiences in Louisiana, Florida, and the territories occupied during the Mexican War. In each case the maintenance of law and order, the respect of local laws and customs, and the benevolent intentions of the United States were stressed. General Merritt or other officers of the expeditionary force undoubtedly were familiar with these previous American attempts at military government.[5] In the Philippines, however, the Americans placed a greater emphasis on the civilizing mission of reconstructing the area under their control in the American image.

The day after his proclamation to the Philippine people General Merritt appointed Brigadier General Arthur MacArthur as Provost-Marshal-General, and MacArthur immediately began the complicated task of restoring order to the city. Shortly after this, MacArthur was promoted to Major General, and Brigadier General R. P. Hughes replaced him in the Provost-Marshal-General's office. A provost guard of three regiments was detailed to serve as a police detachment, and they began patrolling at once to keep order in the city. By the end of August, the army had organized a Superior Provost Court, and by the end of September an inferior branch of the court was set up to deal with minor offenders. The military government's attempt to revive the local courts to try civil cases was a failure. Because Spanish justices refused to serve the American government, all judicial proceedings remained in the hands of the military. Civil cases thus went untried, but the provost courts heard all criminal cases. From the beginning of its work in Manila the Provost-Marshal-General's office operated efficiently to restore order, and both Generals MacArthur and Hughes succeeded in averting what could have been a major crisis in the American government of the city.[6]

The threat of epidemic was as immediate as that of anarchy, and the army instituted a comprehensive public health program to meet it. Provision was made for a Board of Health where both Filipino and American experts worked under the general direction of Major Frank S. Bourns, Chief Surgeon. The city and its environs were divided into ten districts, and within those areas the Board of Health undertook an extensive program that was destined to completely change the face of Manila. Inspectors examined dwellings, markets, slaughterhouses, drug stores, and any other establishments that could possibly affect the health of the community. The board carefully monitored the port against epidemic disease and enforced strict quarantine regulations. It appointed municipal health officials at fixed salaries, and ten local physicians and eight midwives were hired to give free medical care to indigent Filipinos. The Board of Health ran the city leper hospital and arranged with the administrators of the privately operated insane asylum and the charity hospital to admit patients to those institutions. The military government also purchased supplies for hospitals not under direct control of the board.[7]

Smallpox broke out among both the Spanish prisoners and the American troops in November, 1898. The Board of Health vaccinated all of the 13,000 Spanish prisoners in three weeks, while a dozen Filipino vaccinators did the same work among the city's inhabitants. The Board of Health also operated a special smallpox hospital. When vaccines from Japan and Indochina deteriorated in the Manila heat, army medical officers reopened a vaccine farm that had been operated by the Spaniards. The city health officials vaccinated over 80,000 persons, and they succeeded in averting a smallpox epidemic.[8]

Meanwhile venereal disease developed to almost epidemic proportions among the American troops. Prostitutes from throughout the Orient flocked to Manila to ply their trade; many of their houses became the scene of drunkenness and disorderly conduct by American troops. The Provost-Marshal-General and the Board of Health concluded that prostitution could not be ended, but it could be controlled. Doctors inspected known prostitutes weekly and issued certificates of good health to those found free from disease. A regular charge was made for the inspections, and the proceeds were used to support a portion of the hospital of San Lazaro set aside for the treatment of diseased women. Army doctors inspected the troops regularly, and within a few weeks the army had brought venereal disease under control.[9]

Another grave problem facing Major Bourns and his associates was that of supplying the city with potable water. Some 97 percent of the city's inhabitants used water from public hydrants, and it was necessary to restore public water service immediately. The army cleaned the reservoirs into which water was pumped before being distributed to the city but, by necessity, continued to draw the water from the San Mateo River. The Board of Health tried to monitor the water in the city's system to detect any increase in contaminants until the system could be improved, and, fortunately, the water remained free from contamination. Army engineers worked constantly to increase the pressure of the system and eliminate sources of waste.[10]

The Board of Health delegated much of its work to the Department of Sanitation, and the sanitary condition of Manila made that department's task truly monumental. What little sanitation work had been done by the Spaniards had ceased with the siege, and, in addition, the work animals that contractors had used for carrying away refuse had been eaten. The department had to reform the whole sanitation service. The early work of the department was done by city firemen with fire wagons and army quartermaster vehicles. But the sanitation problems created by a foreign culture far overshadowed those caused by the siege. Manila and its inhabitants were, by American standards, just plain unsanitary. The refuse of centuries filled the moat surrounding the city walls and the several open drains that flowed into the *esteros* or tidal inlets edging the city's suburbs and the Pasig River delta. "Horrid beds of ooze and rank swamp vegetation" replaced drains that were improperly designed and inadequately maintained.[11] The sewerage of the city ran into these open drains, accumulated in the dark privy vaults of private dwellings, or, even worse, was deposited in the city streets with the garbage. What was not carried off by rats or other animals was left to the rain and the natural decay that set in so rapidly in the tropics. The Spaniards had hauled some of the refuse out of the city where it was left to rot in the suburbs. According to General Hughes, "had it not been for the daily breezes nobody could have lived in the place at all."[12] The Spaniards had developed excellent laws on municipal sanitation but had not enforced them.[13]

A general cleansing of the city was one of the first projects undertaken by the Board of Health and the Department of Sanitation. The sanitation department increased the number of its workmen from the original 240 to 520. Within the first three weeks of operation the department hired thirty carts and buffalo to augment the existing force of draft animals and vehicles, and it increased the number even more at a later date. Garbage was no longer dumped outside of the city, and the department began instead to haul it to sea in iron dumping scows. Tropical storms and tides frustrated this plan for they drove the refuse back into port and the already filthy *esteros*. Burning proved a better solution, although for a time a lack of funds and facilities forced the army to continue the practice of dumping some garbage at sea. Street refuse and other less offensive waste was used as fill in an attempt to improve the land surrounding the city. The department resorted to the night soil bucket system as a solution to the problem of sewerage disposal, and civilian contractors hauled this refuse off to special dumping grounds well outside of the city.[14]

The American restrictions forced changes in the daily routine of the city's inhabitants. Patrols of the Provost-Marshal's guard were responsible for enforcing the sanitary regulations, and people were fined for such offenses as emptying slops out of windows or allowing refuse to accumulate in front of their residences. The military government required occupants of buildings to clean their sidewalks, and people were to empty their privy vaults at least once a week. The Americans made the people of Manila do those things that they believed were in the interests of the Filipinos' health and well-being. The sanitary measures that the military initiated brought them, according to one observer, "squarely in conflict with the daily life of the great mass of people."[15] The result, however, seemed worth the effort, and in the words of a British traveller in the city, the Americans "worked sanitary marvels" even in a few weeks.[16] General Merritt took pride in reporting that "a stranger to the city might easily imagine that the American forces had been in control for months rather than days."[17]

American efforts to further public education were almost as extensive as those devoted to public health and sanitation.

Most schools, closed during the siege, were in poor condition. Many buildings had been destroyed, and many teachers had stopped holding classes. General Merritt gave the task of reopening the schools to Father W. D. McKinnon, chaplain of the 1st California Volunteers. In accordance with the policy of the military government, most of the courses taught were the same as those given under the Spanish regime. Father McKinnon leased, rented, and repaired school buildings; when he could not obtain a sufficient number of local teachers, he used military personnel as instructors. McKinnon reopened the schools in September, and in a matter of days he had seven in session, with an English instructor, usually a soldier, in each. In keeping with American practice, Father McKinnon deleted courses of religious instruction. Although he was secularizing the education system, he was able to enlist the support of the city's Catholic teaching orders. He allowed them to supervise secondary and higher education and concentrated his own efforts on primary and intermediate instruction. In a short time he increased the schools in operation from 7 to 39 with over 3,700 pupils. The city's inhabitants—Filipino, mestizo, and Spanish—valued education highly, and McKinnon's secularization of education, rather than alienating the parents of most students, increased their support of the American school system. The end of religious education had been one goal of the Philippine revolutionaries.[18]

The military government took a similar interest in the commercial affairs of the city. The increase of trade at the end of the siege presented the American government with a host of problems concerning the regulation of commercial activities and the maintenance of the services that contributed to the city's economic well-being. The blockade and siege had halted inter-island as well as international trade. When it resumed, the army had to administer the customs house and to face the complex problems of tariff rates and ship registry. A revision of the customs and tariff regulations followed, and the new regulations, retaining most of the Spanish rate scale, were placed in effect in November. The American officer in charge of the Internal Revenue Office collected a clerical force consisting of local persons previously employed by the Spaniards, since the latter had refused either to accept employment or to give information on the old methods and regulations. The Americans abolished the *cédula* or head tax and the transportation tax. They retained with slight modifications the stamp taxes, the tax on industrial and commercial operations, and the taxes on rent and property. Their major work was to reform assessments and collections, both of which had been riddled with graft and corruption.[19]

Other work certain to gain friends among the civil population was a widespread program of public works. The Americans repaired street lights and installed new ones; renovated the public water hydrants, fire plugs, and private water systems; and repaired or rebuilt many of the bridges throughout the town. The military government also proposed new bridges and made plans for the development of the city's market and port facilities.[20]

The Provost-Marshal-General had direct jurisdiction over the prisons of Manila, foremost among them the Bilibid jail and the Presidio de Manila (a penitentiary). He at once instituted reforms to alleviate crowded conditions and to rectify the major abuses of the Spanish system of justice. The Americans released some 2,000 unsentenced prisoners for whom there existed no records, no formal charges, or insufficient evidence by American judicial standards to retain them in custody. Soldiers struck heavy irons from the prisoner's limbs and tried to clean up the filth that had accumulated in the cells and corridors. When the American authorities found a $30,000 shortage in the Bilibid prison money chest, they tried and sentenced the Spanish officers responsible for the loss. The Americans ended the practice of allowing prisoners to work outside the prison and draw excess ration money and put them to work manufacturing bamboo cots for the army. A hospital was established within the Presidio to serve it and the adjacent jail.[21]

The American military government even attempted to reform the public morals of Manila's inhabitants. Although the regulation of prostitution and alcoholic beverages was undertaken primarily to protect American soldiers, the army officers in charge of the city regulated other pastimes solely because they deemed them offensive or uncivilized. Cockfighting, the Philippine national passion, was prohibited. Lotteries and gambling houses were closed, and the contracts that the Spaniards had issued for the sale of opium to the city's Chinese inhabitants were discontinued. As might be expected, these attempts on the part of the Americans to remake the Filipino in their own image did not meet with approval.[22]

Under the American military government the city of Manila began to resemble a boom town. With the lifting of the siege and the opening of the port, businessmen, criminals, prostitutes, adventurers, and other assorted camp followers flocked into the city. School construction, public-works projects, and other evidence of the activity of the American government could be seen everywhere. Commerce and trade revived, and for possibly the first time in the city's history the streets were clean. A long-time British resident in the islands had the greatest praise for the Americans and the transformation they had made, writing that "General Otis's able administration wrought a wonderful change in the city. The weary, forlorn look of those who had great interests at stake gradually wore off; business was as brisk as in the old times, and the Custom House was being worked with a promptitude hitherto unknown in the islands."[23]

With the opening of Manila, the entrance of large numbers of Chinese presented General Otis with a problem that demanded his immediate attention. The Chinese had long been a source of friction in the islands. Many Filipinos resented their presence, and local leaders were "decidedly anti-Chinese."[24] General Otis recognized that he had to solve the problems of continued Chinese immigration promptly, and he knew that it would be one means of lessening Filipino resistance to the American presence in Manila. Lacking guidelines from Washington, the General decided on his own to apply United States laws prohibiting the entrance of Chinese immigrants to the Philippines. This action won him support among the city's inhabitants who looked upon the Chinese with enmity and suspicion.[25]

The American army went far beyond the general instructions issued by the President in policing, cleaning, and governing Manila. Not knowing whether their occupation would last a month, a year, or a century, the soldiers had developed a comprehensive program of benevolent government and had placed it in operation promptly, efficiently, and honestly.

The great ability of the army officer corps was one of the reasons for the success in organizing and administering the military government. Although its members represented no special civil affairs branch and often had no specific training for their positions in government, they were well qualified to fill the numerous posts vacated by the Spaniards and to deal with the demanding tasks before them. One foreign observer in the islands remarked that "perhaps no military force is better situated for meeting such a demand than is an army composed of the material which fills the ranks of the American Expeditionary Force." He observed that the force included

> men drawn from every rank of society, lawyers, merchants, postal clerks, tradesmen, office hands of all descriptions, university men; and, indeed, it would be difficult to say what trade or calling is not represented. From amongst these men it was possible to draw fairly proficient officials.[26]

Approximately 75 percent of the American troops were volunteers who were only a few months removed from civilian life.

Both regular and volunteer officers contributed to the army's work in Manila. General Otis was extremely interested in the problems of government and spent long hours personally attending to the task of remaking Manila in the American image. A capable adminstrator, he had graduated from Harvard Law School before embarking on his long military career. The General was particularly concerned with the development of the city's school system, and in this he was fortunate to be aided by Father McKinnon. Although the chaplain had no experience as a school administrator, he was a man of seemingly boundless energy with a talent for enlisting the support of both Spaniards and Filipinos despite his inability to speak Spanish or any local language. Major Bourns, the volunteer officer responsible for efforts in public health, had been in the Philippines twice before for a total of three years on scientific expeditions. He brought with him an intimate knowledge of the islands, fluency in both Spanish and local dialects, and a personal acquaintance with many Spanish and Filipino professional men. His connections helped him obtain the cooperation of Manila physicians in the public health campaign, while his familiarity with the islands and their people was of inestimable value to the American command. Lieutenant Colonel Enoch H. Crowder, a Regular Army officer and lawyer, provided much of General Otis's advice on the judicial problems of the military government. Colonel James F. Smith of the California Volunteers was also a lawyer of great competence to whom General Otis could entrust difficult administrative tasks. These men were just a few of the notable examples among a wide range of officers of greater or lesser ability and dedication.[27]

Many of the officers in the Regular Army had served in the southwestern United States, and they had not only acquired a functional knowledge of Spanish, but also a familiarity with a people who were basically Hispanic in culture. Some, like Major J. Franklin Bell, had travelled extensively in portions of Central or South America. Although the army often seemed isolated from the civilian community around it, the peaceful period of the 1880s and 1890s, lacking in military emergencies, provided a favorable environment for the development of contact between soldiers and civilians. Many officers taught military science in civilian institutions, and some of them undertook the study of law or other professions in their spare time. Colonel Crowder, for example, not only practiced law privately while serving in the army, but also taught in the law school of the University of Missouri while a military science instructor there.[28] These kinds of experiences had prepared many soldiers for the difficult task in Manila.

Because of the importance of the work the army began in Manila and the fact that the army's activities had obviously gone beyond both its instructions from Washington and purely military considerations for the health and well-being of its men, the motives prompting the military to such great efforts demand attention. In many ways the expeditionary force sent to the Philippines was a rather heterogeneous group composed of regulars, militia, and volunteers. Even within a single, seem-

ingly homogeneous group, such as the officer corps of the
Regular Army, many differences could be noted in the experience and training of the members. Some regular officers had
spent almost their entire career in field service at isolated
army posts in the West. Others had served primarily with the
staff bureaus on duty much of the time in Washington. Some of
the more able or intellectually inclined officers had had a
career of varied but rewarding service including advanced
schooling, foreign service in embassies or attachment to foreign
armies, and both staff and line work in Washington and the
West.

In the volunteer and militia units the officer corps
included not only men recruited from the officer ranks of the
Regular Army, but a good cross section of American professional and business personnel as well. The enlisted ranks of
both regulars and volunteers contained a combination of the
dregs of society for whom there was no place in the United
States, soldiers of fortune, adventurous youths, and truly
dedicated individuals who viewed the war with Spain as a war
for humanity and Cuban independence. Yet, out of this diverse
contingent came the energy and the will to undertake the
monumental job of not only governing, but also reforming and
reconstructing Manila.

Little in the strictly military duties of the members of the
Regular Army had prepared them for their role as governors.
The last difficulties that had even resembled those facing them
in the Philippines, the Indian wars, had ended over a decade
before, and for the younger men and officers the only connections with that past were the stories of the older soldiers. The
demands of military government during the Civil War and the
army's role during Reconstruction were part of an even more
distant past. Only the oldest members of the expeditionary
force could have drawn upon previous military experience for
their work of military government in the Philippines. Still, in its
contact with the American Negro and the Indian, the army had
acquired a reputation for fair treatment and efficient administration of peoples far different from those filling its ranks.
Many officers during Reconstruction and the Indian wars had
exhibited the same humanitarian traits and reform impulses in

the 1860s, 1870s, and 1880s as those shown in the Philippines in 1898.[29] These impulses could have been passed from older to younger officers, although there was no evidence that tradition or past military experience motivated the widespread reforms undertaken by the military government.

The great similarity between many American army officers in the Philippines and reformers at work in the United States at the same time seems to provide the key to understanding the motives of the American in Manila. At home, reformers were striving for changes that would alleviate the ills of society and afford greater economic, political, and social justice to a larger segment of the American people. These were, in the main, the goals of the men in control of Manila. The only major difference seemed to be that while one group was working for the betterment of the United States, the other was concerned with the Philippines. The army's work to promote public health, judicial reform, tax equalization, honest government, and public education often mirrored work done in these same areas by progressive reformers in America.[30]

Aside from the distinct similarity in their actions, reformers in the United States and army officers in the Philippines were similar in a number of other ways. Although good quantitative profiles of both groups are not available, the research that has been done shows a marked resemblance between urban reformers in America and the officer corps of the army in 1898. A majority of both groups had Anglo-Saxon family backgrounds and upper middle-class origins. When compared with the rest of the nation, they were well above average in their level of educational attainment. Also, most of them claimed a Protestant religious affiliation.[31] Although the exact significance of these shared characteristics is yet to be determined, the fact that they were shard by these two groups is obviously of more than passing interest. Unfortunately, much more research must be done on the fascinating question of the relationship between group characteristics and motivation before we can properly assess the importance of the relationships evident here.

Domestic reformers and army officers held a number of ideas and attitudes in common which seemed to nurture their interest in reform activity. Both groups placed considerable emphasis on what they sometimes referred to as "character," that nebulous term that included such tangible elements as truthfulness, honesty, attention to duty, self-discipline, strength of will, and the acceptance of individual moral responsibility for one's actions. The maintenance of personal honor and integrity was also important. Of perhaps greatest significance, both groups had a keen sense of fair play and a geniune concern for their fellow men.

Officers and reformers alike had an intense faith in America's democratic mission, and, with few exceptions, they were not opposed to American imperialism. Instead, they believed that their nation had a duty to uplift the world's "retarded" peoples and bring them the joys of law, order, and "civilization." Although they often assumed an attitude of Anglo-Saxon superiority mixed with true benevolence, they exhibited a strong desire to assist the dispossessed. The actions of Americans in the Philippines clearly portrayed this faith in the moral and intellectual superiority of the Caucasian and, at the same time, the willingness of officers to assume the role of stewards for what many of them considered "the lesser breeds." Members of the army, like the reformers at home, had a great faith in man's ability to change other men and the environment in which they lived. They believed that progress was both desirable and possible. The ideas of reform popular in late nineteenth-century America were as evident among army officers in the Philippines as among other select groups in the United States.

In their willingness to use the power of government to effect change, army officers proved to be more radical than most of their domestic counterparts. Although they were firmly committed to the concept of democratic government, they were often impatient with the whimsical nature of local control. To them the proper utilization of the great power of the central government was a much more efficient method for the regeneration of society. As a consequence, the army's work in the Philippines aimed at the development of a centralized bureaucracy with broad powers in such areas as public education and public health. The Corps of Engineers undertook public-works projects directly rather than assigning them to an agent of the private sector of the economy as was the common practice of American municipalities at the time. The extent to which the military government was willing to use its power to change the daily habits of the Filipinos under its protection represented an attitude toward the role of government in social change that was greatly advanced from that held by all but the most radical reformers in the United States. To interpret the army's action solely as the result of military discipline and authoritarianism would be a grave error. The emphasis was always on reform rather than control.[32]

Herbert Croly, a well-known theorist of American reform, wrote in 1910 that the Spanish-American War gave "a tremendous impulse to the work of national reform."[33] He could easily have included the international aspects of such work evident in the Philippines. The reform spirit was as much imbued in the army as in any other body in America. Army officers acted like reformers, shared many common characteristics with them, and held many of the same ideas. This, probably more than any other single factor, accounted for the work done in Manila. Contrary to the stereotype often drawn of them, army officers were neither reactionary nor out of the mainstream of American thought. They were, in fact, a leading force for reform in many of the same areas as the progressives in America. At the turn of the century the United States was beginning an era of reform, and this spirit was transmitted to the Philippine islands by the members of the American expeditionary force.

The success of the military in Manila, however, could not hope to compensate entirely for its diplomatic failure in dealing with the Filipino revolutionaries. As other colonial powers were beginning to observe in their holdings, a policy based on the assumption that the local population was not fit to rule itself was incompatible with the desires of a self-assertive, partially Westernized elite and middle class.[34] The revolutionaries in the Philippines had led the people to expect independence, and they had received a new colonial master instead. The thoughtless actions of some American soldiers had given credence to Spanish and Filipino propaganda claims that the Americans were barbarians seeking to enslave the Filipinos, and the statements of the opponents of imperialism in the United States encouraged the Filipinos in their resistance to American demands. Even American reform efforts had been misunderstood, and many Filipinos looked upon changes such as those in sanitary regulations as an unwarranted interference with their daily lives. The population of Manila met with decided opposition acts such as those designed to supervise the public markets, and the evasion of many public health codes was common.[35] It would take time to overcome such resistance and to convince the Fillipinos that the American government would be truly benevolent. The military government of Manila, no matter how beneficent, efficient, or progressive, could not effect a change overnight. What was needed was time, but time was the one resource not available as January 1899 drew to a close.

The work done in Manila did prepare the army for the job that would face it in the months to come. The efforts of the military government made Manila a firm base for the extension of American control to the remaining area of the archipelago. The Americans restored the city as a port and set up the administrative facilities of a complete colonial government. In spite of the poor conduct of some American troops and the inevitable friction caused by attempts to impose American standards on a people of a different culture, the actions of the military government did exhibit the benevolence, efficiency, and honesty necessary to gain the confidence of the Filipinos and their acceptance of American sovereignty. The first efforts of the military government in Manila thus included some of the most important steps in the slow development of the American Philippine policy and in the army's role as the advance agent of American culture and government.

NOTES

1. John R. M. Taylor, "Compilation," 14-16AJ; F. V. Greene, "Memoranda Concerning the Situation in the Philippines on August 30, 1898," *A Treaty of Peace, Between the United States and Spain*, SD 62, 55th Cong., 3d sess., 418-19; Otis to AG, Sept. 16, 1898, *Correspondence Relating to the War with Spain, April 15, 1898-July 30, 1902*, II, 791.

2. McKinley to Merritt, May 19, 1898, *Correspondence*, II, 676-78.

3. General Orders No. 3, Aug. 9, 1898, Headquarters Department of the Pacific and 8th Army Corps, *General Orders and Circulars, Philippine Islands Expeditionary Forces, 1898*.

4. *Annual Reports of the War Department for the Fiscal Year Ended June 30, 1898*, HD 2, 55th Cong., 3d sess., 49-50.

5. One could assume, for example, that many American officers in the islands had read works like William E. Birkhimer, *Military Government and Martial Law* (Washington, 1892). For a good summary of American military government in territories acquired prior to the Civil War see David Yancey Thomas, *A History of Military Government in Newly Acquired Territory of the United States* (New York, 1904), 25, 66, 101-102, 161, 193-94.

6. *Annual Reports of the War Department for the Fiscal Year Ended June 30, 1899*, HD 2, 56th Cong., 1st sess., V, 257-59;

U.S., Congress, House, *Annual Reports of the War Department for the Fiscal Year Ended June 30, 1901,* HD 2, 57th Cong., 1st sess., 1901, VIII, 77-79.

7. *War Department, 1899,* HD 2, 56th Cong., 1st sess., V, 260-61. *War Department, 1901,* HD 2, 57th Cong., 1st sess., VIII, 247-49 has a set of ordinances published at a later date showing the type of regulations eventually developed by the board. See also testimony of Hughes in *Affairs in the Philippine Islands,* SD 331, 57th Cong., 1st sess., pt. 1, 513-15.

8. *War Department, 1899,* HD 2, 56th Cong., 1st sess., V, 260-61; testimony of Hughes in *Affairs in the Philippine Islands,* SD 331, 57th Cong., 1st sess., pt. 1, 520-21.

9. *War Department, 1899,* HD 2, 56th Cong., 1st sess., III, 453-61; *War Department, 1901,* HD 2, 57th Cong., 1st sess., VIII, 183-84; testimony of Hughes in SD 331, 57th Cong., 1st sess., pt. 1, 514.

10. *War Department, 1899,* HD 2, 56th Cong., 1st sess., V, 266-67; *War Department, 1901,* HD 2, 57th Cong., 1st sess., VIII, 91, 96, 179-80, 206-15.

11. *War Department, 1901,* HD 2, 57th Cong., 1st sess., VIII, 90.

12. *Affairs in the Philippine Islands,* SD 331, 57th Cong., 1st sess., pt. 1, 512.

13. U.S., Congress, House, *Annual Reports of the War Department for the Fiscal Year Ended June 30, 1900,* HD 2, 56th Cong., 2d sess., 1900, III, 609. See also *War Department, 1899,* HD 2, 56th Cong., 1st sess., V, 262-64; *War Department, 1901,* HD 2, 57th Cong., 1st sess., VIII, 90-94.

14. *War Department, 1899,* HD 2, 56th Cong., 1st sess., V, 262-64; *War Department, 1901,* HD 2, 57th Cong., 1st sess., VIII, 93, 174, 240-43.

15. Karl Irving Faust, *Campaigning in the Philippines* (San Francisco, 1899), 111.

16. G. J. Younghusband, *The Philippines and Round About* (New York, 1899), 53.

17. *War Department, 1898,* HD 2, 55th Cong., 3d sess., 45.

18. *War Department, 1899,* HD 2, 56th Cong., 1st sess., V, 271-72; *War Department, 1901,* HD 2, 57th Cong., 1st sess., VIII, 98; V. Edmund McDevitt, *The First California's Chaplain* (Fresno, 1956), 100-102; Manuel G. Lacuesta, "Foundations of an American Educational System in the Philippines," *Philippine Social Sci-*

ences and Humanities Review 23 (1958): 129, 132; Cesar Adib Majul, "Political and Constitutional Ideas of the Philippine Revolution," *Philippine Social Sciences and Humanities Review* 21 (1956): 109-112.

19. On customs see *War Department, 1899,* HD 2, 56th Cong., 1st sess., V, 313-33. On taxes see V, 297-302. See also V, 12-15, 45-49.

20. Ibid., 264-69.

21. Ibid., 12-13, 272-73; testimony of Hughes in *Affairs in the Philippine Islands,* SD 331, 57th Cong., 1st sess., pt. 1, 516-19.

22. Younghusband, *Philippines,* 55-56; Otis to AG, Sept. 16, 1898, *Correspondence,* II, 791.

23. John Foreman, *The Philippine Islands,* 627. See also *War Department, 1899,* HD 2, 56th Cong., 1st sess., V, 15.

24. Thomas S. Fonacier, "The Chinese Exclusion Policy in the Philippines," *Philippine Social Sciences and Humanities Review* 14 (1949): 12n.

25. Ibid., 7-9; *War Department, 1899,* HD 2, 56th Cong., 1st sess., V, 15, 31-36. The best work on the Chinese in the Philippines is Edgar Wickberg, *The Chinese in Philippine Life. 1850-1898.*

26. Younghusband, *Philippines,* 52.

27. For further material on these American officers see for Otis, *DAB,* 14, 94-95; for McKinnon, V. Edmund McDevitt, *The First California's Chaplain*; for Bourns, U.S., Congress, Senate, *Report of the Philippine Commission to The President, January 31, 1900,* SD 138, 56th Cong., 1st sess., 1900, I, 347-68; for Crowder, David A. Lockmiller, *Enoch H Crowder: Soldier, Lawyer, and Statesman* (Columbia, 1955), 70-78 in particular; for Smith, *War Department, 1899,* HD 2, 56th Cong., 1st sess., 123-24, 128, and *DAB,* 17, 287-88. Other extremely capable officers included Henry W. Lawton, Dean C. Worcester, "General Lawton's Work in the Philippines," *McClure's Magazine* 15 (1900): 19-30; Arthur MacArthur, *DAB,* 21, 521-22; and J. Franklin Bell, *DAB,* 21, 67-68.

28. Ibid.

29. For examples of army humanitarianism in the Indian wars see George Crook, "The Apache Problem," *Journal of the Military Service Institution of the United States* 7 (1886): 257-69; Richard Henry Pratt, *Battlefield and Classroom: Four Decades with the American Indian, 1867-1904* (New Haven, 1964). See also Gil-

bert C. Fite, "The United States Army and Relief to Pioneer Set-
tlers, 1874-1875," *Journal of the West* 6 (1967): 99-107, and James
T. King, "George Crook, Indian Fighter and Humanitarian,"
Arizona and the West 10 (1968): 333-48. On the Army during
Reconstruction see John and LaWanda Cox, "General O. O.
Howard and the Misrepresented Bureau," *Journal of Southern
History* 19 (1953): 427-56, and James E. Sefton, *The United States
Army and Reconstruction, 1865-1877* (Baton Rouge, 1967).

30. For a good short summary of the work being done by
reformers in the United States, see George E. Mowry, *The Era
of Theodore Roosevelt and the Birth of Modern America, 1900-1912*
(New York, 1958), 59-84.

31. This profile of the officer corps stems from the work
of Richard C. Brown, "Social Attitudes of American Generals,
1898-1940" (Ph.D. diss., University of Wisconsin, 1951), 3-40.
See also Samuel P. Huntington, *The Soldier and the State* (Cambridge, Mass., 1964), 227, 266-67. For the similarity to reformers in the United States see George E. Mowry, *Era of Theodore
Roosevelt and the Birth of Modern America, 1900-1912*, chap. 5, and
Allen F. Davis, *Spearheads for Reform: The Social Settlements and
the Progressive Movement, 1890-1914* (New York, 1967), chap. 2.

32. Compare the ideas evident in Otis' Aug. 31, 1898 report
in *War Department, 1899*, HD 2, 56th Cong., 1st sess., V, *passim*;
testimony and depositions of American army officers presented
to the peace commissioners in Paris in *A Treaty of Peace* SD 62,
55th Cong., 3d sess., 362-86; "The Mission of the Army," *The
United States Army and Navy Journal* 36 (July 15, 1899): 1097;
"Army as an Instrument of Reform," *The United States Army and
Navy Journal* 37 (Aug. 18, 1900): 1208; the constitution prepared
by the military government for the island of Negros in HD 2,
56th Cong., 1st sess., V, 124-27; and recent studies of the military by Brown, "Social Attitudes," 40, 84-124, 374-76, 391-404;
Morris Janowitz, *The Professional Soldier* (Glencoe, 1960), 104-
224; Huntington, *Soldier and State*, 266-68; and Allan R. Millett,
*The Politics of Intervention: The Military Occupation of Cuba, 1906-
1909* (Columbus, 1968), 124-25, 133, 192-93, 262-63 with the
profiles of American reformers and reform ideas found in such
works as Ralph Henry Gabriel, *The Course of American Democratic
Thought: An Intellectual History since 1815* (New York, 1940),
chaps. 17-25; Mowry, *Era of T.R.*, chap. 5; Eric F. Goldman,
Rendezvous with Destiny (rev. & abridged ed., New York, 1956),

chap. 5-10; Richard Hofstadter, *The Age of Reform: From Bryan to F.D.R.* (New York, 1955), 82-85; Robert H. Wiebe, *The Search for Order, 1877-1920* (New York, 1967), chap. 5-7; William E. Leuchtenburg, "Progressivism and Imperialism: The Progresive Movement and American Foreign Policy, 1898-1917," *Mississippi Valley Historical Review* 39 (1952): 500; Daniel Levine, "The Social Philosophy of Albert J. Beveridge," *Indiana Magazine of History* 58 (1962): 101-16; and Arthur S. Link, "The Progressive Movement in the South, 1870-1914," *North Carolina Historical Review* 23 (1946): 172-95. For civilian acceptance of that supposedly military virtue of efficiency see Samuel Haber, *Efficiency and Uplift: Scientific Management in the Progressive Era, 1890-1920* (Chicago, 1964) and Samuel P. Hays, *Conservation and the Gospel of Efficiency: The Progressive Conservation Movement, 1890-1920* (Cambridge, Mass., 1959).

33. Herbert Croly, *The Promise of American Life* (New York, 1910), 169.

34. An excellent example of this phenomena in an existing colony was in India. See Percival Spear (ed.), *The Oxford History of India* (3d ed., Oxford, 1964), Book IX, chap. 1, 681; Book X, chap. 2, *passim*.

35. Younghusband, *Philippines*, 55-56; *War Department, 1899*, HD 2, 56th Cong., 1st sess., V, 260-62, 268-69.

3

OPTIMISM AND THE ILLUSION OF VICTORY

On the evening of February 4 1899, Private William Grayson of D Company, 1st Nebraska Volunteers, fired at a small group of Filipino soldiers who failed to heed his challenge and were approaching the American defenses. Within a few minutes, firing was coming from both the American and Filipino lines. War had begun.

The friction between the American and Filipino troops had increased in the first days of February. On February 2, revolutionaries commanded by Colonel L. F. San Miguel had moved across the boundary between themselves and the Americans and had occupied a small barrio or hamlet, immediately in front of the American outposts. When General MacArthur protested, the Filipinos withdrew,[1] and he occupied the area with troops of the Nebraska regiment. It was this group that fired at the Filipino soldiers approaching their position on the night of February 4. They had been ordered that no armed revolutionaries were to enter the barrio or its vicinity. If such trespassers could not be arrested or driven back, General MacArthur had given his troops authority to fire.[2]

The Filipinos had not planned to inaugurate an attack on February 4. It was a Saturday, and many officers were absent from their units to be with their families on Sunday. Some were in Manila when the fighting began, and the Filipino troops surrounding the city did not act in concert when the hostilities continued throughout the night. An uprising inside Manila, in preparation by the revolutionaries since January, did not materialize, and the militia in the city probably had no idea that hostilities would commence when they did. Aguinaldo, upon hearing that war had begun, ordered an investigation to determine the cause of the fighting. General Otis also realized that the fight had not been started intentionally.[3]

Military diplomacy and the bid to achieve a recognition of American sovereignty in the Philippines by peaceful means had failed, and General Otis thought that the only course of action remaining was to prosecute the war that had begun so unexpectedly. The army's contingency plans for a Filipino attack contemplated immediate offensive operations, and the plans were put into effect on February 5. Aided by gunfire from the ships of Dewey's squadron in the bay and gunboats on the Pasig River, American troops secured the city water works, and generally extended the American lines around Manila.[4] The Filipinos, although entrenched, could not withstand the American offensive. General Otis estimated that in the first two days of battle his men had killed over 500 Filipino soldiers and captured about the same number. American casualties, although much lighter, were heavy enough to give the General pause in any plans he might have had for a large-scale offensive. In four days the Americans had suffered 59 killed and more than 200 wounded, over 1 percent of their entire force.[5]

When hostilities began, the army was still the only representative of the American government in the islands. The commissioners appointed by the President had not yet arrived. Although the Senate had ratified the treaty with Spain on February 6, Congress had made no provision for the administration of the territory. The work of securing and governing the archipelago was wholly in the hands of the military. The army had been unable to solve the problem of obtaining the Philippines without violence, and it was faced with the new problem of establishing American sovereignty there through military action.

The objective of war according to the master theorist on the subject, Carl von Clausewitz, is to impose one's will on the enemy. The American force in the Philippines, however, was involved in a colonial war, and the problem facing it implied a different kind of objective. General Otis and his men were required not only to defeat the revolutionaries in the most decisive manner, but, at the same time, to guarantee permanent pacification. They would have to organize the territory gained for the development of a colonial government, avoid destruction as much as possible, and create conditions favoring the maintenance of peace in the future. It was not enough to convince the Filipinos that the Americans were going to stay and could not be defeated militarily. The army had to make them want United States rule, or at least tolerate it peacefully. President McKinley's policy of "benevolent assimilation" placed a further burden on the army. The President not only expected the army to set up the basis for a beneficent colonial government, but also to serve as a transmitter of American civilization, culture, and values.[6]

General Otis acted very cautiously in February. His lines were greatly extended, and he was short of troops. When hostilities began, he had about 5,000 regulars and 15,000 volunteers, but when ratification of the Treaty of Paris ended the war with Spain, the volunteers became eligible for discharge. Also the size of the Regular Army was to be reduced. Of Otis's total force of over 20,000 only some 3,500 men were not eligible for discharge under provisions of the wartime legislation. Of the troops in Manila, 3,000 were needed as a provost guard in the city; leaving some 11,000 for combat duty in the fortifications on its outskirts. Almost all of these men were to be returned to the United States as soon as possible.[7]

Approximately 30,000 Filipino soldiers, about half of them armed with some type of rifle, surrounded the city. Their numbers were being augmented by reinforcements arriving from the surrounding countryside. Lacking artillery, ammunition, and firearms, however, they were unable to take Manila by a frontal assault, although an attack coordinated with a popular uprising inside the city would have presented the Americans with a serious problem. Behind the Filipino force around Manila stood a large but unknown number of troops and militia spread throughout the other portions of the archipelago. These men had somewhere between 10,000 and 20,000 more rifles, most of them also on Luzon.[8] Though not a formidable force by American standards, the revolutionary army was of sufficient size to prevent General Otis from undertaking any great offensive movements until he was reinforced.

General Otis did not want to become overextended, and his army was certainly too small to undertake a conquest of the Philippines. He concentrated on operations to make his Manila base more secure and to establish as good a foothold as was possible with the limited number of troops at his disposal. He refused to release the volunteers to return to the United States. Most of the men eligible for discharge, including the volunteer units, consented to remain on duty in the islands until a sufficient force could be raised in the United States to relieve them. Using the troops on hand, the General proceeded to extend the American lines around Manila and improve his defensive position. On February 22, the army quelled an uprising in the city, and offensive thrusts during March, April, and May kept the revolutionaries off balance and prevented their unhindered buildup of fortifications and troops in the surrounding countryside.

Shortly after the war began, other American units had secured footholds on islands south of Luzon. General Miller's command, kept on board ships off Iloilo since December, landed and took the city. The navy took the city of Cebu on the island of the same name, and by the end of February a battalion of the 23rd Infantry occupied it. On the island of Negros, some of the wealthier Filipinos took it upon themselves to raise the American flag and send emissaries to General Miller requesting his protection. They were forwarded to General Otis, who dispatched a battalion of the California Volunteers to the city of Bacolod. The island was placed under the command of Colonel James F. Smith. By the end of May, American forces also occupied the city of Jolo in the Sulu Archipelago, and relieved the Spanish garrison there. In all cases the Americans occupied purely defensive positions, and only the key ports were in their hands. The revolutionaries, for their part, proceeded to organize the interior regions of the occupied islands, and the American units in the Visayas found themselves in a situation similar to that of General Otis in

Manila, lacking troops and surrounded. A blockade by the navy did succeed in keeping the revolutionary forces from increasing their arms supplies.[9]

Throughout these early months of 1899 the Americans continued to believe that benevolent action could overcome the resistance of the Filipinos. General Otis and many of his subordinates subscribed to the theory that the group opposed to United States sovereignty was a minority consisting only of Tagalogs, the primary ethnic group in the Manila area. The General reported to Washington in March that the revolution was only a Luzon affair. This idea that only a single faction was organized against the Americans persisted for many months. Assuming their assessment to be correct, the Americans tried to win the support of the Filipino leadership elements and sought to bring about the collapse of the revolution with a minimum of fighting. This seemed not only the most sensible course of action to follow in seeking to establish a lasting peace and settled basis for a colonial government, but also the only one possible because of the shortage of troops.[10]

The civilian commissioners appointed by President McKinley arrived in the Philippines at the end of March. The chairman, Jacob G. Schurman, president of Cornell University, was accompanied by Charles Denby, former American minister to China, and Dean C. Worcester, a professor of zoology from the University of Michigan who had some knowledge of the Philippines gained through scientific expeditions there. Admiral Dewey and General Otis were the other members of the five-man commission. The President's instructions to the group, issued on January 20 before the beginning of the war, stated that they were "to facilitate the most humane, pacific, and effective extension of authority throughout these islands, and to secure, with the least possible delay, the benefits of a wise and generous protection of life and property to the inhabitants."[11] The commissioners arrived too late to prevent hostilities, if indeed anything could have accomplished that feat, but they were of great help in the attempt to gain Filipino support for the Americans.[12]

The commission sought to convince the Filipinos of the benevolent intentions of the Americans, and to this end the commissioners published a proclamation on April 4, 1899, that reiterated the ideas developed by President McKinley regarding future American policy in the Philippines. The proclamation spoke of the intention of the Americans to "promote the best interests of the inhabitants" and their desire to enhance the "well-being, the prosperity, and the happiness of the Philippine people." The pronouncement included a list of eleven "regulative principles" that the commission said would guide the United States in its relations with the Filipinos. The commission pledged (1) to enforce United States supremacy; (2) to grant "the most ample liberty of self-government . . . reconcilable with the maintenance of a wise, just, stable, effective, and economical administration of public affairs"; (3) to guarantee the civil rights of the inhabitants, including religious freedom and equal standing before the law; (4) to forbid exploitation of the Filipinos, and, instead, to provide for their welfare and advancement; (5) to give the islands "an honest and effective civil service" in which natives would be employed; (6) to insure sound, honest, and economical collection and distribution of tax revenue with local funds used for local purposes; (7) to establish "a pure, speedy, and effective administration of justice"; (8) to construct an island network of transportation and communication; (9) to conduct the economic life of the islands in the interests of the inhabitants; (10) to provide educational facilities for the people; and (11) to institute "reforms in all departments of the government . . . without delay." The commission set forth the fullest statement of American purposes in the Philippines to that date, and the proclamation did not go unheeded.[13]

The revolutionaries reacted immediately to the commission's proclamation. In Manila, copies were thrown into the sewers or mutilated as soon as they had been posted. Elsewhere, the revolutionaries took great pains to insure that the populace did not hear about the liberal framework for the insular government that the commission had outlined. The revolutionaries could not, however, prevent the news about the intentions of the Americans from spreading.[14]

Despite the efforts of Aguinaldo's men, the members of the commission were convinced that the proclamation had good effect. In Manila, the proclamation brought the commissioners into closer contact with Filipinos of wealth and education who valued order and stability above independence. This conservative group was encouraged by the American announcement, and they seemed to prefer good colonial government to that of Aguinaldo. These Filipinos, after frequent consultations with the members of the commission, wrote letters to their friends among the revolutionaries urging them to submit and apprising them of the hopelessness of resisting. They willingly gave advice to the Americans as to how best to deal with their recalcitrant countrymen. Many of the educated and highly respected Filipinos who were collaborating with the Americans had been members of the largely appointive Filipino Congress, and their swing to the Americans represented a serious division in the ranks of the revolutionaries.[15]

While the commission was at work, the army was not idle. In its administration of Manila and the development of the insular military government, the officers of the army made a real effort to show the Filipinos what American rule might be like. In 1898, however, the Americans had been motivated by humanitarian instincts and a reform impulse divorced from the necessities of a military campaign. In Manila, their actions had been those of an army at peace. After February 4, 1899, this was no longer the case, and the benevolent actions and humanitarian work begun in Manila took on a military significance. Such efforts became an explicit part of the army's campaign to pacify the islands.

One Filipino drawn to the Americans by the April 4 proclamation had advised them that the only way to deal with Filipinos was "with a rattan in one hand and a lump of sugar in the other."[16] Many members of the army already understood this concept, and they recognized the value of benevolence as a technique of pacification. General Otis knew that the conduct of the American troops toward the Philippine people was important. He was convinced that kind treatment and continued efforts in such fields as school development and governmental reform could help win support for the American presence in the islands. He personally encouraged his subordinates to act in accordance with President McKinley's policy of benevolence, and he was instrumental in involving the army in educational work.

The actions and orders of many other officers showed that

they too were in sympathy with the ideas expressed by President McKinley, the commission, and General Otis. Major General Henry W. Lawton reportedly remarked to a subordinate that to pacify the Philippines "we should impress the inhabitants with the idea of our good intentions and destroy the idea that we are barbarians or anything of that sort."[17] Lawton thought that if the army acted in a kind manner toward the Filipinos they would soon realize that the American government was there to operate in their own interests. General MacArthur explained the "beneficent" purpose of the United States in the islands to his troops, and in his field orders he impressed upon them that it was "one of the most important duties of American soldiers to assist in establishing friendly relations with the natives by kind and considerate treatment in all matters arising from personal contact." To act otherwise, in his eyes, would only tend "to impede the policy of the United States and to defeat the very purpose which the army is here to accomplish."[18] Orders issued by commanders of units in the field in the first half of 1899 showed that many officers recognized the important connection between their mission of pacifying the islands and the way in which American fighting men treated the inhabitants.[19] Enlisted men who violated these orders were punished swiftly, and in 1899 at least sixty-seven soldiers were punished by courts martial or military commissions for crimes against Filipinos. Officers made great efforts to insure that enemy propaganda about the barbarous nature of the American troops would have no basis in fact.[20]

Although enunciated by some military writers after the Civil War, the concepts of total war implied by William T. Sherman's March to the Sea had not been assimilated into the mainstream of American military thought.[21] The officers in the Philippines still saw a place for humanity in war. Captain John Bigelow, Jr., whose study of the battle of Chancellorsville would later earn him a national reputation, had developed the theoretical basis for a benevolent pacification campaign in his *Principles of Strategy*. Bigelow noted the advantages in war of a policy directed toward detaching the belligerent population from its allegiance to the enemy and organizing it to one's own ends. He observed that "even a government imposed upon a hostile people for the purpose merely of controlling it during the course of operations should be made as acceptable to it as possible. . . . [and that] the maintenance of a military despotism in the rear of an invading army must generally prove a waste of power."[22]

Major General John M. Schofield had been a powerful force for moderation in war during and after his tenure as Commanding General of the Army from 1888 to 1894. Although Schofield had been one of Sherman's trusted subordinates during the Civil War, his ideas on the need for severity in warfare differed markedly from those of Sherman. Schofield was critical of Sherman's march through Georgia and the Carolinas, and he favored, instead, the limitation of war whenever possible. He noted that just as wars differ in their objectives, the means of fighting them could and should also differ.[23]

The army's past experience, the makeup of its officer corps, and instructions emanating from both the United States and headquarters in the Philippines helped form the basis for the humanitarian campaign of 1899. In the Indian wars some officers had recognized that fair treatment and benevolence were as much a solution to the Indian problem as was the brutal dictum that the only good Indian was a dead one. Added to this experience were the humanitarian qualities and reform impulses exhibited by the army's leaders in the administration, not only of Manila, but of all of the territory falling within the army's jurisdiction as a result of the Spanish-American War.[24] Officers with experience in civil government naturally thought in terms of a campaign of pacification designed to win over the alienated population through acts of kindness rather than brutality. The repressive measures used by Spain in Cuba had, after all, led to American intervention there in 1898, and similar actions by Americans in 1899 would have been neither in keeping with the spirit generated by the war nor acceptable to the American people and government. The President's instructions on the policy to be followed in the Philippines were clear, and a number of ranking officers there, including Generals Otis, Lawton, and MacArthur, were completely in sympathy with them.

The army's desire to bring a quick end to the war and at

the same time follow a benevolent course of action toward the Filipinos was closely connected to the development and extension of military government in the Philippines. The work begun in Manila in such fields as public health and school organization was of a type that not only promoted the well-being of the inhabitants, but also showed them the benevolent character of the American government. As a result, the experience gained in the adminstration of Manila gave many officers an insight into how to deal with similar problems of military government that presented themselves when, with the outbreak of hostilities, the Americans extended the area under their control. They had already faced the problems of the adminstration of justice, public education, municipal affairs, internal revenue, sanitation, and commerce, and evolved methods for dealing with such problems. In 1899 however, the army's work in the development of a government for the Philippines was in its formative stages. Most of the efforts visible in the first months of the year were done, most often, on an ad hoc basis to alleviate some specific need. [25] These efforts were also restricted to an extremely limited area, for in the early months of 1899 the Americans only held a perimeter around Manila, portions of the islands of Negros, and a few port cities, such as Iloilo and Cebu on islands south of Luzon.

One of the first problems the Americans had to face in the territory they held was that of maintaining law and order, with the concurrent problem of dispensing justice. Trying always to work within the existing framework of the Spanish laws and institutions already familiar to the Filipinos, the army sought to reestablish the normal routine of justice that had broken down when the Spaniards left the islands. After conferring with prominent Filipino lawyers in Manila, General Otis reconstituted the Spanish Audiencia as an insular supreme court. Cayetano Arellano—a mestizo who, until January 1899, was a member of Aguinaldo's government—was influential in this work. In June the military government reestablished the courts of the city and province of Manila and gave them both civil and criminal jurisdiction. Because civil cases had not been heard since the American occupation began, the provost courts in Iloilo and Cebu were given temporary civil jurisdiction and instructed to try cases in accordance with existing Spanish legal principles. In Negros, Colonel Smith developed a court system, and elsewhere in American-occupied territory military courts tried civilian cases. In all of this work American commanders recognized the connection between dispensing impartial justice and the campaign underway to pacify the islands.[26]

When the army moved out from Manila, officers found sanitary conditions in the towns and villages "execrable," and they began an immediate cleanup campaign similar to that in Manila. Army doctors examined Filipinos for communicable diseases, and they introduced quarantine procedures to prevent their spread. Vaccination of the local population was a continuing process, and surgeons used army medical supplies for treatment, although such action was prohibited by regulations. In areas where crops and supplies had either been destroyed by the ravages of war or confiscated by the retreating revolutionaries, the Americans distributed food to the villagers. In addition, the army regularly gave food to lepers, hospital patients, and destitute Filipinos. Filipino prisoners of war received the same care as American soldiers, and this also helped the army develop an image as a benevolent force seeking to aid rather than harm the Filipinos. The charitable work undertaken in the early months of 1899, although not systematized, was extensive and a vivid example of American humanitarianism.[27]

School building and development was probably the one action of the army that was most appreciated by the Filipinos. General MacArthur observed that the establishment of schools "was one of their first-expressed wishes," and the soldiers responded "instantly" to that desire.[28] There was considerable agreement between the aims expressed by both the Filipinos and the Americans on the question of education; and, although there was a regular systematized program of instruction only in Manila, Filipinos everywhere received the schools developed by the army with enthusiasm.

The army recognized from the very beginning that the school work could be an important factor in the pacification campaign. General Otis encouraged his subordinates to open as many schools as possible, and he took a personal interest in the selection and ordering of texts. Education became a primary interest of the army, and commanders detailed officers and enlisted men as superintendents and teachers. In many cases a school was the first thing established by the army in a town, even preceding the rudiments of municipal government. Soldiers were always available for teaching assignments, and, though lacking equipment and books, they improvised sufficiently to begin classes, including instructions in English. Ponchos served as blackboards, lumps of starch as chalk, and tin can labels as teaching aids.[29] The soldiers involved in this work and the officers in charge took pride in what they were doing. General MacArthur noted that it was "one of the easy and pleasant subjects of administration." An enlisted man, regarding his assignment as a teacher, said: "I enjoyed it more than anything else; in fact, those are the best six months of my life."[30]

Because the Filipinos wanted it and the Americans entered into it so willingly and enthusiastically, the army's school work generated a great deal of goodwill between the military and the Filipinos who came in contact with each other in the municipalities. This action on the part of the soldiers, taken in the midst of war, helped to soften the bitterness that normally accompanied such a conflict and also laid the foundations for the more systematic work that followed at a later date. In December 1899 Phelps Whitmarsh, an American journalist in the islands who was not noted for his favorable commentaries on the army, summed up the importance of the school work.

> At no very distant date, I hope, when the suspicious nature of these people is satisfied, the work being done in the schools here will have its effect. It will then be one of the most potent forces in bringing about a reconciliation, and go far toward convincing the natives that American sovereignty means enlightenment, progress, civilization, and the fullest measure of independence consistent with their safety and well-being.[31]

Wartime conditions obstructed the development of local government in the limited areas under American control, but both Filipinos and American thought some form of organization desirable. Both the civilians of the commission and military officers, such as General Otis and General Lawton, recognized the advantages to be gained from the development of municipal governments in which the Filipinos participated as much as possible. General Lawton established the first such government under United States jurisdiction at Baliuag in May. The order organizing it was hastily drawn and obviously meant to be temporary. Elsewhere other officers took it upon themselves to do whatever they thought necessary to revive the life of the towns that they occupied, and it soon became evident that some form of detailed plan was needed for the development of municipal government in the areas occupied by American troops.[32]

North of Manila, Colonel William A. Kobbé was very worried about the condition of the towns along the railroad line. Kobbé had been charged with the responsibility of securing that area, and he was convinced that peace was impossible without the immediate organization of some form of municipal government in the towns. He spoke to both General MacArthur and General Otis concerning his desire for some scheme of local government that he might implement in the towns under his jurisdiction. He also attempted to acquire information not only about conditions in the towns of his region, but also about the form of municipal government that had been in effect under the Spaniards. He had seen a copy of the order issued by Lawton, but he decided that a more detailed plan was needed. When, on July 18, he finally received the request of General Otis to submit his suggestions for developing municipal government, he worked all day on his proposal, and he submitted it the following day.[33]

Although General MacArthur was convinced that Colonel Kobbé's plan was much too complicated considering the disorderly state of the towns occupied by the Americans, General Otis thought that the plan was excellent. If anything, Otis feared that the plan might not be detailed enough for an important town such as Malabon. Otis was so enthusiastic about Kobbé's proposal that he had the order printed and returned with his endorsement of the plan. He noted that he planned to take Kobbé's work "as a sort of model for municipal government at Corregidor, Calamba and some of the other towns south."[34]

The order published by Otis included a statement on the reasons for the development of the governments, provided a format for their organization, and specified the powers and duties of their officers. According to the order, published on July 31, 1899, the municipal governments were developed to promote peace and tranquility, to establish equality before the law, "to impress proper respect for property . . . to permit all inhabitants to devote themselves to their accustomed civil pursuits and to reopen churches and schools; in fine, to render life, property and individual liberty secure."[35] Each town had a municipal council composed of a president and as many members as there were barrios. The town-at-large elected the president, and the barrios elected the council. The duties of the officers included establishing a police force, collecting and disbursing tax and license money, regulating local commerce, enforcing sanitary measures, establishing schools, and lighting the village. The commanding officer of the American troops stationed in the community had to approve the election and the ordinances and decrees of the council. Almost immediately, General Otis made this form of government outlined by Colonel Kobbé the example to be followed by all American commanders in the establishment of temporary municipal governments, and this uniform pattern for the organization of towns was published as General Order No. 43 on August 8, 1899. The general organization and function of these governments was in keeping with existing Spanish decrees and customs.[36]

American soldiers began the work of forming municipal governments with the same enthusiasm, sincerity, and dedication that they devoted to school organization. This was revealed in a rather humorous, although undoubtedly exaggerated, tale of an incident taking place in the town of Polo, eight miles north of Manila. Captain Beaumont B. Buck set the election in Polo, the town under his jurisdiction, for September 3. Upon being questioned by one of the municipal elders, he gave his assurance that he would personally guarantee that the person elected would be installed in the office of president, no matter who that person might be. With this assurance, the election took place as scheduled. Ricardo Roco, the only announced candidate and one of the wealthier members of the town, seemed bound for an easy victory. To Captain Buck's sur-

prise, when the ballots were counted, one Pío Dorte Valenzuela had thirty-nine votes to Roco's twenty-two. The Captain
was doubly surprised when, upon requesting the new president
to step forward, he found that Valenzuela was not present in
the town, nor had he been for several months. The townspeople
told Buck that the new president could be found in Manila and
that Señor Valenzuela would be honored if he received the
news of his election from a member of the American army.
Buck agreed, and he proceeded to the capital on the following
day. To the Captain's surprise, he found that the address given
him by the elders was the Bilibid prison. The Spaniards had imprisoned Polo's new president because of his support of the
revolutionaries in the rebellion of 1896. True to his word, Captain Buck obtained Valenzuela's release and returned with him
to Polo, thus scoring a victory for American-style democracy
and, one could surmise, winning Filipinos over to the American
cause. Obviously this isolated event was of minor significance
in the overall campaign for the support of the Philippine people. Nevertheless, this type of personal involvement with
municipal problems contributed to the increasing success of the
Americans in 1899.[37]

The army intended to make the government of the island
of Negros an example of American benevolence on a grand
scale, a showplace for Filipinos in other parts of the
archipelago. Conditions were favorable for the immediate development of a government in which Filipinos could play a
major role. The citizens of Negros had requested American
troops, and the revolutionary movement on the island was extremely weak. Prominent people on Negros had even drafted a
constitution providing for autonomous status under American
sovereignty and sent it to Washington. While waiting for action
on their request, they organized a government in accordance
with a plan devised by the military and the civil commission.

General Otis issued General Order No. 30 on July 22,
1899, as the organic act for the government of Negros. The
provisional government was to be one under which the people
could enjoy "the largest measure of civil liberty compatible
with prevailing conditions and which shall conform to their
desires as expressed in their proposed constitution."[38] Col-

onel Smith was appointed a brigadier and became the military governor of the island. A civil governor and an advisory council were elected. Secretaries of the treasury, interior, agriculture, and public instruction, an attorney general, and an auditor were appointed by the military governor. General Order No. 30 limited suffrage to males over twenty years of age who were literate in English, Spanish, or the local dialect; who owned real property valued at a minimum of $500; or who paid rent on property valued at $1,000 or more. Free public schools in which the English language would be taught were to be established throughout the island, and the burden of taxes was to be equitably distributed among the island's inhabitants. A force of 200 native police was organized to keep order, because the problem of banditry had been long-standing on Negros and the island was too large to be effectively garrisoned by the troops at General Smith's disposal. The Americans recognized that the work on Negros was of great importance to the overall scheme of pacification. General Otis viewed it as an "example to the inhabitants of the other Philippine Islands." He knew that affairs on Negros were being closely watched by Filipinos elsewhere, and he wrote that "a successfully conducted government there—one which will protect individual rights and give a fair measure of individual liberty—will be a most important factor in the pacification labors of these islands."[39]

The civilian commissioners thought that the campaign of benevolent pacification was having great success. When American units went into the area a few miles south of Manila, some prominent Filipinos from the capital accompanied them to propagandize for the Americans, explaining to the inhabitants the purposes of the United States in the islands and endeavoring to persuade them to cease fighting. They reported back that "they found the people both surprised and pleased at the treatment accorded them" by the American soldiers.[40] This was in contrast to the conduct of the revolutionary troops who had looted the area before leaving it. Writing on the work of forming municipal governments, one commissioner said that

the result of the work . . . has been to create confidence in the intentions of the United States while large num-

> bers of people have been induced to return to their
> homes and to resume their ordinary occupations; the
> leading men of the towns visited have been persuaded
> to co-operate with our forces in the restoration of
> peace, and the maintenance of public order; each of
> these towns has become a centre of attraction for
> underfed and underpaid insurgent soldiers, a con-
> siderable number of whom have already deserted,
> and come in to rejoin their families.[41]

The preliminary report of the commission noted that when
General Lawton organized municipal governments in Cavite
Province his work was met with great enthusiasm on the part of
the inhabitants.[42]

General Otis was as optimistic as the commissioners
regarding the results of the early months of his campaign of
benevolent pacification. He noted in June, even before the
organization of the municipal governments, that the mass of
people "no longer flee" when approached by American troops;
and he was convinced that, "unless forced by the insurgents" to
act otherwise, the people would "gladly welcome" the
Americans.[43] The General's assessment of the situation
became even more optimistic as additional territory came under American control, and by the end of August he wrote that
with little difficulty he could take and temporarily hold any section of the country. He thought that, if it were not for his lack
of troops, "formidable opposition to American supremacy
would cease."[44]

The Americans had reasons for optimism in mid-1899,
because real problems had developed in the revolutionary
camp. Many Filipinos were reluctant to fight against the
Americans, and several desired to come to some accord with
the United States. The annexationist party on Negros was probably the most active group, but similar sentiment existed
among the more conservative and wealthy men of property on
other islands.[45] Even within the revolutionary government
there was a split between those seeking to prosecute the war
against the Americans and those willing to accept American
sovereignty. Shortly after the American proclamation of April
4, at a meeting of the revolutionary congress at which only fif-

teen members were present, the delegates voted unanimously for a settlement with the United States. As a result, Mabini was replaced by Paterno as the head of the cabinet. Only forcible intervention by elements of the Filipino military led by General Antonio Luna stopped this peace move. Luna seized the members of a committee appointed to confer with the Schurman Commission in Manila, and they were replaced with irreconcilables like himself and Mabini. Meanwhile, continued warfare between American and Filipino troops enhanced the power of the nationalist leaders opposed to any accord with the United States.[46]

Among the masses of the Filipino population and the rank and file of the revolutionary movement, people were growing dissatisfied with Aguinaldo's government. In particular, in areas under Filipino control, the inhabitants reacted to abuses committed by the occupying revolutionary troops. Reports arrived from many areas complaining about the conduct of Filipino soldiers and officers, and townspeople accused them of various crimes including robbery, rape, and murder.[47] Localities refused to pay their taxes or render any other aid to the revolution, and in one instance a municipality raised its own militia force to protect itself from the abuses of revolutionary soldiers.[48] General Luna threatened to resign unless discipline was restored to the revolutionary army, but he only gained the enmity of other commanders when he sought to change the situation by summarily executing troublemakers.[49]

Some revolutionary leaders actually feared an uprising, and disorder was apparent in many areas. The hill peoples of central Luzon refused to pay tribute to the revolutionaries, choosing to raid the lowland villages instead. Bandits ravaged the countryside, and groups dressed in military uniforms terrorized villages. The situation seemed to be approaching anarchy, and some revolutionaries feared that the Americans would foment rebellion behind their lines.[50]

Ethnic divisions throughout the Philippines made unity difficult. Aguinaldo and most of his associates were Tagalogs from central Luzon. In the Visayan Islands to the south, although there was sentiment for independence, the populace had little desire for independence under Tagalog rule. On the island of Panay, for example, Tagalog troops under Lieutenant Colonel Timoteo Marella were forced to concentrate and withdraw from the area they occupied because of, as Marella observed, "strained relations with the immense majority of the people." He feared the existence of "a profound antagonism" between the Visayans and the Tagalogs. In Antique Province of Panay there was friction between General Leandro Fullon, a Tagalog, and Visayan civil officials. Tagalog officers accused many Visayans of being *Americanistas,* and Visayans complained of abuses suffered at the hands of the Tagalogs.[51] The whole situation developing in the southern islands was a source of great worry for the revolutionary government on Luzon.

Filipinos in the few towns under the control of the Americans seemed willing to cooperate and even aid them against the revolutionaries. This was perhaps the greatest problem facing Aguinaldo and the major reason for American optimism in 1899. Some Visayans showed their willingness to accept American authority at an early date when the merchants of Iloilo on Panay requested that American troops be sent to that city and when the wealthy landowners of Negros willingly accepted an American government. In Cebu there was also a movement toward the Americans, and the revolutionary commander on that island requested authority to institute a military government because he thought that Filipino civil officials were ready to accept American sovereignty.[52] Prominent professional men of Manila, like Judge Arellano, Felipe Calderón, Benito Legarda, and Dr. T.H. Pardo de Tavera, did great damage to the nationalist cause through the support and aid they gave the Americans. De Tavera, for example, founded the newspaper *La Democracia* in May 1899 to persuade Filipinos to lay down their arms and accept American sovereignty. He also circulated a petition asking the United States government to expel the Spanish friars, although the revolutionaries believed that the act of signing such a document was tacit recognition of American rule.[53] The work of Arellano and Calderón on court and municipal government organization also aided the Americans. The revolutionaries recognized that these men were doing harm to their cause, and one group of revolutionaries even advocated an attack on Manila in July to capture the collaborators, many of whom, like Arellano and Calderón, had been members of Aguinaldos government at one time.[54]

Apolinario Mabini observed that Filipinos served the Americans as spies, scouts, and government officials. In Manila, collaboration of local spies led to the arrest of many revolutionaries including organizers of the February 22 uprising and members of a secret organization among the employees of the waterworks. Local spies also helped the Provost-Marshal-General's guard locate an illicit revolutionary post office operating in the district of Binondo.[55] Many Filipinos had worked for the Americans as civil servants in Manila since the beginning of the occupation, and the number of these officials increased as municipal governments were organized throughout 1899. In the countryside Filipinos acted as interpreters and guides for American units, and the American troops began to form units of Filipino scouts and police on Luzon as they had on Negros. The first of these units was formed from inhabitants of the town of Macabebe. They had long been enemies of the Tagalogs, and they had remained loyal to Spain throughout the earlier revolt.[56] General Otis was reluctant to use the Macabebes against their Tagalog enemies, and at first their role was confined to patroling the rivers and nipa swamps near their homes. The Americans thought, however, that the scouts might be useful to General Lawton when he pushed north at the end of the rainy season.[57]

The propaganda efforts of the Americans were also partially responsible for the growing support that the Filipinos gave them in 1899. Proclamations of American intentions in the islands, in particular that of the Schurman Commission on April 4, appealed to many natives, and the benevolent actions of the army in the field gave proof of the sincerity of those statements. Both the revolutionary leaders and the Americans recognized that the benevolent approach to pacification accounted for some of the support given the army by the islands' inhabitants. One Filipino officer in Cebu wrote that, "unhappily, the occupation of this city by the North Americans makes felt the pernicious influence of the policy of attraction that they

have established," and he noted that "it is not strange that they
continue attracting many sympathizers."[58] The benevolence
of the Americans was too marked to go unnoticed by those
coming in contact with them, and Filipino troops even left their
own wounded to fall into American hands, knowing that good
care would be given to them.[59] American goals and Filipino
desires were so close in many cases that the army was bound to
meet with success. Schools, law and order, municipal government, and other reforms desired by the Filipinos were an important part of the American program. This similarity of mutual aims and aspirations was one good reason for the growing
support of the Americans by the Philippine people, limited,
however, to the relatively small area under American control.

The adverse reaction of many Filipinos to revolutionary
rule was another factor accounting for the swing of support to the
Americans. The Chinese inhabitants of the islands, for example, were poorly treated by the revolutionaries, and some, as a
consequence, collaborated with the Americans. The Chinese
performed much of the army's manual labor and "Chinos" acted
as guides and spies.[60] The members of the Schurman Commission observed that in areas where revolutionary rule had
been severe the people were "thankful for the considerate treatment they had received from our troops, and willing to aid us
against the insurgents."[61] The fears that the revolutionaries
exhibited over their loss of authority in the towns were well
founded.

The Filipinos were also short of ammunition. This problem and that of disorder within the areas they controlled led
them to request a truce from General Otis early in April. They
hoped that the time gained could be used to "reorganize" and
"re-stock."[62] General Otis doubted the sincerity of the
Filipino negotiators, and he refused to grant an armistice. The
Filipinos tried to obtain a cease-fire again at the end of the
month, but the result was the same. It was on that occasion that
the war party among the revolutionaries forestalled the attempt
of the revolutionary congress to negotiate with the Schurman
Commission. Commissioner Schurman thought that negotiation was the best course of action, but his colleagues Denby,
Worcester, and Otis overruled him. They all recommended to

the government in Washington that the war be prosecuted until the revolutionaries recognized American sovereignty. They agreed that General Otis should have complete control over the pacification campaign and the arrangement of terms for surrender. They rejected the Filipino bid for time, and the only real accomplishment of the short-lived truce negotiations was to deepen the cleavage in the revolutionary ranks between those favoring an accord with the Americans and those desiring to continue the war.[63]

As the Filipino inability to withstand the American army in regular warfare became apparent, some revolutionary leaders gave considerable thought to the possibility of changing their strategy. Less than a month after the war began one Filipino wrote General Luna advocating the adoption of guerrilla warfare in a plan designed to harass the Americans until a reaction in the United States should force abondonment of the islands. Mariano Ponce, Aguinaldo's representative in Japan, noted the advantages of a guerrilla war in April 1899, and General Tomás Mascardo recommended it after his units suffered defeat at the hands of the Americans in May. Felipe Buencamino, Aguinaldo's Secretary of Foreign Affairs, favored collecting the regular Filipino army in northern Luzon and leaving guerrilla units behind to harass the enemy. He observed that regular warfare acted to cut off the areas held by Aguinaldo from the economic center of the islands, Manila. Other commanders also saw that regular warfare was failing and spoke of the advantages of a guerrilla campaign.[64]

Revolutionary leaders naturally thought in terms of guerrilla warfare. In 1896 their units had fared badly at the hands of regular Spanish troops but had been successful in guerrilla actions. Using the example of the Cuban guerrilla movement, many revolutionaries recognized the advantages of irregular warfare in 1897, and the events of 1899 only reinforced the lessons that had been learned in the early years of the revolt and seemingly forgotten in the intervening months.[65] Even though many Filipinos saw the futility of resisting American arms directly, they were not yet willing to stop resisting American sovereignty.

Even when faced with a loss of popular support, friction within their own ranks, and a lack of unity between the divergent cultural groups in the islands, Aguinaldo and his associates were determined to continue the fight against the Americans. They hoped that the pressures generated by the Democratic party and the Anti-Imperialist League would lead the American people to demand an end to the war. They also believed that in time some European powers, perhaps Germany, might champion their cause. Independence was the goal, and Aguinaldo saw no other means of achieving it short of continued resistance. In the face of powerful odds, he did what he could to check the popular movement of support away from the revolution and prevent the total defeat of his forces in the first year of the war.

Filipino propagandist were active in attempting to prevent the people of the Philippines from supporting the Americans. They depicted the Americans as "turbulent, undisciplined, and given to gross and licentious excesses upon helpless people."[66] They stressed the treatment that had been accorded the Indian in the United States, and they exploited religious and cultural differences between Americans and Filipinos. Claiming that the Americans would suppress Catholicism and destroy the property of the natives, they depicted American benevolence as a "deceit to enslave."[67] The revolutionaries spread fictional accounts of great victories in which the American army was said to suffer enormous casualties. In fact, in one instance, they reported an American casualty figure larger than the total number of American troops in the islands at the time.[68]

In an attempt to gain support for their movement the revolutionaries also aimed their propaganda at American and foreign opinion. Aguinaldo proclaimed that he was making war not upon the United States, but upon the imperialist party, thereby encouraging his anti-imperialist supporters in America. Revolutionary propaganda told American soldiers that they should give up their arms and come over to the Filipino side where they would be treated like gentlemen. It stressed the intelligence of the Filipinos and their ability to govern themselves. The propaganda also protested to foreign consuls in Manila against "constant transgressions of the laws of war" such as the use of explosive bullets.[69] No charge was too great for the propagandists to make, and they overlooked few tricks of propaganda in their bid for support.

To forestall defections caused by the poor conduct of revolutionary troops and officials, Aguinaldo ordered his commanders to repress all abuses "lest the pueblos should get tired and accept American autonomy." He instructed the commissioners collecting the war tax to render detailed accounts of their operations and ordered that new elections be held in the province of Nueva Vizcaya to give local offices to Ilocanos rather than Tagalogs. The revolutionaries also tried to eliminate the roving bands in military uniform that were terrorizing villages in some areas.[70]

Events in the United States encouraged the Filipinos in their resistance. They watched American and foreign press accounts of the anti-imperialist movement and thought that, if they could possibly resist a few months longer, the American people would repudiate McKinley's imperialist policies.[71] In addition, American anti-imperialists corresponded with the revolutionaries and gave them encouragement. For example, S. Dansinger, secretary of the Single Tax Club of Cincinnati, wished "for General Aguinaldo and his patriotic army the greatest success against our army of subjugation, tyranny, and oppression."[72] While this type of correspondence gave Aguinaldo and his followers a distorted picture of American public opinion, Americans, such as anti-imperialist Montague Leverson, recommended that Aguinaldo publicize any evidence he might have concerning American atrocities committed in the islands. Leverson implied that the American people were not being told the truth about conditions there.[73] Only the quick action of American postal authorities and military officials in both the United States and the Philippines forestalled industrialist Edward Atkinson's attempt to send anti-imperialist pamphlets to American troops in the islands. General Otis viewed these letters and defamatory newspaper articles published in the United States and Europe as one of his "chief difficulties." The revolutionaries used such material as propaganda, giving their people reason to hold out against the American troops and prolonging the war, and these items certainly deceived the Filipino leaders in their assessment of American policy and will.[74]

The revolutionaries viewed the Democratic party as their champion. In the Philippines they advised their people to resist, promising that the election of 1900 would prove the undoing of McKinley and the imperialists. They even planned a meeting in honor of William Jennings Bryan, whom they assumed would be the Democratic candidate in 1900, and a propaganda document printed in Manila stated that "the triumph of Bryan is a triumph of the cause of the Filipinos."[75]

The revolutionary junta in Hong Kong was a center for propaganda, intelligence data, and liaison with the anti-imperialists in the United States and Filipino agents throughout the world. This junta encouraged the revolutionaries in the Philippines with promises of overwhelming support for their independence in America, the ultimate triumph of the revolutionary movement, and a Democratic victory in the election of 1900. It forwarded correspondence and newspaper clippings to the revolutionaries, kept alive the idea of European intervention and foreign support, and produced propaganda for use by the anti-imperialists in the United States. Because it operated in Hong Kong, the Americans could do little to restrict its activities.[76]

The Filipinos had some foreign support from both the Chinese revolutionaries and the Japanese, and the Hong Kong junta convinced them that more would be forthcoming. Sun Yat-sen aided Ponce in his mission to Japan, and Aguinaldo was convinced that the Chinese revolutionary movement would further his cause.[77] Galicano Apacible, a junta member, urged the revolutionaries to be firm and wrote that in the spring of 1900 hostilities would begin between China and the European powers.[78] The Filipinos hoped that this would draw American troops away from the Philippines. At the same time, negotiations were underway with the Japanese for firearms and munitions. The Japanese army favored aiding the Filipinos, but the foreign office opposed it. Ponce, with the help of Sun, obtained sufficient support from the military and a few Japanese politicians to enter into an agreement for the purchase of arms and ammunition in the spring of 1899. At the same time, arrangements were made for "retired" Japanese officers to go to the Philippines as advisors to the Filipino army. The officers, a relatively small contingent, did serve with the Filipino forces, but the attempt to ship arms to the islands was a complete failure. The *Nunobiki Maru* carrying 10,000 rifles, 6,000,000 rounds of ammunition, and other military supplies was sunk in a typhoon, and a second attempt was stymied by the threat of the effective American blockade. On the whole, the Japanese contributed little to the Filipinos. Their officers arrived at a time when regular warfare was proving impossible, and no substantial shipments of weapons ever arrived. The Japanese government, not willing to alienate the Americans, gave no formal support to Aguinaldo's government or the nationalist cause.[79]

The Filipino revolutionaries worked hard to prevent the collapse of their government, and the contest between them and the Americans was by no means decided by mid-1899. Aguinaldo and his followers did their best to prevent the Filipinos from supporting the Americans and continued to hope for foreign intervention or a reaction in the United States that would cause the withdrawal of American forces. Most important of all, Aguinaldo continued to control a greater amount of Philippine territory and population than the Americans. The Americans continued to hope for a collapse of the revolution and retained faith in their benevolent policy. The Americans did have some reasons for optimism, but they, too, had problems which prevented them from gaining an immediate advantage in the developing conflict.

At a time when extra effort and continuing military pressure was of the utmost importance, General Otis found himself unable to take offensive action. By deciding not to negotiate or accept Aguinaldo's bid for an armistice, Otis had committed the Americans to a military solution without sufficient strength to pursue it. By the end of May, the coming rainy season prevented a continuation of even small offensive operations. Movements against Filipino troop concentrations south of Manila and General MacArthur's successful thrust against the revolutionary capital of Malolos in March had left the American troops physically exhausted. Supply facilities had broken down completely, and the difficulties of weather and communications made it impossible to press home any attack against the revolutionaries on Luzon. The railroad running north from Manila enabled the Filipinos to retreat and to regroup their forces in the face of any American advance.[80]

Insufficient numbers, more than any other single factor, hampered the American operations. The thousands of men sent from the United States to Manila during the first half of the year had only replaced the volunteers going in the opposite direction. In the Visayas, the Americans could do little more than hold Iloilo, Cebu, and key points on Negros. On Luzon, General Otis commanded an exhausted army. Most of his offensive movements were only calculated to keep the revolutionaries off balance, and he was unable to garrison adequately the small area north of Manila already under his control.[81]

Unable to furnish protection to the Filipinos living in the areas held by the army, the Americans could not prevent the revolutionaries from exerting undue pressures on the population. In the region south of Manila and other areas, American units had conquered and abandoned many towns. Each time, the revolutionaries would reoccupy the region and punish the inhabitants who had collaborated with the Americans. On Panay, General Hughes had told some Filipino municipal presidents to stay away because he could not give them protection if they took the oath of allegiance to the United States.[82] General Otis summed up the general problem facing the Americans in his annual report of August 31, 1899.

> Little difficulty attends the act of taking possession of and temporarily holding any section of the country. A column of 3,000 men could march through and successfully contend with any force which the insurgents could place in its route, but they would close in behind it and again prey upon the inhabitants, persecuting without mercy those who had manifested any friendly feeling toward the American troops.[83]

Influenced by revolutionary propaganda, many Filipinos feared that the Americans would not remain in the islands permanently. Unable to give the assurance of continued protection against revolutionary reprisals, the Americans found it difficult to organize any form of Filipino secret service or to obtain intelligence data. Officials in the hastily organized American municipal governments cooperated with the revolutionaries or were even active in the revolution. General Otis recognized the problem, but the American commanders tolerated such duplicity because, until they received sufficient garrison troops, they could do nothing about it.[84]

Threats and reprisals became a real obstacle to the American pacification effort. American officers trying to organize municipal governments found that the traditional community leaders were often unwilling to serve them for fear that the revolutionaries would destroy their property or harm their persons. Even on Negros, where pro-American sentiment was high, General Smith reported that the inhabitants were afraid to come over completely to the Americans. Some feared that the Americans would eventually withdraw and leave them to an independent Philippine government of Tagalogs; others believed that the benevolent policy of the Americans was only a temporary ruse to gain control over the inhabitants of the island.[85] Also on Negros the Americans were troubled by guerrilla bands infiltrating from Luzon, as well as propaganda and threats keeping the people from giving wholehearted support to the American sponsored government.[86] Elsewhere, Filipinos living in American areas actively cooperated with the revolutionaries and supplied them with data on American movements and troop dispositions. Filipino clergymen were one important source of intelligence data for the revolutionaries.[87] And many officers of American municipal governments were followers of Aguinaldo. At San Pedro Macati, for example, the municipal president used his town as a central recruiting station for the revolutionary army. American soldiers found that in most of the Philippines the populace had never heard of the pronouncements of the government in Manila.[88]

Other American problems could hardly be traced to the Filipino revolutionaries. Few American soldiers spoke Spanish; almost none spoke any of the numerous dialects used by most of the Philippine people. In many cases the Americans responsible for organizing the towns were young and inexperienced junior officers. Their primary tasks were military; and many of the reforms they began in the municipalities interfered with local customs. American rule represented a threat to Filipino culture in some ways and an annoyance in others. American health regulations forced the Filipinos to be much more sanitary than they really wanted to be; and in the name of morality the Americans had outlawed traditional Filipino pastimes such as gambling and the favorite sport of cockfighting. In an attempted tax reform the Americans had stopped issuing the *cédula* or head tax receipt and then found it necessary to reissue it at a nominal fee, because Filipinos looked upon it as an important document of indentification. As one correspondent observed, the American had "frowned upon some long-established customs, . . . set up his own standards of right and righteousness and . . . suppressed or sought to suppress diversions that had become an integral part of the life of the people."[89]

The Filipinos were often not ready for the democratic local government that the Americans sought to develop. Municipal presidents feared to act on their own initiative lest they offend the military authorities. Although the towns had a rudimentary form of democratic rule dating back to pre-Spanish times, the Filipino masses were easily controlled by the educated minority. In some cases presidents ruled as tyrants, and there was a notorious lack of public responsibility on the part of officials. Graft and corruption were prevalent, and municipal governments organized by the army fell far short of the standards envisaged by their founders. The report of the Schurman Commission summed up the problem facing the Americans seeking to develop truly democratic government in the region surrounding Manila. A large amount of supervision had to be given the new municipal governments. Local officials were reluctant to assume responsibility and slow to comprehend their duties. "At many of the elections voters went in succession to the commissioner present, the military representatives, and the native priest, asking whom they were expected to vote for, and it was only with great difficulty and by dint of much argument that they were persuaded to exercise the right of free suffrage."[90] In seeking to change Filipino society, the Americans were faced with cultural problems that could not be solved in the few short months that the army had been at work in the municipalities.

Some members of the American force did not understand the value of benevolence and civil affairs work as an adjunct to the pacification campaign. When American units undertook offensive operations outside of Manila, their officers had difficulty maintaining effective control over some of the troops, and the resulting incidents furnished Filipino propagandists and anti-imperialists in the United States with material which could be used against the army. The term "nigger" was in general use in reference to Filipinos and was even used in the English-language newspapers published in Manila. American soldiers incurred debts to Filipino merchants under assumed names and then refused to pay. Looting, arson, and robbery all demanded official attention during 1899. General orders published during the offensive to the north declared that something had to be done about the general misconduct evident in the American ranks. Commanders promised strict enforcement of the existing regulations, but the problems persisted. The looting of churches, although an infrequent activity indulged in by only a small minority of Americans, doubtless convinced many deeply religious Filipinos that the Americans were, in fact, barbarians, as the revolutionary propaganda stated. Other looting took place in the process of souvenir hunting or in attempts to augment the standard army ration by, as one soldier reminisced, "acquiring a viscious chicken."[91] Although, as revealed subsequently in Senate investigations, most of these practices were the exception and not the rule, such acts nevertheless tended to negate the image that the army was trying to develop in its application of a policy of benevolence.[92]

Other actions which worked in opposition to the army's policy were officially sanctioned and done out of military necessity. Troops often took the best village homes for their own quarters and forced the owners to seek other lodging. The army used large private dwellings and churches for headquarters, hospitals, or other administrative and logistical functions.[93] Army foragers seized carabaos, the native water buffaloes that were the primary draft animal of the islands, to replace losses in the supply trains. In one case they ripped banana trees from the fields to serve as fill in a road building project.[94] Benevolent pacification was a policy that took a great deal of effort, and the army found it impossible to pre-

vent all acts that made the task of winning Filipino support difficult.

Among the Americans there was a serious division of
opinion concerning the Philippine policy. In the United States,
anti-imperialist opposition to President McKinley's policy
caused anxiety among those in the administration thinking
about the election of 1900, and the government wanted to end
the war in the islands as soon as possible. In Manila, General
Otis and the Schurman Commission disagreed almost from the
arrival of the commissioners. The General claimed that they
had no status, since they had been appointed before the fighting
began, and he refused to be bound by any action they might
take. Their recommendation that a board of civilians be appointed to take over much of the work of the military government only made the commission more distasteful in the
General's eyes.[95] Their talks and discussions with the revolutionaries annoyed him, and he reported to Washington that
such conferences "cost soldiers' lives and prolong our difficulties." The General pledged, however, that he would publicly
support the commission so that to the outside world "gentle
peace shall prevail."[96] By the middle of 1899, at least commissioners Denby and Worcester had come to an accord with
the General. These three agreed on the necessity for a military
decision within the framework of a benevolent program of
pacification, and they stubbornly opposed Schurman's proposal
for negotiation and concessions to the Filipino nationalists.
The General and the other commissioners deemed such a
course "fatal."[97]

Although General Otis had come to an agreement with a
majority of the commissioners, his relations with American
press representatives in the Philippines were strained by censorship. The Associated Press charged that the General and his
censor discriminated against it and had accused it of working
with the revolutionary junta in Hong Kong. Robert M. Collins,
an Associated Press correspondent in the Philippines, wrote
that "the only way to get anything like news through the censorship was to give it a sort of editorial bias."[98] Other correspondents charged that news was being withheld from the
American public and joined together in June in what was to be

termed in the United States "The Manila Round Robin." The round robin was a thorough condemnation of General Otis's censorship. The correspondents claimed that

> owing to official dispatches from Manila published in American newspapers which have reached here the people of the U. S. have not received a correct impression of the situation in the Philippines, that these dispatches have presented an ultra optimistic view which is not shared by the general officers in the field. We believe the dispatches misrepresent existing conditions among the Filipinos in respect to internal dissensions and demoralization resulting from the American campaign.[99]

The reporters claimed that censorship compelled them "to participate in this misrepresentation by excising or altering uncontroverted statements of facts on the plea that, as General Otis stated 'They would alarm people at home' or 'have the people in the United States by the ears.' " Newsmen alleged that General Otis was at odds with all his generals and almost all of the American and European population in Manila over the question of the number of troops needed in the islands. According to reporters, Otis wanted 40,000 to 50,000, the rest estimated 75,000 to 125,000.[100]

The government supported General Otis but insisted that all newsmen should be treated alike. When the Adjutant General cabled Otis on June 30 that the government did not desire to interfere with his censorship of matter sent from Manila, he replied that he had not practiced any discrimination but stated his certainty that an Associated Press correspondent had used his position to send dispatches in the interests of the revolutionaries in 1898. Three weeks later General Otis wrote that he was "not conscious of sending misrepresentations" and that he was "willing to remove censorship and let them cable anything."[101] The administration upheld General Otis in the controversy and issued a public statement prepared by McKinley's cabinet stating that "when the correspondents were asked . . . wherein General Otis's dispatches were misleading they offered nothing tangible except that his conclusions were unwarranted."[102] The Adjutant General told Otis that, although the Secretary of War advised a more liberal censorship policy, the requirement for material to be submitted to military authorities in advance should be retained. This was to be done without a public announcement.[103] The issue of censorship subsided, but it was not completely forgotten.

American newsmen had been correct in discerning some differences of opinion between General Otis and some of his field commanders. The General proceeded too cautiously for many of his subordinates, and they did not like the policy of offensive action followed by withdrawal. They thought that he was a poor commander, although they recognized his ability as a military governor. Brigadier General S. B. M. Young confided to Theodore Roosevelt that, although he thought Otis "the best equipped General we have for the handling of the civil political affairs out here" the necessity for "vigorous action" made it imperative that command of the actual conduct of military operations be given to a more aggressive officer, such as Lawton.[104] Young thought that a force of 2,500 to 3,000 cavalry and 5,000 infantry under Lawton's command could disperse the "insurgents" in thirty days. Brigadier General Joseph Wheeler, in a letter to President McKinley, intimated that General Otis was delaying an active and final campaign against the revolutionaries without good cause. Theodore Roosevelt wrote to Elihu Root, the newly appointed Secretary of War, that in addition to the letter received from Young, he had the opinions of two generals, one captain, and two other officers that Otis lacked the aggressiveness called for by the situation in the islands. In the Philippines, soldiers complained that "Otis is too old" and that his campaign had been "humane to the point of military weakness."[105]

The administration, although aware of the criticism of General Otis, stuck by him in the face of opposition and, viewed in retrospect, probably made the correct decision. General Otis recognized as well as General Young that a large column of American troops could easily destroy any revolutionary opposition in the islands. He knew, however, that such destruction would be temporary, at best, and that American sovereignty in the islands depended on the ability to hold rather than to clear territory. Cautious advance, the policy Otis was criticized for most, seemed the only course of action open to the Americans that did not court disaster at the hands of a Filipino guerrilla movement, should it develop.

Otis had his champions as well as his critics. Brigadier General Theodore Schwan, his chief of staff, sent a very favorable assessment of Otis's performance to the Adjutant General. After looking at both Otis's civil and military correspondence, Schwan was convinced "that he has handled this delicate and most difficult situation with consumate skill, and that there is no officer in our Army who could have done as well as he." The only criticism voiced by Schwan was that the General failed to delegate work to his subordinates. Brigadier General Henry C. Corbin, the Adjutant General, answered Schwan that he too thought Otis had met the situation in the Philippines "as fully and completely as was possible for any mortal man to do."[106] The President and Secretary of War agreed with Corbin and refused to recall General Otis or place another man in command of the military campaign. Even Theodore Roosevelt changed his opinion of Otis at a later date and wrote that the views he had seen concerning the General in 1899 were "one-sided."[107] Though the General was overoptimistic in his assessment of the situation in the islands, the administration was already taking precautions against further trouble.

The War Department had begun mobilizing a force of volunteers and increasing the strength of the Regular Army in case General Otis's opinion on the number of troops needed should prove too low. The messages received in the United States from the Philippines pointed to the need for more troops, and Secretary of War Root proceeded to raise a volunteer force superior to any group previously in American service. General Otis himself tried to form two volunteer regiments with men enlisted from units returning home. To escape political pressure in the choice of officers, the War Department stressed the importance that experience and merit would play in the selection process. Colonels and lieutenant colonels were taken from officers in the Regular Army, and the appointment of line officers was made primarily to men who had seen service in the

Spanish-American War. This policy insured that officers in the newly formed units would have a high level of experience. Adjutant General Corbin was even convinced that the enlisted ranks consisted of a better class of men than those in the regular service. The result was to develop an experienced force that would soon be on hand to augment the regulars already serving under Otis. In addition, the troops in the Philippines were increased by the enlistment of two additional companies of Macabebe scouts and local police units in the Visayas and Manila. By the end of September, General Otis was in a position to begin a powerful offensive against the Filipino army on Luzon.[108]

General Otis planned his offensive to begin in October when he would be receiving his new replacements and the rainy season would be ending. In the first week of the month, however, Filipino operations south of Manila forestalled any American attempt to attack to the north. Otis's first move was to send another expedition south of the city to break up the Filipino concentration. The expedition resulted in a temporary demoralization of the revolutionaries in Cavite Province, the capture of their supplies and money, and the destruction of much contraband of war. Since he deemed this area to be without strategic value, Otis withdrew his units as soon as they accomplished their purpose.[109]

The American plan for the dry season offensive involved the northward movement of three separate forces. One column under General MacArthur would proceed up the railroad line on the western side of the central Luzon plain. A second under General Lawton would move up the eastern side of the plain and occupy the mountain passes that led to the north and east. A third force under Brigadier General Loyd Wheaton would go by sea to Lingayen at the northern extremity of the plain to act as a blocking force. The two columns advancing from Manila would drive the revolutionaries before them and, through the use of flying columns of scouts and cavalry, prevent the escape of large bodies of Filipino troops into the mountains bordering the plain. These operations unfolded as planned in November, and the advancing American units completely dispersed the Filipino army. Swift movement was the key to the success of the campaign, and the army used mounted troops effectively to seize strategic points, to break up Filipino concentrations, and to capture their supply depots and adminstrative facilities. Aguinaldo's army retreated or broke into small units capable of eluding the advancing Americans. When hard pressed, they buried their arms and returned to their homes.[110]

Then the American offensive began to slow because of terrain, climate, and transport problems. American horses and mules could not subsist on native grasses; the carabao could not travel more than two miles an hour on the march. The rainy season had not ended completely before the offensive began, and the country that Lawton's men advanced through was literally submerged. Wheeled transport could not move, and Lawton had to rely on his cavalry, a few infantry, and local scouts, all living off the countryside. The whole campaign became an example of complete improvisation in the important areas of transport and supply. Engineers made do with what was at hand, and using banana trees, bamboo, Chinese coolies, local draft animals, and anything else they could beg, borrow, and steal they built roads and bridges throughout the area of advance. They also worked endless hours trying to get the railroad running north in operation to help sustain the American advance. Still, the American offensive ground to a halt.[111]

The troops were completely exhausted. Units of Lawton's column reported as many as 50 percent of their men sick with fever, and General Schwan, in Manila, received messages asking for any kind of supplies to be forwarded immediately. The American soldiers had gone to the limit of their endurance. One enlisted man wrote in his diary that in one battalion "half the men have no shoes" and that in Lawton's division no one "except the Cavalry have blankets or ponchos."[112] The Oregon Volunteers, upon their return to Manila, were an example of the state of the American army at the end of the campaign. According to the regimental history there were

fifty per cent of them so weak that they would have been unable to remain in the field much longer. Nearly all were suffering from some kind of stomach or bowel

complaint, due to the water, food, and heat, and
from sore feet and ringworms. . . . The medical officer's investigation called out over half of the regiment as unfit for duty.[113]

Marching, rain, poor diet, extreme heat, diarrhea, and dysen-
tery had done what Aguinaldo's troops could not do. The
American offensive ended with the United States Army in a
state of, as General MacArthur described it, "general enerva-
tion."[114] But it had accomplished its goal. The Filipino army,
as a regular fighting force, ceased to exist. Aguinaldo had
escaped capture but was in flight in the mountain vastness
north of the plain. American troops occupied all of the
populated areas of northern Luzon, and it would be only a matter of time before reinforcements coming from the United
States would occupy southern Luzon and the Visayas.

As 1899 drew to a close, the Americans were convinced
that the war had ended in an American victory. Most of them
thought it inconceivable that the revolutionaries could present any further threat to American sovereignty. A dispatch
from Lieutenant Colonel Robert L. Howze was typical of those
coming into the various American headquarters throughout
November: "The natives . . . are pretty well discouraged. They
report that the Filipino army at Tavloe is starving. . . . also that
Colonel or General Emilio's command is deserting him
now."[115] In the town of Vigan the Americans published a
proclamation declaring that the war was over and stating that
Aguinaldo was a fugitive.[116] General Otis cabled Washington
that the "claim to government by insurgents can be made no
longer under any fiction" and that the revolutionaries had been
completely dispersed.[117] From the American viewpoint the
war was finished. General MacArthur observed that there was
"no organized insurgent force left to strike at" and recommended to General Otis that those Filipinos continuing to fight
be declared outlaws and that the killing of American soldiers be
regarded as murder rather than an act of war.[118]

Throughout 1899 most Americans in the Philippines had
been firmly committed to their policy of benevolent pacification, and, from all appearances, it had proven itself by the end
of the year. General Otis declined to initiate General MacAr-

thur's recommendations that the remaining revolutionaries be outlawed. He feared that such a policy would interfere with the army's mission, which he viewed as conquering the Filipinos "by acquainting them with a knowledge of our pacific intentions."[119] Other officers also professed sentiments that showed a firm commitment to the benevolent and humanitarian policy the army had followed. Colonel Lyman W. V. Kennon wrote General Corbin that the way to pacify the Filipinos was through a convincing conquest to make them realize the futility of armed resistance combined with efforts to win them over by "fair and just treatment."[120] Captain Joseph B. Batchelor, Jr., summed up much of the thinking on the advantages of a benevolent policy. Speaking of the Filipinos, he wrote:

> What their feelings may be hereafter will depend on the treatment they receive. It would be easy to make them now faithful, loyal, and law-abiding subjects by a policy of kindness and firmness, in which every promise given shall be inviolably fulfilled. If they be treated with weakness or cruelty; if bad faith be shown; if they be exposed to a course of insult and robbery, a fire will be kindled which it will take thousands of men to extinguish.[121]

Captain Batchelor was not alone in his thoughts, and both in Washington and in the Philippines the policy of benevolent pacification had many adherents.[122]

At the year's end both President McKinley and Secretary Root made statements that reinforced the nation's and the army's commitment to a benevolent and humane policy in the Philippines. Secretary Root's ideas were communicated to the army in the Philippines by General Corbin, who mailed out several copies of a speech given by Root in October.[123] In the speech Root left no doubt that a continuation of the benevolent and humane policy begun in the islands would find favor in the War Department. He lauded the American soldier as one who "the moment that the enemy ceases to fire . . . is ready with open hand, . . . to heal the sick, to succor the poor, to teach the ignorant, to set up the arts of peace and to turn the scene of warfare into the smiling land of

114 SCHOOLBOOKS AND KRAGS

plenty." Root showed that he was prouder of a commander firmly committed to the development of good, benevolent military government than he ever could be "of a hero on the ramparts amid the hail of shot." He preferred to claim for the American soldier the "higher honor" that "he brings the schoolbook, the plow, and the Bible. While he leads the forlorn hope of war, he is the advanced guard of liberty and justice, of law and order, and peace and happiness."

The President's annual message to Congress on December 5 praised the beneficent work of the military government, and McKinley singled out the island of Negros as an example of what could be expected to develop as the insular government spread its control throughout the archipelago. There could be no doubt that he wanted the army to continue the work begun in 1898 and 1899 when he stated:

> no effort will be spared to build up the vast places desolated by war and by long years of misgovernment. We shall not wait for the end of strife to begin the beneficent work. We shall continue, as we have begun, to open the schools and the churches, to set the courts in operation, to foster industry and trade and agriculture, and in every way in our power to make these people whom Providence has brought within our jurisdiction feel that it is their liberty and not our power, their welfare and not our gain, we are seeking to enhance.[124]

Benevolent pacification had become the official policy of the American government in the islands. It was based on the beneficent intentions expressed by the President as early as 1898 and reinforced by the statements of McKinley and Root as the first year of the war ended.

NOTES

1. The barrio was clearly within the territory that Aguinaldo and his troops recognized as being under American control. *Annual Reports of the War Department for the Fiscal Year Ended June 30, 1899,* HD 2, 56th Cong., 1st sess., V, 423-24.

2. A good summary of these events is Philippine Information Society, "The Outbreak of Hostilities," *Facts about the Filipinos,* I (Nov. 6, 1901), 6-36.

3. Buencamino to Secretary of War, Feb. 7, 1899, PIR 65.2; Otis to AG, Feb. 5 and 7, 1899, *Correspondence Relating to the War with Spain, April 15, 1898-July 30, 1902,* II, 894, 896; Instructions to the Brave Soldiers of Sandatahan in Manila, Jan. 9, 1899, J. R. M. Taylor, "Compilation," 8KU, see also 85AJ.

4. These initial American operations and others taking place throughout 1899 will only be covered in most general terms. More detailed coverage of the campaign of 1899 can be found in *War Department, 1899,* HD 2, 56th Cong., 1st sess., V, VI, *passim;* James A. LeRoy, *The Americans in the Philippines,* II, 1-156; William Thaddeus Sexton, *Soldiers in the Sun: An Adventure in Imperialism* (Harrisburg, 1939), 79-220.

5. Otis to AG, Feb. 7 and 9, 1899, *Correspondence,* II, 896, 899.

6. An excellent statement on the objectives and problems of colonial warfare is Jean Gottmann, "Bugeaud, Galliéni, Lyautey: The Development of French Colonial Warfare," in Edward Mead Earle (ed.), *Makers of Modern Strategy: Military Thought from Machiavelli to Hitler* (Princeton, 1941), 234-40. McKinley's use of the term "benevolent assimilation" is found in his Dec. 21, 1898 letter to Otis.

7. *War Department, 1899,* HD 2, 56th Cong., 1st sess., II, 3-7.

8. Taylor, "Compilation," 20-22AJ, 75AJ, 91-93AJ covers the development of the revolutionary force and its arms. The estimate placing the total arms held by the Filipinos at 30,000 was probably correct, although one American estimate placed it as high as 39,500.

9. For a short but good summary, see Philippine Information Society, "Taking the Southern Islands, February, 1899 to July 31, 1900," *Facts about the Filipinos,* I (Nov. 8, 1901).

10. Otis to AG, Mar. 16, 1899, *Correspondence,* II, 935; Joseph Wheeler, "Tranquilizing the Philippines," *Independent* 52 (1900): 3044; Dean C. Worcester, *The Philippines, Past and Present,* 2 vols. (New York, 1914), I, 252.

11. *Report of the Philippine Commission to the President, January 31, 1900,* SD 138, 56th Cong., 1st sess., I, 185.

12. Almost nothing has been written recently on the work of the first commission. See Kenneth E. Hendrickson, Jr.'s excellent article "Reluctant Expansionist—Jacob Gould Schurman and the Philippine Question," *Pacific Historical Review* 36 (1967): 405-21.

13. The proclamation is in *Report of the Philippine Commission,* 3-5.

14. Commander, Conquering Regiment of *Armas Blancas* to President of Philippine Republic, Apr. 7, 1898, Philippine Insurgent Records (PIR) 72.10; HD 2, 56th Cong., 1st sess. V, 149.

15. Schurman to John Hay, Apr. 25, May 1, 1899, Records of the U. S. Commission to the Philippine Islands, E-739 in General Records of the Department of State. Cited hereafter as Commission Records. See also *Report,* SD 138, 56th Cong., 1st sess., I, 6; Otis to Alger, May 29, 1899, *Correspondence,* II, 998.

16. Schurman to Hay, May 1, 1899, Commission Records, E-739.

17. Testimony of Jesse Lee Hall, *Affairs in the Philippine Islands, Hearings before the Committee on the Philippines of the United States Senate,* SD 331, 57th Cong., 1st sess., pt. 3, 2430.

18. Field Orders No. 26, Headquarters 2d Division, 8th Army Corps, Apr. 22, 1899, *Affairs in the Philippine Islands,* SD 331, 57th Cong., 1st sess., pt. 2, 893. See also Field Orders No. 2, Apr. 2, 1899.

19. Ibid., 982-88; *Congressional Record,* 57th Cong., 1st sess. (1902), XXXV, pt. 6, 6143.

20. Testimony of George T. Boardman, *Affairs in the Philippine Islands,* SD 331, 57th Cong., 1st sess., pt. 3, 2322. See also Field Orders No. 2, Apr. 2, 1899, pt. 2, 893. Statistics on punishments in pt. 3, 2073-96.

21. Russell F. Weigley, *Towards an American Army: Military Thought from Washington to Marshall* (New York, 1962), 100-101.

22. John Bigelow, Jr., *The Principles of Strategy* (rev. ed., Philadelphia, 1894), 263-64. Bigelow enlarged both his book and the comments on the role of benevolence from the original 1891 edition. See also Russell F. Weigley, *Towards an American Army,* 97-98.

23. John M. Schofield, *Forty-Six Years in the Army* (New York, 1897), 313-15; Weigley, *Towards an American Army,* 169-70.

24. *Annual Reports of the War Department for the Fiscal Year Ended June 30, 1901,* HD 2, 57th Cong., 1st sess., VII covers the army's occupation of Cuba and Puerto Rico.

25. For a truly excellent example of an officer responding to the problems of a municipality, see A. Williams to Colonel William A. Kobbé, May 31, 1899 in which Williams gives a detailed account of his work in the town of Malabon, William A. Kobbé Papers, a part of the U.S. Military History Research Collection being organized at Carlisle Barracks.

26. Charles Denby to Hay, June 21, 1899, Commission Records, E-739; *War Department, 1899,* HD 2, 56th Cong., 1st sess., V, 145-48; *Annual Reports of the War Department for the Fiscal Year Ended June 30, 1900,* HD 2, 56th Cong., 5 HS. 2d sess., V, 449-69; Taylor, "Compilation," 5 H.S.

27. An interesting army view of what should be done to establish a regular public health system is in *Philippine Commission,* SD 138, 56th Cong., 1st sess., I, 262-64. On work in

progress in 1899 see *War Department, 1900,* HD 2, 56th
Cong., 2d sess., III, 617, IX, 294-95; Frank L. Dodds to
Joseph Wheeler, Sept. 22, 1899, William McKinley Papers; Albert G. Robinson, *The Philippines: The War and the People, A
Record of Personal Observations and Experiences,* 307-308.
Food distribution is covered in *War Department, 1899,* HD 2,
56th Cong., 1st sess., V, 228, VI, 169-70; *War Department,
1900,* HD 2, 56th Cong., 2d sess., VI, 313; Frederick J. Herman, *The Forty-Second Foot: A History of the 42d Regiment
of Infantry, United States Volunteers, Organized for Ser-
vice in the Philippine Insurrection* (Kansas City, Mo., 1942),
168; Henry Porter Williams, "Iowa's First Overseas Expedition,"
Annals of Iowa 32 (1955): 568.
    28. Testimony of MacArthur, *Affairs of the Philippine
Islands,* SD 331, 57th Cong., 1st sess., pt. 2, 872.
    29. Dorothy Della Swendiman, "The Development of
Education in the Philippine Islands since 1898" (M.A. thesis,
Duke University, 1942), 4-5.
    30. Testimonies of MacArthur and George T. Boardman,
Affairs in the Philippine Islands, SD 331, 57th Cong., 1st sess.,
pt. 2, 872, pt. 3, 2318-19. On army school work, see also, *War
Department, 1899,* HD 2, 56th Cong., 1st sess., V, 152; tes-
timony of David P. Barrows, SD 331, 57th Cong., 1st sess., pt. 1,
703; U. S. Department of the Interior, *Report of the Commissioner
of Education for the Year 1900-1901,* 2 vols. (Washington, 1902),
II, 1320.
    31. Phelps Whitmarsh, "Conditions in Manila," *The
Outlook* 63 (1899): 921. See also *Census, 1903,* III, 641.
    32. For a copy of Lawton's order see *War Department,
1899,* HD 2, 56th Cong., 1st sess., VI, 88. For an example of
an officer of lower rank working on his own to revive the town
of Malabon see Williams to Kobbé, May 31, 1899, Kobbé
Papers.
    33. See Kobbé's endorsements on the reports of Capt.
Alfred Morgan, June 13, 1899 and 1st Lt. E. M. Conrad, June
18, 1899 concerning conditions in and around Malabon; Kobbé to CO, Polo and CO, Malabon, July 5, 1899; unsigned to
Kobbé, July 17, 1899 explaining the Spanish system of
municipal government; Kobbé draft of a plan for municipal
government dated July 18, 1899; and William A. Kobbé,
"Diary of Field Service in the Philippines, 1898-1901," 74-79,
all in Kobbé Papers.

34. See MacArthur's endorsement to Kobbé's plan, July 21, 1899; Otis to MacArthur, July 31, 1899; Otis to Kobbé, Aug. 1, 1899; and Kobbé, "Diary," 80-84, Kobbé Papers.

35. Order No. 2, Headquarters U. S. Troops Guarding Railroad, July 31, 1899, Commission Records, E-738.

36. *War Department, 1899,* HD 2, 56th Cong., 1st sess., V, 144-45 contains the substantive portion of this order. The best summary of the Spanish system is R. L. Packard, "Political Organization of the Filipinos," *Scientific American Supplement* 69 (1900): 20459-60. A summary of the changes is in Carl C. Plehn, "Municipal Government in the Philippine Islands," *Municipal Affairs* 5 (1901): 793-801.

37. Beaumont B. Buck, *Memories of Peace and War* (San Antonio, 1935), 77-83. See other evidence of personal involvement in *War Department, 1900,* HD 2, 56th Cong., 2d sess., IX, 294-95; Dodds to Wheeler, Sept. 22, 1899, McKinley Papers; Robinson, *Philippines,* 302-308; Kobbé, "Diary," 90-94, Kobbé Papers.

38. General Orders No. 30, July 22, 1899, Office of the U. S. Military Governor in the Philippine Islands, *War Department, 1899,* HD 2, 56th Cong., 1st sess., V, 125-27.

39. *War Department, 1899,* HD 2, 56th Cong., 1st sess., V, 128. See also V, 122-28; VI, 342-43; Denby to Hay, July 25, 1899, Commission Records E-739; *War Department, 1900,* HD 2, 56th Cong., 2d sess., XI, 250-56.

40. Denby to Hay, July 7, 1899, McKinley Papers.

41. Ibid.

42. "Preliminary Statement of the Commissioners Appointed by the President of the United States to Investigate Affairs in the Philippine Islands," Records of the Bureau of Insular Affairs, 300, Incl. 3. Cited hereafter as BIA.

43. Otis to AG, June 26, 1899, *Correspondence,* II, 1019.

44. *War Department, 1899,* HD 2, 56th Cong., 1st sess., V, 162.

45. Arcadio Maxilom to Mabini, May 1, 1899, PIR 144.4.

46. Schurman to Hay, June 3, 1899, McKinley Papers; Denby to Hay, June 30, 1899, Commission Records, E-739. See also Teodoro A. Agoncillo, "Malolos: The Crisis of the Republic," *Philippine Social Sciences and Humanities Review* 25 (1960): 397-404.

47. Mabini to Aguinaldo, Apr. 8, 1899, PIR 62.2; Leandro Fullón to Aguinaldo, May 31, 1899, PIR 117.2; Bonifa-

cio Arevalo to Aguinaldo, Apr. 18, 1899, PIR 182.4; L.
M. Lacandola to Aguinaldo, Apr. 18, 1899, 192.3; Felipe
Rendon to Aguinaldo, Aug. 2, 1899, PIR 1017.4; Taylor,
"Compilation," 4HS.
    48. Aguinaldo to Secretary of War, June 15, 1899, PIR
289.4; José Ignacio Paua to Aguinaldo, June 20, 1899, PIR
355.1; Rendon to Aguinaldo, Aug. 2, 1899, PIR 1017.4;
Taylor, "Compilation," 4HS, 42AJ.
    49. Mabini to Aguinaldo, Feb. 28, 1899, PIR 512a.3;
Mabini to Aguinaldo, Mar. 6, 1899, PIR 512a.2; Mabini to
Aguinaldo, Apr. 8, 1899, PIR 62.2
    50. Taylor, "Compilation," 4HS; Martin Delgado, edict,
Oct. 14, 1899, PIR 881.4; Trías to Political Military Chief of
Infanta, Apr. 6, 1899, PIR 896.9; Serapión Atres to
Macabulos, Mar. 31, 1899, PIR 47.5.
    51. Marella to Delgado, Apr. 9, 1899, Taylor, "Compila-
tion," 26HK, 26-37HK, 65-70HS.
    52. Maxilom to Mabini, May 1, 1899, PIR 144.4, May
30, 1899, PIR 144.2.
    53. Agoncillo, "Malolos," 564-65; Matibay to Aguinal-
do, Sept. 16, 1899, PIR 102.2.
    54. Unsigned to Aguinaldo, July 18, 1899, PIR 72.6.
    55. Mabini, "Seamos Justos," Nov. 4, 1899, in *La
Revolución Filipina (con otros documentos de la época)*,
108; unsigned to Mabini, Apr. 6, 1899, PIR 56.5; Romeo V.
Cruz, "Filipino Collaboration with the Americans, 1899-
1902" (M.A. thesis, University of the Philippines, 1956), 100-
31.
    56. The thesis has been put forth that the original inhabi-
tants of the village of Macabebe were the progeny of Filipino
mothers and Indian soldiers brought by the Spaniards from
Mexico and California in the seventeenth century. William
Cameron Forbes, *The Philippine Islands* (Boston, 1928), I,
103*n*.
    57. *War Department, 1900*, HD 2, 56th Cong., 2d sess.,
V, 209.
    58. Maxilom to Mabini, May 15, 1899, PIR 144.5.
    59. Joseph I. Markey, *From Iowa to the Philippines: A
History of Company M. Fifty-First Iowa Infantry Volunteers*
(Red Oak, Iowa, 1900), 211.
    60. John Clifford Brown, *Diary of a Soldier in the Philip-*

pines (Portland, Me., 1901), 47; Taylor, "Compilation," 43AJ, 91AJ; Kobbé "Diary," 51, 97, 173. A different view of the reaction of the Chinese community can be found in Edgar Wickberg, *The Chinese in Philippine Life, 1850-1898*, 202. According to Wickberg, "as a general rule, the Chinese seem to have refrained from overt commitment to either side. Their method was simply to wait and be prepared to do business with whoever might be victorious." The limited evidence available, however, supports the opposite tentative conclusion that the Chinese suffered at the hands of the revolutionaries and were disposed to support the Americans.

61. "Preliminary Statement of the Commissioners," BIA 300, Inc. 3, 13.

62. Buencamino circular letter to Agoncillo, Apacible, and Ponce, Mar. 27, 1899 in Taylor, "Compilation," 55GR. See also 95-99AJ and unsg. to Luna, Apr. 11, 1899, 51 GR.

63. Denby to Hay, June 2 and 30, 1899, Commission Records, E-739; Schurman to Hay, June 3, 1899, Denby, Worcester, and Otis to Hay, June 7, 1899, McKinley Papers.

64. A. Guzman to Luna, Feb. 22, 1899, PIR 580.2; Ponce to Y. Yamagata, Apr. 11, 1899, in *Mario Ponce: Cartas sobre la revolución*, 328; Mascardo to Ruperto Arce, May 23, 1899, PIR 923.3; Taylor, "Compilation," 53MM; opinion of Pío del Pilar in Aguinaldo to Secretary of War, Sept. 19, 1899, PIR 57.4; and Vlease to Esprindión Borgia, Oct. 17, 1899, PIR 57.3.

65. Aguinaldo, proclamation, Sept. 6, 1897 taken from W. E. Retana, *La Política de España en Filipinas*, VII (1897) in Taylor, "Compilation," 48LY.

66. This was an American analysis of Filipino propaganda. See Field Orders No. 2, Headquarters, 2d Division, 8th Army Corps, Apr. 2, 1899, *Affairs in the Philippine Islands*, SD 331, 57th Cong., 1st sess., pt. 2, 892.

67. Quesada to Local Chiefs, Mar. 29, 1899, PIR 887.6. On propaganda see also report of Acting Assistant Surgeon Henry du R. Phelan, Mar. 4, 1899, in Robert H. Noble (comp.), "A Compilation of Insurgent Documents consisting chiefly of letters and orders issued by insurgent officials during the Insurrection in the Philippine Islands from 1898 to 1902 pertaining chiefly to the Visayan group, comprising the islands of Panay, Negros, Cebu, Bohol, Leyte and Samar," 34 vols.

(1902), XV, 2456-57. The original of this document could not be found either in Washington or Manila. A copy is contained on microfilm in the United States National Archives. Cited hereafter as Noble, "Compilation." See also *War Department, 1900,* HD 2, 56th Cong., 2d sess., V, 361-65.

68. This was a Mar. 27, 1899 report of a loss of 28,000 men recorded in Worcester, *Philippines,* I, 282. See also I, 281-85; Army of the Visayas to Local Presidents of Iloilo Province, Apr. 6, 1899, PIR 886.13.

69. Aguinaldo, proclamation, Aug. 31, 1899, PIR 457.12; Aguinaldo, undated propaganda letter, Records of the Adjutant General's Office, 317876, incl. 3, cited hereafter as AGO; Buencamino to Foreign Consuls, Oct. 7, 1899, PIR 442.9.

70. Mabini to Maxilom, Apr. 11, 1899, PIR 1079.1; Aguinaldo to Secretary of War, June 15, 1899, PIR 289.4; Taylor, "Compilation," 4HS; Delgado to Province of Iloilo, Oct. 14, 1899, PIR 881.4.

71. Examples of collected press clippings are in PIR 343, 394, and 395. See also John R. Thomas, Jr., "Collection Relating to the Insurrectionist Government of the Philippines, 1898-1899."

72. Dansinger to Hong Kong junta, Mar. 8, 1899, PIR 16.1.

73. Leverson to Apacible, July 17, 1899, PIR 391.4.

74. Fred H. Harrington, "The Anti-Imperialist Movement in the United States, 1898-1900," *Mississippi Valley Historical Review* 22 (1935): 224-25; Alger to Otis, Apr. 25, 1899, *Correspondence,* II, 973; Otis to AG, Dec. 8, 1899, *Correspondence,* II, 1115-16; Otis to AG, Dec. 1, 1899, BIA 141, incl. 15; Frederick Palmer, *With My Own Eyes* (Indianapolis, 1932), 160.

75. Ambrosio Flores to Generals, Chief Officers, and Soldiers of the Filipino Army, Oct. 5, 1899, PIR 106.1; Buencamino to Secretary of Interior, Oct. 26, 1899, PIR 16.2 and Secretary of Interior to Provincial, Local, and Military Commanders in Tarlac, Murcia, Capas, Bangbang, Gerona, Panique, and Victoria, Oct. 27, 1899, PIR 16.5; untitled document, Nov. 14, 1899, PIR 1159.

76. Wildman to David J. Hill, Aug. 19, 1899, AGO 287205; Buencamino and Aguinaldo to Chief of Bureau of Information in Manila, July 26, 1899, PIR 78.10; Faustino [of the junta] to "Sir," May 2, 1899, PIR 16.1.

77. Isidoro de los Santos to Aguinaldo, Mar. 29, 1899, PIR 455.8.

78. Apacible to Mabini, Mar. 13, 1899, PIR, 493.12.

79. Marius B. Jansen, *The Japanese and Sun Yat-sen*, 68-73; Enrique J. Corpus, "Japan and the Philippine Revolution," *The Philippine Social Science Review* 6 (1934): 286-96; James K. Eyre, Jr., "Japan and the American Annexation of the Philippines," *Pacific Historical Review* 11 (1942), "Japanese Imperialism and the Aguinaldo Insurrection," *United States Naval Institute Proceedings* 75 (1949). On Japanese officers with the Filipino army documentation is sketchy. See extract of document No. 180, Letters Received Book of the Philippine Secretary of War, PIR 390.3; Manuel Luis Quezon, *The Good Fight* (New York, 1946), 55; extract from Sept. 1, 1899, letter taken by the Americans from Martin García Fermín, PIR 903.3. The Americans only became concerned over the possibility of Japanese aid to the revolutionaries in 1901, long after such aid was a reality. See William Howard Taft to Elihu Root, Feb. 10, 1901, Elihu Root Papers; documents collected in PIR 903.5 concerning the search of the house of Captain Shinoba Narahara of the Japanese army in Manila; Taylor, note, Jan. 4, 1902, PIR 420.1.

80. *War Department, 1899*, HD 2, 56th Cong., 1st sess., V, 120-21; Otis to AG, May 4, 1899, *Correspondence*, II, 981-82.

81. Otis to AG, Apr. 20, June 16 and 26, Aug. 27, Sept. 17, 1899, *Correspondence*, II, 969, 1014, 1020, 1059-60, 1069-70.

82. Testimony of Hughes, *Affairs in the Philippine Islands*, SD 331, 57th Cong., 1st sess., pt. 1, 541.

83. *War Department, 1899*, HD 2, 56th Cong., 1st sess., V, 162.

84. Palmer, *Own Eyes*, 143; Whitmarsh, "Conditions in Manila," 918-19; testimony of Bourns, *Philippine Commission*, SD 138, 56th Cong., 1st sess., II, 350-51; testimony of Otis, *Affairs in the Philippine Islands*, SD 331, 57th Cong., 1st sess., pt. 1, 736; Dodds to Wheeler, Sept. 22, 1899, McKinley Papers.

85. *War Department, 1900*, HD 2, 56th Cong., 2d sess., IX, 294-95 and XI, 254-55.

86. Otis to AG, Dec. 19, 1899, *Correspondence*, II, 1123; Dionisio Papa, orders, Dec. 1899, PIR 970.5; Taylor, "Compilation," 73-75HS.

87. See all enclosures to PIR 99; Taylor, "Compilation," 71-72HS, 68AJ.

88. Robinson, *The Philippines,* 297; Denby to Hay, July 7, 1899, McKinley Papers.

89. Robinson, *The Philippines,* 301-302, see also 298; Palmer, *Own Eyes,* 160; the material covering similar problems in Manila, *supra,* chap. 2.

90. *Philippine Commission,* SD 138, 56th Cong., 1st sess., I, 178. See also Robinson, *The Philippines,* 297-98; *War Department, 1901,* HD 2, 57th Cong., 1st sess., IX, 20-21.

91. See item 9 of a questionnaire completed by Lawrence Benton, 33rd Infantry as a part of the Spanish-American War, Philippine Insurrection, and Boxer Rebellion Veterans Research Project, U.S. Military History Research Collection. One should probably distinguish between looting and foraging. The latter was accepted by most commanders as a military necessity, and, as Mr. Benton recalled, "acquiring a viscious chicken was not considered theft."

92. For evidence of both misconduct on the part of American troops and actions of the Army to end it see *Charges of Cruelty, etc., to the Natives of the Philippines,* SD 205, 57th Cong., 1st sess., (1902). *Affairs in the Philippine Islands,* SD 331, 57th Cong., 1st sess., pts. 1-3; V. Edmund McDevitt, *The First California's Chaplain,* 153-73; Brown, *Diary,* 33, 35, 38, 93, 99; Corbin to Otis, Sept. 18, 1899, Otis to AG, Sept. 21, 1899, *Correspondence,* II, 1070, 1072; *Congressional Record,* 57th Cong., 1st sess., XXXV, pt. 6, 6143; Charles J. Crane, *The Experiences of a Colonel of Infantry* (New York, 1923), 321.

93. The most vivid evidence of this is in the Records of the Office of the Chief Signal Officer, File 93, "Red Book Collection;" File 96, Signal Corps "Historical File." The best single photo is that of a signal corps telegraph station on a church altar, "Red Book Collection," No. 1344.

94. Brown, *Diary,* 84.

95. Schurman to Hay, May 30, 1899, Commission Records, E-739; Denby to Hay, Sept. 13, 1899, ibid.

96. Otis to Secretary of War, June 4, 1899, *Correspondence,* II, 1002.

97. Denby, Worcester, and Otis to Hay, June 7, 1899,

McKinley Papers. See also Hendrickson, "Reluctant Expansionist," 411-13.

98. Collins to Charles S. Diehl, May 9, 1899 quoted in Diehl to Charles A. Boynton, June 28, 1899, McKinley Papers.

99. Copy of the round robin in Collins to Diehl, June 29, 1899, McKinley Papers.

100. Ibid.

101. Corbin to Otis, June 30, 1899, *Correspondence,* II, 1023-24; Otis to AG, July 1, 1899, ibid., 1025 and July 20, 1899, ibid., 1036.

102. *New York Tribune,* July 22, 1899, 1.

103. Corbin to Otis, Sept. 9, 1899, *Correspondence,* II, 1065.

104. Young to Roosevelt, Aug. 7, 1899, Root Papers.

105. Wheeler to McKinley, Oct 29, 1899, McKinley Papers; Roosevelt to Root, Sept. 25, 1899, Elting E. Morison (ed.), *The Letters of Theodore Roosevelt* (Cambridge, Mass., 1951), II, 1078-79; William G. Haan, MS Diary, Feb. 20, 1899, William G. Haan Papers; Frederick Palmer, "White Man and Brown Man in the Philippines," *Scribner's Magazine* 27 (1900): 85; Robert Dexter Carter to sister, May 7, 1899, Robert Dexter Carter Papers, Rutherford B. Hayes Memorial Library.

106. Schwan to Corbin, Aug. 21, 1899, Henry C. Corbin Papers; Corbin to Schwan, Oct. 6, 1899, ibid.

107. Roosevelt to John Henry Parker, May 16, 1900, Morison, *Letters,* II, 1297-98.

108. On raising of the volunteer force, see Corbin to Otis, Aug. 12, 1899, Otis to AG, Aug. 14, 1899, *Correspondence,* II, 1051-53; *War Department, 1899,* HD 2, 56th Cong., 1st sess., II, 3-8; Root to McKinley, Aug. 15, 1899, McKinley to Root, Aug. 19, 1899, McKinley Papers; Roosevelt to Lodge, Aug. 10, 1899, Henry Cabot Lodge, *Selections from the Correspondence of Theodore Roosevelt and Henry Cabot Lodge, 1884-1918,* I, 416; Philip C. Jessup, *Elihu Root,* 2 vols. (New York, 1938), I, 228-29; Root to J. R. Hawley, Sept. 13, 1899, Root to Franklin Bartlett, Oct, 24, 1899, Root Papers; Corbin to Schwan, Oct. 6, 1899, Corbin Papers. On the native scouts see Otis to AG, Sept. 29, 1899, *Correspondence,* II, 1076; *War Department, 1900,* HD 2, 56th Cong., 2d sess., V, 209-10, VIII, 123-29.

109. *War Department, 1900,* HD 2, 56th Cong., 2d sess., V, 207, 214; Otis to AG, Oct. 4, 7 and 11, 1899, *Correspondence,* II, 1079, 1082, 1084.

110. *War Department, 1899,* HD 2, 56th Cong., 1st sess., II, 9-12; W. L. Sibert, "Military Occupation of Northern Luzon," *Journal of the Military Service Institution of the United States* 30 (1902): 404-408; Otis to AG, Nov. 13, 1899, *Correspondence,* II, 1100. On use of scouts see John W. Ganzhorn, *I've Killed Men: An Epic of Early Arizona* (New York, 1959), 147-49, 159; T. H. Slavens, *Scouting in Northern Luzon, P. I., 1899-1900* (n.p., 1947), *passim.*

111. *War Department, 1899,* HD 2, 56th Cong., 1st sess., II, 12; Sibert, "Military Occupation," 408; Edward B. Clark, *William L. Sibert: The Army Engineer* (Philadelphia, 1930), 46-75.

112. Brown, *Diary,* 110. Donald F. Carmony et al., "Three Years in the Orient: The Diary of William R. Johnson, 1898-1902," *Indiana Magazine of History* 63 (1967): 279-81 contains a similar observation.

113. State of Oregon, *Official Records of the Oregon Volunteers in the Spanish War and Philippine Insurrection,* 94.

114. *War Department, 1899* HD 2, 56th Cong., 1st sess., III, 467.

115. Howze to Kennon, Nov. 12, 1899, Kennon Papers.

116. James Parker, *The Old Army* (Philadelphia, 1929), 282-83.

117. Otis to AG, Nov. 24, 1899, *Correspondence,* II, 1107.

118. *War Department, 1900,* HD 2, 56th Cong., 2d sess., V, 275-76.

119. Ibid., 286.

120. Kennon to Corbin, Oct. 25, 1899, Corbin Papers.

121. *War Department, 1900* HD 2, 56th Cong., 2d sess., VII, 379.

122. Ibid., V, 306-307; Howze to Kennon, Nov. 12, 1899, Kennon Papers; T. M. Anderson, "Our Rule in the Philippines," *North American Review* 170 (1900): 282-83.

123. Corbin to Schwan, Oct. 19, 1899, Corbin Papers. Quotations in this paragraph are taken from Root's speech in Robert Bacon and James B. Scott (eds.), *The Military and Colonial Policy of the United States: Addresses and Reports by*

Elihu Root (Cambridge, Mass., 1916), 11-12. Root's ideas on colonial government are best expressed in *War Department, 1899*, HD 2, 56th Cong., 1st sess., II, 24-27.

124. James D. Richardson, ed., *A Compilation of the Messages and Papers of the Presidents* (New York, 1917), XIII, 6399.

4

THE ROOTS OF COLONIAL GOVERNMENT

The American command in Manila believed that the offensive at the end of 1899 had been a complete success. Commanders in the field were equally optimistic, and there was a general view among members of the American force that the revolution was at an end. General Hughes, commanding in the Visayas, thought that signs there pointed to a speedy termination of the war. He was more interested in reconstructing the war-torn areas than in further operations against the Filipinos. General Schwan, operating in southern Luzon, believed that "before many months the guerrilla warfare now waged by the old insurgent element will be ended, and the pacification of the country accomplished." In a similar report from northern Luzon, General Wheaton wrote that the local populace seemed well disposed toward the American occupation and that they would acquiesce to it if protected from the remaining guerrilla bands roaming the countryside. General Otis was also optimistic. He thought that only a short mop-up campaign remained before a stable colonial rule would be developed in the islands. Any threat of renewed revolution would end if all strategic points in the island were garrisoned. American protection, schools, local government, and other features of a benevolent rule would be sufficient to maintain the peace.[1]

Throughout the first half of 1900 the army focused on actions calculated to pacify the people and to extend American authority as rapidly as possible. The war, as far as the Americans were concerned, had ended with the destruction of Aguinaldo's army in 1899. Reconstruction and the establishment of a well organized government were uppermost in the minds of General Otis and his immediate subordinates. A new series of proclamations, such as that issued by General Schwan in Batangas, outlined the American policy to the Filipinos. Schwan proclaimed that the United States had come into the area "not in the spirit of ruthless invasion, but in the spirit of peace and good will to all good citizens, and with the object of establishing good government amongst you, which will secure to individuals the protection of their persons and property and the peaceful pursuit of industry and happiness." He enjoined "all citizens to continue in or return to their homes and to pursue their peaceful avocations, in which they will not be molested." He also stated that he or local commanders would be "glad to receive the people's representatives for the purpose of advising with them as to the measures necessary to promote prosperity and contentment under the authority of the United States Government."[2]

Continued resistance on the part of the Filipinos was unthinkable to American commanders such as General Schwan. The task at hand was to establish rapport between Filipino and American and get on with the work of organizing the islands under American control in accordance with the promises made to the inhabitants by the army and the government.

During 1899 the colonial government operating in Manila worked from day to day on an ad hoc basis. With few precedents to follow, administrators based their procedures and decisions on a combination of Spanish custom and American experience. Filipino employees of the Spanish government and American military personnel cooperated to run the various arms of colonial government inherited from the Spaniards. In 1900, following the defeat of the regular Filipino army, the Americans attempted to regularize and systematize their military government to provide a firm basis for the eventual establishment of a more permanent colonial administration.

In their attempt to organize a court system, American officers found that the substantive body of Spanish law was excellent and adequate for the American purposes. The real prob-

lem was in applying it. In 1899, the Americans had reestablished the Audiencia as the Supreme Court and opened civil
courts in the major cities under American control. In 1900, the
Americans concentrated on making necessary changes in judicial procedure and continued their efforts to reorganize the civil
courts. They developed a system under Filipino judges in a
uniform hierarchy of justices of the peace, lower courts at the
municipal level, and higher courts at the provincial level. The
Supreme Court remained the capstone of the system. The office
of solicitor was combined with that of lawyer, as was common
in the United States. At the end of 1899 the Americans had also changed the marriage laws to legalize civil marriage.
Filipinos had long complained that Spanish marriage laws
were too restrictive and that the expense of the religious marriage ceremony encouraged concubinage.[3]

The Americans instituted a second major legal reform in
April 1900 with a complete revision of the Spanish criminal
code. The new code provided the safeguards of individual
rights so prominent in American practice, including the concepts of the official complaint, a speedy and public trial,
defense through witnesses and appeal, the right of defendants
to separate trials, the plea of insufficient complaint or prior
jeopardy, and the rights of retrial, bail, habeas corpus, and
search warrants. The Americans revoked Spanish rules admitting hearsay evidence and prohibiting the accused, his relatives,
and his employees from testifying. In developing the new laws
the Americans were aided by Florentino Torres, a Manila
lawyer, but the new code was such a departure from previous
practice that the army appointed special American aides to
help Filipino lawyers and judges operate within the framework
of the new procedures.[4]

Because judges, prosecuting attorneys, and lawyers en-
countered many initial difficulties due to their unfamiliarity
with American principles of justice, the Americans found that
continued use of military courts in criminal cases was a
necessity. They also continued to use them in areas where civil
courts were not yet organized. Civil cases, however, were handled almost exclusively in the reorganized system, and no matter how difficult the administration of justice seemed in 1900
there was at least the framework of a complete court system

based on legal principles and statutes compatible with those in the United States. When conditions became more settled, the transfer from the dual system of military and civil courts to a completely civil system was relatively simple.[5]

In addition to reorganizing the courts, the military government undertook to equalize and reform the internal revenue system. The Americans had been forced to reinstate the *cédula* or head tax that they had abolished in 1899, but the new *cédula* was sold at an extremely low price. It no longer represented an important form of revenue and was only retained because of its widespread use as a means of identification. The original Spanish tax structure was exceedingly complex, and the Americans streamlined it by abolishing numerous taxes. They ended the vassalage tax, the 10 percent discount on certain classes of official salaries, the lottery tax, monopoly contracts, and numerous surtaxes and provisional taxes. The remaining assessments were divided into the revised industrial tax, amounting to a levy on income and profits; the *urbana* or dwelling tax, revised to exempt the majority of private houses; and a stamp tax on contracts, legal documents, and other official paper. Although General Otis noted that the collection of revenue within the new framework proceeded slowly, he added that "haste in these matters was not intended, as the majority of the people are in poverty, having suffered severely . . . during several years of almost constant warfare."[6] American officers had seen the inequity of the Spanish system that taxed houses and shops but did not tax land, but remanded the difficult problem of developing a new system of land taxation to the civil government which they knew would eventually rule the islands.[7]

The other departments of the military government were also busy reorganizing for the eventual transfer to civil control. The Mining Bureau, for example, refused to grant new concessions; the officers in charge devoted their time to a study of the Spanish archives, the examination of claims pending before the American occupation, and the preparation of laws and regulations to be placed into effect at a later date. Similar work was done in the Forestry Bureau, where employees and military personnel devoted their time to the work of classification, translation, and revision of regulations. The army stressed the development of a system that could be used as the basis for continuing American rule in the islands. The work done in reorganizing the government was detailed and obviously not intended to be temporary.[8]

In an attempt to link all of the islands into administrative units connected to the central colonial government being developed in Manila, General Otis ordered his commanders in the field to organize municipal governments and to develop district offices to carry out such functions of the central government as the collection of customs duties and taxes.[9] General Order No. 43, 1899 series, had proven adequate for the organization of small towns or centers of population in areas greatly disturbed by the war, but it was not sufficient for large municipalities. Therefore, General Otis appointed a board under the presidency of Cayetano Arellano to formulate a more detailed plan of municipal government "as liberal in character as existing conditions permit."[10]

The plan for the new municipal government organization was set forth in General Order No. 40, March 29, 1900. According to General Otis, it was intended to be "experimental" and to "furnish the foundation upon which can be erected a stable civil government."[11] The order provided for a government closely resembling that used by the Spaniards in the towns. The Americans hoped that this would make the implementation of the system easier. As in the Spanish plan, suffrage was limited, but the Americans broadened its base by lowering the requirements. The electorate included owners of property valued at more than 500 pesos; those paying over 30 pesos in taxes; those who spoke, read, and wrote English or Spanish; and those who had served previously in an elective municipal office. Each town was to elect a president and a council for administering municipal affairs. The municipalities were to be self-supporting and were to be supervised by administrative officers appointed at the provincial level.

The military tried to develop a system that was neither completely autonomous nor unduly centralized. One of General Otis's subordinates, Enoch H. Crowder, viewed it as "a conservative system which . . . gave the necessary impulse and initiative to municipal life and at the same time permitted the necessary inspection by, and subordination to, the military

authorities."[12] General Otis thought that "a reading of the provisions of the law clearly demonstrates the purposes, tenden-
cies, and beneficent intentions of the United States Government." The Americans hoped that the municipal governments
would serve a tutorial as well as an administrative function,
and General Order No. 40 stated that the law was to be "educating . . . calculated to urge on the people in the path of true
progress."[13]

Convinced that their wartime role was ending, American
troops in the field embarked rapidly on efforts to institute
municipal governments and develop their military government
in other ways. In the process of organizing the provincial and
municipal governments, they built schools, initiated public
health work, and generally continued all of the actions that they
had begun earlier in Manila, Negros, and the other areas that
had fallen to them in 1899. Reports from the commanders involved in this work spoke of "satisfactory progress," schools
"well attended," towns "remarkably quiet," and conditions
"encouraging" or "improved" throughout the regions under
American jurisdiction.[14] There were minor problems, such as
the lack of interpreters and the poverty of the municipalities,
but progress seemed rapid.

In the towns the Americans garrisoned, they tried to improve the political, economic, and social conditions in which
the great mass of Filipinos had lived for years. Perhaps even
more important, their work was calcualted to impress upon the
Filipinos the benefits of American rule and gain popular acceptance of United States sovereignty. In the *pueblo* of Lagonoy, for example, two companies of American soldiers con-
structed roads, built and repaired bridges, fed the people during
a short famine, organized civil government, and established a
local police force. In short, they did all they could to "gain the
people's confidence."[15] On the island of Leyte, men of the
43d Regiment of Volunteers completely cleaned the town of
Tacloban and instituted sanitary measures resembling those
begun in Manila in 1898. The officers of the regiment viewed
the money spent to employ men to clean the streets as doing
"as much if not more than anything else in bringing about the
comparatively good feeling that has ever since existed in the
town."[16] They developed the town budget with a view toward

equalization of taxation, obtained buildings for a public school system, and established both a municipal government and a police force. The regiment built and repaired bridges and roads, appropriated $250 for the erection of a market, and worked to show the local inhabitants that American intentions in their municipality were truly humanitarian. Members of the army elsewhere on Leyte were instructed to follow similar procedures in the villages under their command, and Captain W. L. Goldsborough in Dagami reported that "the amount of good work to be done with this town as a base is only limited by the number of men in the garrison."[17]

The army was particularly active in public health work, as it extended, increased, and systematized the efforts begun in 1898 and 1899. The Manila Board of Health continued to operate in that city. In addition to its massive sanitary efforts, it instituted a system of house-to-house inspection and quarantine to prevent epidemics of plague, cholera, and smallpox. The army opened a dispensary where prescriptions given to paupers were filled free of charge. It operated bacteriological laboratories and institutes to develop vaccines and serums and to monitor the city's water supply. The Americans sent a medical officer to cities in Japan and China to study measures used to prevent bubonic plague epidemics. All of this work led to a decided diminution in the city's death rate. By June 1900, deaths were about half of what they had been in October 1899, although the steady decrease took place in the face of increasing heat and the approach of the rainy season. The medical officers had successfully combated a plague outbreak in the first few months of 1900. Colonel Charles R. Greenleaf, Chief Surgeon for the Philippines, recommended to Washington that not only should the projects already in progress be continued, but that a more permanent public health organization should be formed in Manila, which should adopt health regulations comparable to those in effect in the larger cities of the United States.[18]

In areas under American control outside of Manila, public health work progressed under the general direction of the Manila Board of Health, which acted throughout 1900 as a public health organization for both the city and the provinces. Immense problems faced the American medical officers as they moved into the municipalities. The war had impoverished the Filipino population; all available medical supplies and many Filipino physicians had been drawn into the revolutionary army. Even the simplest medical remedies were absent in most towns, and the army began a comprehensive program of medical charity. It supplied essential drugs and surgical dressings for use in treating the local populace in the towns. Army surgeons, when not actively engaged in treating American soldiers, devoted considerable time to the health needs of the immediate areas under their supervision. The army allotted them $150.00 Mex. every three months for each 1,000 sick persons in their charge. As in Manila, the army distributed medicine to the indigent. In addition, although against regulations, surgeons continued to treat the local people with medical supplies allotted for the American troops. Such work, combined with efforts to better sanitary conditions in the towns, did much to improve the general level of health. In the town of Mexico, for example, an active program of sanitation and fifty ounces of quinine ended a malaria epidemic that had previously killed as many as twelve people in one week. An emergency hospital was established in Manila, and in places where doctors were not available, enlisted members of the Hospital Corps often saved lives. In one case, in the absence of the regimental surgeon, two Hospital Corps privates successfully operated on a woman badly cut by a bolo. They replaced the woman's eyeball and successfully amputated her gangrenous arm.[19]

Vaccination was one of the army's most important public-health projects. Large-scale vaccinations were conducted under the supervision of the Manila Board of Health. The army manufactured the vaccine locally and distributed it throughout the islands. It instructed medical officers in the procedures of mass vaccination and authorized them to hire an unlimited number of local vaccinators to aid in the task. The Spaniards had practiced vaccination for years, and few persons objected when the army's public vaccinations began. The army vaccination program reduced smallpox to such an extent that the disease was no longer a serious menace in the islands, although, before the arrival of the Americans, it had on occasion reached epidemic proportions.[20]

Although army public health efforts in the provinces were

beset with the same problems as those which had accompanied similar work in Manila, they were, on the whole, extremely successful. The Filipinos had no concept of municipal sanitation, although they were extremely clean personally, and they viewed disease rather fatalistically.[21] The army, already forcing them to dispose of refuse and to clean up around their dwellings, was encouraged to find that they readily accepted vaccination and medical treatment. The Filipinos could not overlook the tremendous drop in mortality that accompanied the initiation of American public health measures. The statistics in the provinces followed the trend evident in Manila; and in the area around the town of Baliuag, for example, the monthly death toll dropped from 206 in October 1899 to 84 by February 1900. One officer, commenting on the efforts of his unit in one municipality, credited the work of his medical officer as being "an important element in the pacification of the district."[22]

At the insistence of the chief surgeon in the Philippines, the number of medical officers in the islands had been increased markedly, and the resulting high ratio of army doctors to troops meant that medical and public health programs were brought to most towns garrisoned by the Americans. In Northern Luzon, where there were eventually 274 military posts, the ratio was one surgeon for every 176 men.[23] General Otis stated in his annual report for 1900 that the "unremitting labors of the officers of the Medical Department . . . in administering to the wounded of the enemy and attending native citizens requiring medical treatment, can not be too highly commended."[24] Because of the widespread distribution of doctors and the immediate statistical evidence of their effectiveness, the army's public health work was an important force for pacification, bringing to the Filipinos vivid evidence of the humanitarian and benevolent intentions of the United States.

When American units occupied a town in 1899, one of their first actions was to organize a school. This pattern continued in 1900. The army tried to expand its work in education and to provide a certain uniformity and coordination for local educational programs throughout the islands. In the field, army units worked to build and organize schools, but there was no comprehensive program of education. Work in early 1900, as in 1899, was done hurriedly and under extremely unfavorable conditions. There were not enough local teachers, and the soldiers detailed to teach in the schools could not retain those positions indefinitely. The towns had difficulty obtaining school supplies; shipments from Manila consisted of items available, not necessarily those most needed. The soldiers made no attempt at placing pupils in grades, and there was little professional supervision. Without a land tax, most towns were too poor to develop schools without assistance from the central government. Materials, including texts, were outdated. The army recognized that its school work in early 1900 was of little intrinsic value except as a way to show the goodwill of the American governent in the municipalities.[25]

Under wartime conditions, the army did accomplish a great deal in the field of public education. It had spent some money on school supplies in 1899, but at the start of 1900 the army's school work was only beginning to develop to its full potential. As in its other civil affairs projects, the military government moved to systematize the school work by establishing an office to coordinate education efforts for the whole of the Philippines. On March 30, 1900 a department of public instruction was organized under the direction of Captain Albert Todd. Almost immediately Captain Todd sent a circular letter to military commanders in the provinces requesting information on school development and on their needs to help him plan an educational program. He also asked for suggestions from those officers directly involved in the school program at the municipal level. After a study of the old Spanish system, Captain Todd concluded that the Americans would have to begin anew.

Within five months from the time of the Department of Public Instruction's organization, the progress seemed remarkable. Over 100,000 pupils were enrolled in about 1,000 schools. The army had distributed over $100,000 of school material, including texts in arithmetic, geography, United States history, English, and English readers, as well as ink, copy books, pens, paper, chalk, blackboard slating, slates, and American flags. Perhaps most important in the long run, Captain Todd formulated a plan for a comprehensive system of education for the Philippines based on the recommendations he received from American commanders in the provinces.

Todd proposed a system organized, supervised, and supported by the central government. He remarked in his report to the military governor that "as yet our Government is but at the threshold of public education in the Philippines, and . . . the future will demand large outlays of money and the labor of experienced and competent educators."[26] Todd recommended compulsory school attendance and primary grades that would represent a "comprehensive modern school system for the teaching of elementary English." He also suggested that English be the language of instruction throughout the islands, with Spanish or native dialects used only during the period of transition. Teachers would be brought from the United States to help develop the system. Also, Todd sought the organization of industrial schools and a well-equipped normal school. He wanted the school structure thoroughly modernized, and he thought that it should be completely divorced from the church. "I am well aware," he wrote, "that some of these recommendations imply the expenditure of considerable sums of public money, but I can think of no expenditure which will have greater influence in developing peace and progress in these islands than public schools."[27]

Todd's ideas of the relation between school development and pacification agreed with those of many other American officers. The Filipinos were enthusiastic about the educational work being done by the army and seemed to appreciate the efforts of the soldiers to build and operate schools. Compulsion was usually unnecessary to get students enrolled; in Iloilo, for example, 438 out of 500 possible students attended school voluntarily.[28] In Laoag, eighty adults met nightly for English instruction given by an American officer. Because of the Filipino interest in education, the officers reporting to Captain Todd recognized that school development was related to pacification efforts and consequently of utmost importance. Major Cornelius Gardener in Tayabas Province believed that "if properly managed hereafter, the bureau of education in these islands . . . can be more beneficial than troops in preventing future revolutions."[29] Colonel E. J. McClernand on Cebu thought that prompt aid from the central government to the municipalities for education would have "an excellent political effect, and materially aid in establishing towns under American orders and laws." On Negros, General Smith thought that the schools and the soldier instructors were "a potent factor in bringing the lower classes, by means of the children, into more cordial relations with Americans."[30] The army regarded school work as a tool of pacification as well as evidence of American benevolence, and throughout 1900 it tried to improve its efforts in the development of municipal schools.

The development of public works projects was another American policy that the Filipinos themselves thought important. One of the original demands of the Propaganda Movement and of the revolutionaries in 1896 was that Spain end its neglect of the islands and institute projects to improve transportation and communications. The American programs went beyond these demands. Public works projects were most evident in Manila. There the army was simultaneously building markets, bridges, and incinerators; reclaiming swamp areas, macadamizing roads; and extending street lighting. Special projects included the repair of the sea wall and the improvement of the harbor facilities. Work in the provinces was not as extensive, but the repair and building of roads and bridges took place continuously. Although such work had a military significance, it represented American interest in the progress of the islands as far as the local inhabitants were concerned. General Otis thought road building and repair had a triple purpose. It improved the military transport and supply system, gave the Filipinos a means of transporting their products to market, and furnished them with employment. The General wrote in his report for 1900 that "no former public proceeding so favorably impressed the inhabitants of the provinces in which the work was being carried on of the kindly intentions of the United States as these highway repairs at the public expense," and he observed that the Filipinos "gave all the assistance they could to expedite the work."[31] In the Visayas, General Hughes used public works as a means of alleviating poverty and supplying the natives with enough money to buy the necessities of life. He thought that throughout the Philippines "some measures

should be taken to provide occupation for the men who have
been idle for a long time."[32] Understanding that each island
had its own specific needs, he favored public works projects
devoted to those facilities most important to each locality.

As in 1899, Negros was still the showplace of the American military government. The Americans viewed it as the
best example of America's good intentions in the Philippines,
and General Smith was intent on making a success of the ex-
periment that had been undertaken there. Negros had an experimental farm and agricultural societies to find ways of
developing the island's agricultural potential, and the army
began new industries for making bamboo fishing rods, chairs,
and fish nets. By distributing free rice to the indigent, the army
prevented a famine that could have accompanied a local
drought and the destruction of the rice crops on other islands
in the Visayas by the revolutionaries. General Smith reported
that "in many of the towns there is a great boom in building"
which he viewed "as a favorable indication that disturbances
of the public order are not expected in Negros." He noted that,
although the Filipinos on the island still feared that what had
been conceded them by the Americans might be taken away,
the nationalists were unable to foment successful revolt there.
Negros was definitive proof that peace could be maintained
through benevolence and humanitarian action in the field of
civil affairs. General Smith was confident that, if the Americans
continued their policy and proceeded cautiously and slowly,
they would not have to worry about a rejection of American
sovereignty.[33]

By the middle of 1900, the army had shown the Filipinos
in the towns under American control a truly impressive array of
benevolent and humane works. Writing on soldier rule in the
Philippines, Captain D. H. Boughton summed up in grand style
the accomplishments of the military government. "It is probable," he wrote, "that the civil administrative work done by
the army in these islands will never be thoroughly appreciated,
but it is safe to say that never again will the pueblo affairs be
administered throughout with the same integrity, same
economy and thoroughness, as when under the supervision of
the United States army."

Taxes were honestly collected and municipal dis-
bursements carefully scrutinized. Public works were

undertaken and carried through, roads and bridges built, schools opened and attendance enforced, enlisted men being detailed as teachers, and officers themselves often conducting classes. Streets were graded, towns drained, and a condition of sanitation introduced that, in the Philippine Islands, is only possible under military rule. The pueblos became models of neatness and a spirit of wholesome rivalry was engendered. Vaccination was made compulsory, and smallpox instead of recurring as a yearly epidemic has now lost its terrors. Interference in Church matters was strictly avoided, and little by little the people were led to understand what was meant by the separation of the Church and State. Nor were these efforts spasmodic or confined to particular localities, but were general throughout the islands wherever and whenever the work of pacification permitted.[34]

Operating through the central military government in Manila, the army developed the basis for a colonial regime strictly in keeping with the desires of the President. In the process, individual members of the officer corps showed a high degree of humanitarian dedication, honesty, and efficiency.

In February 1900, President McKinley began the formation of a second Philippine commission to transfer the government of the islands from military to civil rule. The President thought that the time was right to begin such efforts, since, from all reports received in Washington, the revolt in the Philippines seemed in its last days. Accordingly, on March 16, he appointed a five-man commission with Judge William Howard Taft at its helm. The commission included General Luke E. Wright, a Civil War veteran and Memphis lawyer; Henry Clay Ide, a leading Vermont lawyer who had been Chief Justice of Samoa in 1891; Bernard Moses, a professor of history and political economy at the University of California; and Dean C. Worcester of the first Philippine Commission. Unlike the Schurman Commission, which had been primarily a fact-finding and recommending body, the Taft Commission was charged with the task of establishing civil rule in the Philippines. To help the members carry out their mission, Secretary of War Root supplied them with a detailed set of instructions.

Phillip Jessup, Root's biographer, has called the instructions "the most important single document in American colonial history,"[35] and they represented the outline and framework for the civil government to be established in the islands.

In the instructions to the commission, Secretary Root did not neglect the work that the army had already accomplished in the islands. He told the commission to build on that base rather than to begin anew in structuring the civil government. He thought that the transfer of authority would be gradual and occupy a considerable period of time. According to the instructions, the continued development of municipal governments was foremost, followed by the organization of government in the larger administrative divisions. By September 1, 1900, the commission would exercise legislative authority in the islands, and the military government would exercise executive power in the colonial government. The commission was to give immediate thought to legislation on the collection, appropriation, and expenditure of public funds; the extension of the system of public education; the establishment of a civil service system; and the continued development of the civil courts. The army's work in the organization of municipal governments was to be the basis for work in that area; the work on Negros was presented as a model for provincial organization. Root stressed the benevolent purposes of the United States in the islands and urged the commission to bear in mind that the government being established was to be designed "for the happiness, peace, and prosperity of the people of the Philippine Islands" and not for the satisfaction of the Americans nor the expression of their theoretical views.[36] In principle and tone, the instructions served to reinforce those already issued by the President to the army and to the Schurman Commission in 1898 and 1899. The Taft Commission would reinforce the campaign of pacification, which Washington thought was drawing to a close, and the work of the commissioners would serve to strengthen the impact of the work already under way by the army.

Like President McKinley, many American army officers in the Philippines remained committed to a policy of benevolent pacification. They still believed that, if treated properly, the vast majority of Filipinos would be loyal to the Americans. General Otis was convinced of this and encouraged his subordinates in their work of school building, government organization, and public works. In order to placate the inhabitants of the towns, he refused to allow the return of the Spanish friars to the parishes or to allow them to resume farming their large estates. He knew that opposition to the friars had been a motivating force in the original Philippine revolt in 1896, and on the question of allowing the friars to minister to the Filipinos, the General realized that "no act of the United States Government would so excite, irritate, and cement them in rebellion."[37] For the General, it was important that the Americans do nothing that might interfere with the benevolent policy being carried to the municipalities.

General Otis relinquished command over the army in the Philippines to General Arthur MacArthur on May 5, 1900, but the new commander was as committed to the policy of benevolent pacification as his predecessor. In particular, MacArthur looked upon the army s school work as being an integral part of the pacification campaign. For him, it formed "an important factor in the military situation," and he was pleased that there was such a point where Filipino and American desires came "into complete and harmonious focus." General MacArthur recommended that "the archipelago be submerged immediately under a tidal wave of education," and he was pleased that considerable progress in that direction had been made before he took command.[38] He was very optimistic about the accomplishments and value of the humanitarian actions manifested by the army throughout the period of American rule in the Philippines.

In the early months of 1900, statements of American officers left no doubt that the army was firmly committed to its policy of benevolent pacification. The general thinking of many of them was summed up by these words of an officer of the 29th Infantry stationed in Pasig. "If the idea that we are acting in good faith towards them could be firmly impressed on their minds I am sure they would welcome our presence."[39] Certainly many events in late 1899 and 1900 reinforced this belief.

General Otis had noticed that following the successful American offensive at the end of 1899 the Filipinos, in increasing numbers, united with the American troops to destroy the revolutionary bands, and he was convinced that the confidence of the inhabitants in the American troops was steadily increasing as a result of humane treatment. Brigadier General Frederick Funston also noticed the trend, writing that in 1900 the Filipinos began to flock to the garrisoned towns for shelter. There was a noticeable change in the conduct of the people toward the Americans. Filipinos acted as guides for American troops; captured guerrillas attempted to induce their compatriots still fighting to surrender; and other Filipinos kept American commanders informed concerning the state of the revolutionaries' morale or the propaganda efforts of the guerrillas. The army enlisted local scouts in larger and larger numbers, and their service proved so satisfactory that some American officers asked constantly for increases in the number of local troops under their command. By June 1900, the American headquarters in Manila issued orders for the development of a systematized police organization in the municipalities, and some officers even suggested that Filipino units be enlisted officially into the American army. In mid-1900, many Americans thought that not only had the revolution collapsed, but benevolence had won a convincing victory in gaining popular support for American sovereignty.[40]

Many Filipinos gave widespread support to the Americans. The revolutionaries noted with disappointment and increasing worry the evidence that numerous Filipinos were accepting American municipal government and even serving the Americans against the revolutionaries. In Iloilo, an insurgent document remarked on "the disastrous moral effect produced in the situation of the country by the innumerable voluntary and other surrenders of prominent persons who filled important offices under the revolution."[41] Another document spoke of the many "Americanistas who seem to have forgotten what they owe their country," and still another observed that the inhabitants of Naga, Sibong, and Argao on Cebu were "all" annexationists.[42] The revolutionaries were convinced that what they called the American "policy of attraction" was succeeding.[43] Perhaps the best evidence of the changing attitude of the Filipinos toward the Americans was in Aguinaldo's own province of Cavite. There an American agent reported that, although the people still had a great desire for independence, they did not hate the Americans as they had the Spaniards. American conduct, prompt payment for supplies, humane care for the wounded, and good treatment of prisoners made the people respect the Americans, and the inhabitants of some towns were friendly or even loyal to them.[44] This observation could have been made of many areas of the Philippines in 1900.

An American correspondent in the Philippines interpreted the change in the behavior on the part of many Filipinos as evidence that the people were tired of the war, but undoubtedly their motives were deeper. The correspondent spoke with some accuracy when he said that "there are Filipinos who are tired of war and there are those who have never been keenly desirous of war,"[45] but his explanation overlooked the effect of the American campaign of benevolent pacification on the Filipino townspeople. The Americans had appealed to Filipino desires for economic progress and reform. The army had brought the townspeople what they wanted most: schools, roads, commercial development, and protection. The Schurman Commission, in its final report, observed in its conversations with both friendly Filipinos and representatives of the revolution that the desire of the Filipinos for education was foremost among the opinions voiced. The commissioners also observed the wish for governmental reform, public works, and the separation of the church from the state.[46] General MacArthur was confident that the "earnest desire to learn the English language," manifested by many Filipinos, could be regarded as a "sincere expression of friendship" that amounted to "a declaration of confidence in American motives and ulterior aims."[47] Filipinos were probably sincere when they stated, as did the president of San Pablo to his town council, that they should cooperate with the Americans to bring their country "all the benefits of civilization and contribute thereby to its happiness."[48]

The work of American officers in the municipalities did much to convince Filipinos of the advantages of American rule, and in some cases townspeople became genuinely attached to officers stationed among them. The president of San Miguel de Mayumo in Bulacan Province praised the work of the provost marshal there. He wrote that even though the Filipino guerrillas

146   SCHOOLBOOKS AND KRAGS

had placed a 300 peso reward for the officer's death, "no one is
willing to kill him, as he is beloved by all."[49] Lieutenant Colonel James Parker, if his memory served him well, formed a
similar bond with the people under his care in Lagonoy.[50] In
1900, many American commanders in the Philippines received
petitions from towns requesting that units be sent to organize
municipal governments or asking that troops already stationed
in towns not be removed. The petitions were filled with praise
for the American work in the municipalities and acknowledged
the debt of the townspeople for the security, justice, and progress brought to them by specific American officers.[51]

Captain John R. M. Taylor, translator and compiler of
captured revolutionary documents, thought that the presence of
American garrisons did more than any other single thing to
gain adherents to the United States government. He observed
that

> towns which had them were tranquil, the regimental
> band played, intimacies grew up between the mem-
> bers of the garrison and the natives, and . . . the
> people of the towns came back. Only the more rest-
> less ones remained outside; but they were friends and
> relatives of the people who had returned to their nor-
> mal lives, and constant intercourse was kept up
> between them. . . . Every town where there was an
> American garrison became the center of a prop-
> aganda against the guerrillas, for the people in them
> were protected and lived measurably free from the
> exactions to which the unfortunate inhabitants of the
> places where there were none were exposed.[52]

Revolutionaries coming into the towns to plot against the
Americans began to realize the great benefits that the
Americans were bringing to the Philippines, and many of the
native leaders, in Taylor's words, "came to see that they were
fighting against the light."[53] Cases of pretended loyalty
became sincere as the Filipinos realized that the often brusque
and direct deportment of the Americans was accompanied by
what General MacArthur termed "friendliness and a
neighborly disposition."[54] The humanitarian and benevolent
actions of American officers and men in the islands could not

go unnoticed by the Filipinos with whom they had daily contact.

Other reasons existed for the increasing support gained by the Americans and the evidence coming to them daily that the revolution was failing. Throughout 1899 General Otis and the Schurman Commission commented on the support given the Americans by men of wealth, property, and education. Obviously such men feared the anarchy and destruction of property that might accompany a nationalist victory. Some members of the Katipunan held radical ideas about agrarian reform and the redistribution of farm land that undoubtedly made many wealthy Filipino landowners favor the American cause. Other Filipinos looked down on the masses and, because of their Spanish heritage and education, favored a conservative government under American sovereignty over the more popular rule that the revolutionaries promised.[55] The Chinese aided the Americans in 1900 for the same reason that they had been such willing collaborators in 1899—their fear of the Filipinos and desire for American protection. The Macabebes continued to be motivated in their support of the Americans by their intense hatred of the Tagalogs. Elsewhere, abuses committed by the revolutionary army or bands of robbers prompted towns to seek the protection of the Americans. The revolutionary leaders had tried to solve this problem in 1899, but it still plagued them in 1900.[56]

For some Filipinos, aid to the Americans meant immediate monetary gain. Municipal officials, teachers, policemen, and other employees of the military government received rather high wages by Philippine standards. Also, the army and individual soldiers were well supplied with money and spent it liberally in the municipalities. This contributed to the desire of towns to have American garrisons and no doubt led businessmen to return to their shops when their towns were occupied by American troops. The American policy of paying $30 Mex. for the surrender of rifles caused many Filipino soldiers to desert and return to their homes. F. M. Soliman, a guerrilla leader, wrote his wife that if he could be assured that none of his men would be imprisoned his whole command would willingly surrender themselves for the bounty on their weapons.[57] In one area of Luzon the purchase of arms brought in over 1,000 weapons and almost 40,000 rounds of ammunition between November 1899 and April 1900. One American regiment bought more than 800 firearms in a three-month period, and the payment of money for guns was a highly successful and extremely inexpensive method of denying the revolutionaries what they needed most. Furthermore, the act of surrendering a weapon almost insured that the bearer would be an adherent of the Americans, for protection if for no other reason.[58]

In the first months of 1900 the American command in Manila thought that the revolution could not possibly continue in the face of such evidence of defection of the Filipinos in the towns. General Otis had been very optimistic, and he was certain that matters in the islands would be "in quite satisfactory condition" by the time he left Manila. When the War Department queried him in April about a pessimistic report made by the Associated Press concerning a shortage of American troops and continued revolution, Otis answered that the troops in the islands, if kept to full strength, were sufficient "to meet any anticipated emergencies."[59] By that date the General had approximately 60,000 men, double his strength in 1899, and was confident that most of the unrest remaining in the islands represented brigandage rather than revolt. He thought that it was only a matter of time before all the towns and villages would lend their support to the Americans.[60] When General MacArthur assumed command, he too was optimistic. He found great significance in the surrender in May of seven Filipino officers with 163 men and 168 weapons and observed that it was the first surrender of a complete guerrilla unit. By the end of the month, MacArthur was planning for the day when the American force in the Philippines would be reduced and consolidated in a few garrisons. His confidence in the Filipinos was such that he proposed the immediate organization of a native constabulary.[61]

The first impression of Judge Taft upon his arrival in the Philippines was that the revolt was indeed at an end. He wrote Secretary Root on June 15 that "the backbone of the Revolt as a political war is broken and the generals in the field are looking about for some excuse to stop the fighting and to come in."[62] In a statement made upon his arrival in the United

States General Otis said that "the natives are learning slowly to trust us, and my idea of quelling the insurrection is simply to keep scrupulous faith with these people and teach them to trust us."[63] Both Taft and Otis were certain the war was over and confident in the power of the program of benevolent pacification that had been carried out during the General's period of command.

General MacArthur thought that the time was right to issue a general amnesty offering complete immunity for past deeds and liberty for those revolutionaries who had not violated the laws of war. He was confident that such a gesture would be sufficient to bring in most guerrilla bands. Taft concurred with MacArthur in the assumption that the situation was right for a major effort to bring about peace. They decided to issue an amnesty. After ninety days, a supplementary notice would be issued, and, if after the expiration of sixty more days there were still guerrilla bands resisting, all who refused to take advantage of the final amnesty notice could be declared outlaws.[64]

The General issued his amnesty proclamation on June 21, 1900, and he followed it on July 2 with a statement of numerous liberal provisions to be embodied in any form of civil government established in the islands by the United States. These included the concepts of due process of law, just compensation, speedy and public trial, and other rights found in the American Bill of Rights. The Taft Commission supported the General in his issuing of these documents, and the commissioners continued to voice their optimism about the rapid collapse of the insurgents. The General's thoughts on the situation in the islands came out in an interview between him and the guerrilla leader José Alejandrino. MacArthur told General Alejandrino that it was hopeless to continue fighting and that "the rules of modern warfare forbid a continuance of hostilities after the hope of success has vanished."[65] From MacArthur's point of view, continued resistance was simple "murder." In the mind of the General and most other Americans in the islands the war had ended.

NOTES

1. *Annual Reports of the War Department for the Fiscal Year Ended June 30, 1900*, HD 2, 56th Cong., 2d sess., VI, 252-53, 413, 196-97; Theodore W. Noyes, *Oriental America and Its Problems* (Washington, 1903), 3-4.

2. *War Department, 1900*, HD 2, 56th Cong., 2d sess., VI, 425.

3. Ibid., V, 449-57.

4. Ibid., 457-69.

5. Ibid., XI, 19, 154-61; *Annual Reports of the War Department for the Fiscal Year Ended June 30, 1901*, HD 2, 57th Cong., 1st Sess., V, 245-46.

6. *War Department, 1900*, HD 2, 56th Cong., 2d sess., V, 546. For a summary of the Spanish system of taxation see Carl C. Plehn, "Taxation in the Philippines," *Political Science Quarterly* 16 (1901): 680-711; 17 (1902): 125-48.

7. *War Department, 1900*, HD 2, 56th Cong., 2d sess., V, 544-46; XI, 14-16, 145-53.

8. Ibid., XI, 20-22. A summary of the development of the military government in the Philippines is in David Yancey Thomas, *A History of Military Government in Newly Acquired Territory of the United States*, 282-303. See also Robert C. Humber, "Military Government in the Philippines" (MS study, U.S. Army War College, Washington, 1943). For an interesting history of a single government bureau see Lawrence Rake-

straw, "George Patrick Ahern and the Philippine Bureau of Forestry, 1900-1914," *Pacific Northwest Quarterly* 58 (1967): 142-50.

9. See General Orders No. 69 and 70, series 1899, General Orders No. 5, series 1900, Office of the U.S. Military Governor in the Philippine Islands, for instructions on setting up civil government in the provinces. *General Orders and Circulars Issued from the Department of the Pacific and 8th Army Corps and Office of Military Governor in Philippine Islands, 1899* (Manila, 1899) and *Philippine Islands Military Governor: General Orders and Circulars, 1900* (n.p., 1900).

10. *War Department, 1900*, HD 2, 56th Cong., 2d sess., XI, 28.

11. Ibid., V, 488. Copy of order, 477-87.

12. Ibid., XI, 29.

13. Ibid., V, 477.

14. Ibid., IX, 163-64, 236-37, 262-74, 314, 372-74, 428-29.

15. James Parker, *The Old Army*, 342.

16. "Official Reports of the 43rd Infantry, U. S. Volunteers," I, Mar. 28, 1900, Henry T. Allen Papers.

17. Ibid., July 1, 1900. In addition to material found in the Allen Papers, evidence of this type of involvement of American units in the reconstruction of Filipino towns can be found in *War Department, 1900*, HD 2, 56th Cong., 2d sess., IX, 163-64, 236-37, 262-74, 314, 372-74, 428-29, 467; E. C. Bumpus, *In Memoriam: Everett Chauncey Bumpus* (Norwood, Mass., 1902), 41-44; Arthur MacArthur, "Letterbook" (Manila, 1900), 199-201, 280-82.

18. *War Department, 1900*, HD 2, 56th Cong., 2d sess., III, 609-10, 723-31; VI, 132-33; XI, 283-88; *War Department, 1901*, HD 2, 57th Cong., 1st sess., V, 439-48.

19. *War Department, 1900*, HD 2, 56th Cong., 2d sess., VI, 123. See also III, 636, 670, 674; VI, 131; XI, 283-88; General Order No. 91, June 26, 1900, Office of the U.S. Military Governor in the Philippine Islands, *Military Governor: General Orders and Circulars, 1900*.

20. *War Department, 1900*, HD 2, 56th Cong., 2d sess., III, 633-35; VI, 123.

21. See James A. LeRoy, "The Philippines Health Problem," *The Outlook* 71 (1902): 777-82.

22. *War Department, 1900,* HD 2, 56th Cong., 2d sess., IX, 164; Parker, *Old Army,* 335.

23. "Annual Report of Chief Surgeon, Department of Northern Luzon," June 30, 1901, Records of the Adjutant General's Office (AGO) 399549, incl. 22. Whereas the overall ratio of doctors to troops in the Philippines had been 1:233 in December, 1899, it was 1:173 by May, 1900, and 1:125 by the following year. The dispersion of American troops in scattered garrisons placed a continual strain on the resources of the Medical Department. Without rapid transportation, medical personnel had to be with the troops to give effective aid. See *War Department, 1900,* HD 2, 56th Cong., 2d sess., III, 605-607, 615.

24. *War Department, 1900,* HD 2, 56th Cong., 2d sess., V, 447.

25. James A. LeRoy, *Philippine Life in Town and Country* (New York, 1905), 214; "The Soldier Teacher in the Philippines," *Harper's Weekly* 46 (Jan. 18, 1902): 74; U.S., Congress, Senate, *Report of the United States Philippine Commission* [1900], SD 112, 56th Cong., 2d sess., 1901, 106-107; Taft to Root, July 26, 1900, Root Papers; *Commissioner of Education, 1900-1901,* 1320; *War Department, 1900,* HD 2, 56th Cong., 2d sess., XI, 221.

26. *War Department, 1900,* HD 2, 56th Cong., 2d sess., V, 491-92.

27. Ibid., XI, 221-22. See also XI, 26-27, 224-39; HD 2, 57th Cong., 1st sess., V, 257; U.S., Congress, Senate, *Education in the Philippine Islands,* SD 129, 56th Cong., 2d sess., 1901, 3, 44; Circular No. 13, Sept. 25, 1900, Office of the Military Governor in the Philippines, *Military Governor: General Orders and Circulars, 1900.*

28. U.S., Congress, Senate, *Land Held for Ecclesiastical or Religious Uses in the Philippine Islands, Etc.,* SD 190, 56th Cong., 2d sess., 1901, 178.

29. *War Department, 1901,* HD 2, 57th Cong., 1st sess., V, 352, 354.

30. *War Department, 1900,* HD 2, 56th Cong., 2d sess., XI, 231, 233. See also V, 491-92.

31. Ibid., V, 446.

32. Ibid., VI, 253.

33. Ibid., XI, 255, 249-80.

34. D. H. Boughton, "How Soldiers Have Ruled in the Philippines," *International Quarterly* 6 (1902): 225-26.

35. Philip C. Jessup, *Elihu Root*, I, 354. See also *New York Tribune*, Feb 25, 1900, 4; Taft to LeRoy, Dec. 1, 1905, Robertson Papers; *War Department, 1901*, HD 2, 57th Cong., 1st sess., II, 55.

36. *War Department, 1900*, HD 2, 56th Cong., 2d sess., II, 74. Full copy of the instructions on 72-76.

37. Ibid., V, 496, 546.

38. Ibid., VI, 64.

39. Walter K. Wheatly to Wingfield Nisbet, Feb. 11, 1900, Eugenius Aristides Nisbet Papers. Other good expressions of similar sentiments are in *War Department, 1900*, HD 2, 56th Cong., 2d sess., VI, 509; Wheaton to Secretary of Military Governor, Oct, 2, 1900, MacArthur, "Letterbook," 67.

40. *War Department, 1900*, HD 2, 56th Cong., 2d sess., V, 327, 332-35, 400; testimony of Otis, *Affairs in the Philippine Islands, Hearings before the Committee on the Philippines of the United States Senate*, SD 331, 57th Cong., 1st sess., pt. 1, 840; Frederick Funston, *Memories of Two Wars: Cuban and Philippine Experiences* (New York, 1914), 315; Howze to Kennon, Nov. 11, 1899, Kennon Papers; John L. Jordan to Mother, Mar. 10, 1900, John L. Jordan Papers; Taft to Root, July 14, 1900, Root Papers; José Ner to Military Governor, Aug. 8, 1900, AGO 344307; "Diary of Events, 1-14 Nov. 1900," AGO 353532; Taft to J. F. Bell, Oct. 2, 1900, William Howard Taft Papers; "Reports of the 43d," I, Apr. 30, 1900, Allen Papers; Clarence R. Edwards to Matthew A. Batson, Mar. 24, 1900, AGO 317496, incl. 1; General Order No. 87, Office of the Military Governor in the Philippine Islands, *Military Governor: General Orders and Circulars, 1900;* "Diary of Events, 6 May-14 Jun., 1900," AGO 333769; J. T. Bootes to Provost-Marshal, Nov. 30, 1900, Records of the Bureau of Insular Affairs (BIA) 1184, incl. 6; "Diary of Events, 14-29 Dec. 1900," AGO 360651; Taylor to LeRoy, Nov. 14, 1906, Robertson Papers.

41. "National Army of Operation," Oct. 1, 1900, Taylor, "Compilation," 51HK.

42. Bonifacio Morales to Isidoro Torres, Aug. 8, 1900, Philippine Insurgent Records (PIR) 555.3; Juan Climaco to "Cousin," 1900, PIR 1204.5.

43. R. F. Santos, Circular No. 21, Aug. 24, 1900, "Compilation," 58GV.

44. Philippine Information Society, "Progress in Pacification," *Facts about the Filipinos,* I (No. 10, 1901), 21. The original "Memorandum of a Secret Service Agent" is in "Diary of Events, 22-30 Sep., 1900," AGO 349353. Evidence of Filipino support for Americans and worry by the revolutionaries is also in Mateo Luga to Cueva de Guadalupe, Feb. 2, 1900, PIR 1219.5; Maxima to Roque and Hernandez, 1900, PIR 1198.2; remaining documents in PIR 1198; Dom. Gellada to President of Tigbuan, Sept. 20, 1900, PIR 1054.1; Eugracio Peña to Commander of Nueva Caceres Province, Jan. 3, 1900, PIR 457.6; Eustasio Malolos to President of Maugan, Mar. 24, 1900, PIR 1219.7; Dimaguila to Trías, Nov. 30, 1900 and summary of PIR 1084 (Papers of Isidoro Torres), Taylor, "Compilation," 70-72GV, 49HS.

45. Albert G. Robinson, *The Philippines: The War and the People, A Record of Personal Observations and Experiences,* 151.

46. *Report of the Philippine Commission to the President, January 31, 1900,* SD 138, 56th Cong., 1st sess., I, 41-42, 62-63, 82-97.

47. *War Department, 1900,* HD 2, 56th Cong., 2d sess., VI, 64.

48. True copy of entry in Municipal President's Record Book, San Pablo, Aug. 17, 1900, MacArthur, "Letterbook," 514.

49. José Buencamino to Military Governor, Oct. 27, 1900, "Diary of Events, 1-14 Nov. 1900," AGO 353532.

50. Parker, *Old Army,* 342-43.

51. An excellent example of such a petition is that from the village of Apalit, Pampanga Province, Oct. 7, 1900, *Affairs in the Philippine Islands,* SD 331, 57th Cong., 1st sess., pt. 2, 1813-14. Petitions are collected in pt. 2, 1799-1853, pt. 3, 2461-2543. Pp. 1799-1853 contain the same petitions as those printed in U.S., Congress, Senate, *Petitions of Natives of the Philippine Islands,* SD 323, 57th Cong., 1st sess., (1902).

52. Taylor, "Compilation" 45HS.

53. Ibid., 11HS.

54. Testimony of MacArthur, *Affairs in the Philippine Islands* SD 331, 57th Cong., 1st sess., pt. 2, 873. See also Taylor, "Compilation," 43HS.

55. This class conflict among the Filipinos is a basic thesis of Teodoro A. Agoncillo, "Malolos: The Crisis of the Republic," *Philippine Social Sciences and Humanities Review* 25 (1960). See in particular 563-64.

56. Severino Komandán to Ramón Abarea Presbitero Sogod, Feb. 13, 1900, PIR 1204.2.

57. Soliman to Dorothea Pascual, Apr. 27, 1900, in Fred R. Brown, *History of the Ninth U. S. Infantry, 1799-1909* (Chicago, 1909), 378.

58. On the policy of purchasing weapons, see ibid., 391; *War Department, 1900*, HD 2, 56th Cong., 2d sess., VIII, 81; *War Department, 1901*, HD 2, 57th Cong., 1st sess., V, 102-103.

59. Otis to AG, Apr. 3, 1900, Root to Otis, Apr. 9, 1900, Otis to Secretary of War, Apr. 10, 1900, *Correspondence Relating to the War with Spain, April 15, 1898-July 30, 1902*, II, 1156, 1158-59.

60. *War Department, 1900*, HD 2, 56th Cong., 2d sess., V, 448-49. See also the similar optimistic assessment of Schwan, Otis's Chief of Staff, V, 389-90.

61. MacArthur to AG, May 22 and 28, 1900, *Correspondence*, II, 1171-73.

62. Taft to Root, June 15, 1900, Root Papers. See also Taft to Root, Aug. 21, 1900, Root Papers; Taft to John M. Harlan, June 30, 1900, Taft Papers.

63. *The United States Army and Navy Journal* 37 (June 16, 1900): 989.

64. Taft to Root, June 15, Aug. 18, 1900, Root Papers; MacArthur to AG, June 5 and 9, 1900, *Correspondence*, II, 1175, 1177-78.

65. MacArthur to AG, Aug. 25, 1900, AGO 344307; *War Department, 1900*, HD 2, 56th Cong., 2d sess., II, 77-79; Commission to Secretary of War, June 25, 1900, *Correspondence*, II, 1184-85.

5

FROM THE HEIGHTS OF OPTIMISM
TO THE DEPTHS OF FRUSTRATION

Judging from the actions of the Americans in Manila and the statements made by figures like Otis, MacArthur, and Taft, few Americans at the higher levels of command understood conditions in the Philippines in mid-1900. Their assumptions that the Filipino army had disintegrated with the American offensive at the end of 1899 or that the Philippine people were completely won over to the American view were incorrect. It was little wonder that the Americans were disappointed when, after MacArthur's amnesty proclamation, few Filipinos surrendered.

What the Americans thought was the disintegration of the Filipino army in November and December 1899 was only a major change in strategy. Aguinaldo and his staff had decided to go over to guerrilla warfare. What the Americans saw as the collapse of the revolutionary army was the redistribution and reorganization which accompanied its decision to change from large regular formations to small, easily dispersed, guerrilla bands. The American offensive of 1899, rather than showing the Filipinos the futility of resistance, only convinced them of the impossibility of fighting the Americans with a regular force. Much more fighting would be necessary to convince the nationalists that a guerrilla war could not achieve their goal of independence and the withdrawal of American troops from the Philippines. The revolutionaries believed that the effectiveness of guerrilla warfare had been demonstrated both by the Cubans in their second rebellion and also by the Filipinos themselves in 1897.[1]

In the first half of 1900, the revolutionaries spent their time preparing for the new form of warfare. They had certainly not adopted guerrilla warfare in desperation. They understood the implications of their choice and pursued that course of action after giving the matter considerable thought. Instructions issued by insurgent commanders showed a good understanding of guerrilla tactics and strategy. A pamphlet published by Isabelo de los Reyes in Madrid summed up much of their thinking. The objective was to tire the Americans and make their occupation of the Philippines as costly as possible. Guerrillas were not expected to fight pitched battles, but they were to constantly harass the Americans by raids on supply trains, patrols, and small detachments. Disease and the terrain would aid the guerrillas, and the revolutionaries expected that the inhabitants of the towns and villages would also help. Guerrillas were to exercise great care in their treatment of civilians both to force the Americans to recognize the Filipino capacity for self-government and to obtain the sympathies of the people. The pamphlet contained detailed instructions on the setting of ambushes, security on the march and in camp, and the need to exercise extreme caution in all operations to prevent the Americans from bringing their superior strength to bear. Reyes ended his work by reminding his countrymen that the object was only to protract the state of war, something that could be accomplished with little cost to the Filipinos but at great price to the Americans.[2]

Aguinaldo divided the Philippines into guerrilla districts, each under a general officer. The size of districts and the number of men in them varied, but an adequate example of the type of organization used was that in the area of General Vito Belarmino in southern Luzon. The provinces of Sorsogon and Albay were each divided into two zones and Ambos Camarines into four. Each zone was divided into two sub-zones. Provincial forces were commanded by a colonel, zones by a lieutenant colonel, and sub-zones by a major.[3] Overall command was theoretically in the hands of Aguinaldo, but he was unable to exercise complete control. His capture had been one important goal of the Americans on their push into northern Luzon at the end of 1899, and Aguinaldo had fled into the mountainous region far to the north of the island. He was out of direct contact with the guerrilla bands in the more populated areas of the Philippines, and even his ranking field commanders did not always know where he was hiding. Communications from him were infrequent and usually dealt with major policy decisions or more general administrative problems. General Isidoro Torres, commander in central Luzon, might have been an extreme case, but between November 9, 1899 and August 12, 1900 his letter book showed only two incoming communications from Aguinaldo. Because the insurgent junta in Hong Kong was in a better position to communicate with most of the revolutionary leaders in the field, it was responsible for many of the directions given guerrilla commanders from outside.[4]

Filipino guerrilla operations took various forms in 1900. The revolutionaries used all types of techniques to prevent American control of the towns. As a result of the change from regular forces to guerrillas, they became a hidden enemy. Regular Filipino troops had, if possible, worn uniforms and fought in formations on prepared battlefields. The guerrilla did nothing to make himself so visible or so easy to combat. Ambushes, sniping, sabotage, all of these were guerrilla tactics. When the army saw the guerrillas, they were either in superior numbers or simply vanished from sight. One American officer had the rare privilege of seeing through his field glasses the process by which a guerrilla literally disappeared.

It was wonderful and fully explained the ease with which our friends, the enemy, have, when beaten, been able to escape destruction. . . . He has shed all signs of the soldier, grabbed a white flag and some agricultural tool and gone to work, *hard*, in the nearest field and shouted "viva America" when the hot American soldier again hove in sight. I caught many wearing two suits, one military, the other, underneath, civilian, so as to be ready for the quicker transformation.[5]

Such action was, of course, only in keeping with the guerrilla's instructions to harass the Americans without suffering damage himself.

The reports and instructions of the guerrillas contained many examples of the types of harassment given the Americans. A typical attack was reported by Tomás Mascardo on the small American garrison at San Pedro, a barrio of Guagua. Reinforced by twenty-five riflemen, eight Filipinos entered the barrio. The eight had knives concealed in their umbrellas. The American sentries did not have time to use their weapons, and the Filipinos captured four rifles. Pursuit by the American garrison in Guagua came too late to catch the guerrillas.[6] Elsewhere revolutionaries contemplated surrendering a few men to the Americans to lull them into a false sense of security, and instructions were issued that a stratagem of friendship be used to entrap the Americans at a later date. To strike at the Americans without suffering any danger to themselves, guerrillas in some areas built traps consisting of concealed pits filled with sharpened stakes or bows and arrows set to be triggered by a concealed line across a path.[7] Filipinos attacked the Americans indirectly by tearing down telegraph lines or smuggling money, supplies, or information to the guerrillas. The revolutionaries tried to involve as many Filipinos as possible in the resistance movement, fighting in as many ways as they could, in order to wear down the Americans.[8]

In the revolutionary system of guerrilla warfare there was no room for neutrals. The revolutionaries expected all towns and villages to cooperate completely with the guerrillas, aiding them with men, material, and money. To insure this cooperation, the guerrillas developed committees similar to the old Katipunan society and called by the same name. They ordered all centers of population to elect a president, secretary, cashier, treasurer, and six councilmen. In the barrios the committees consisted only of a president, secretary, treasurer, and four councilmen. Membership in the society itself was unlimited, and the members were bound together by a set of oaths and rituals that resembled those used in the earlier Katipunan. The

duties of the new Katipunan committees included the collection
of war contributions and taxes, the sale of *cédulas*, and in
general the preparation of assistance in money and in kind for
the guerrillas in the field. Towns also organized militia and
recruited men for the guerrilla units in their area. Katipunan
committees organized guides, lookouts, couriers, and parties to
destroy railroads, bridges, and telegraph lines. They also furnished the guerrillas with information regarding American troop
strength and disposition and sent reports to the overseas representatives of the revolution to be used as propaganda. The
Filipino general Juan Villamor saw the revised Katipunan committees as a key factor in maintaining morale and the tenacious
resistance evident in 1901.[9]

One extremely important function of the local municipal
committees was to promote and insure the loyalty of the inhabitants to the insurgent cause. Guerrilla leaders instructed the
committees to organize a secret police and, if necessary, arrest
any Filipino who showed himself to be a traitor to his country.
In addition to their work of ferreting out and punishing traitors,
the committees also spread revolutionary propaganda. Unity of
the population in support of the revolution was the goal, and
the committees were probably more important in achieving that
end than the guerrillas in the field.[10]

The revolutionaries continued their propaganda efforts as
an adjunct of the guerrilla war. Throughout 1900, they appealed for support not only to their countrymen, but also to the
American troops in the islands. American soldiers found the
Filipinos using propaganda against them that was very similar
to that being used by the United States Army. The revolutionaries offered $80.00 for each rifle the American soldiers
would surrender and promised to free any American who
voluntarily surrendered with a weapon. The revolutionaries
made a special appeal to black American troops. To discourage
the American command in its efforts to organize municipal
governments, revolutionaries on Cebu had village officers draw
up petitions protesting forced loyalty to American municipal
governments. Petitioners also protested against violence committed by American soldiers.[11]

Filipino overseas propaganda efforts also continued. In

Japan, Mariano Ponce worked for recognition of the Philippine Republic and for military aid, but the Japanese were still extremely reluctant to risk a diplomatic break with the United States. Chances of aid from that quarter diminished, and the help that Filipinos hoped they might obtain from Germany or other European powers never materialized. The most vocal pro-revolutionary movement was in the United States. The Hong Kong junta actively prepared propaganda for this American audience, and statements and tracts of the anti-imperialists in the United States served a similar purpose in the Philippines. To create dissension in America, the junta turned to propaganda stressing atrocities committed by American troops against Filipinos, and this was in turn elaborated upon and disseminated by the anti-imperialists. Both Filipino propaganda and the statements of the opponents of the war in the United States portrayed William McKinley as the enemy who had forsaken all good American traditions. William Jennings Bryan, whom the anti-imperialists supported for president, was the hero of the revolutionaries, who depicted him as the savior of both Filipinos and Americans from the evil of imperialism.[12]

Among their own people the revolutionaries used all types of propaganda, citing American crimes of rape, looting, murder, and the use of exploding bullets. The revolutionaries alleged that the American troops shot all their prisoners whenever attacked by guerrilla bands and portrayed American intentions as those of exploiting the land and exterminating the people. Such exaggerated proclamations were effective, and many Filipinos had a complete lack of understanding of what the Americans were trying to achieve in the Philippines. One native reportedly asked Felipe Calderón if it was true that the Americans intended to levy a *cédula* of $8.00, to pass laws confining Filipinos to a square mile of ground, and to kill all the horses in the islands and use the local inhabitants as draft animals instead.[13] An American correspondent reported that some Filipinos were thoroughly confused, first thinking that the Americans were going to Protestantize them and then fearing that the Catholic friars would be reinstated.[14]

Some revolutionary propaganda was calculated to con-

vince the people that the guerrillas were achieving great successes against the Americans and that independence was near.
On Samar, guerrilla leader Vicente Lukban proclaimed that
Luzon was already independent and that the American troops
in the islands were suffering from disease and hunger. Other
propaganda claims went even further. One set of letters stated
that the death rate among American troops was 70 percent,
that General MacArthur and his entire staff had been taken
prisoner, and that over 400,000 troops with more than eighty
warships from Russia, France, Germany, and Japan were
awaiting orders to intervene against the Americans. Another
revolutionary spread the rumor that an international association of merchants had purchased the votes of twenty-one
United States senators to get favorable consideration of the
question of Philippine independence.[15]

The revolutionaries urged their countrymen to stand firm.
Instructions were issued on the types of answers to be given to
any questions concerning Filipino desires asked by members or
representatives of the Taft Commission, and the revolutionaries issued other proclamations in an attempt to negate the
effect of General MacArthur's amnesty offer. The guerrillas
were even willing to pardon those Filipinos that had already
taken an oath of allegiance to the Americans, and much of their
propaganda stressed the importance of national unity or appealed to Filipino patriotism.[16]

The possibility of an outcome favorable to the Philippine
cause in the American presidential election loomed large as a
theme of Filipino propaganda in 1900. The Hong Kong junta
provided the guerrillas with reports that led them to believe that
William Jennings Bryan, running on an anti-imperialist platform, stood a good chance of defeating McKinley,[17] and the
members of the junta urged the guerrillas to continue their
resistance. Filipinos in the islands took up the theme that the
international situation in 1900 and the election in America
gave the Philippine revolt an excellent chance of success, if the
revolutionaries would only keep active. A proclamation issued
by Teodoro Sandico in June 1900 summed up their analysis of
the situation. He wrote to "True Filipino Patriots" that "the
present campaign has produced in America a political situation

which may defeat McKinley, which means the triumph of our ideals; the Transvaal war and revolution in China have created a critical international political atmosphere which may result in a general war; we should continue the struggle and accept only independence."[18]

Aguinaldo recognized the need to heighten guerrilla activity in the hope of influencing the election. He thought that if the Philippines appeared pacified "it will guarantee the triumph of the imperialists." Therefore he ordered an immediate increase in the frequency of guerrilla operations against the Americans, calling upon his generals "to adopt all means . . . advisable for strengthening our army, in order that, in this manner the imperialists of the United States will have no cause to contribute to their success at the next Presidential election."[19] He assumed that the Americans were tiring of war and that, if they could be led to believe that Filipino resistance would not only continue but become stiffer, they would surely vote to withdraw from the islands. Aguinaldo urged his countrymen to mount a pre-election offensive in which they would give the Americans "some hard fighting" to bring about "the downfall of the imperialist party" and a Bryan victory.[20]

For Aguinaldo, the presidential election was "a ray of hope,"[21] and he and his subordinates made the very most of its value as propaganda calculated to stiffen Filipino resistance. In terms of the long-run consequences of this action, however, the use of such a fixed event as an election as a focus for propaganda was a grave error. Like the leader of a doomsday cult, Aguinaldo left his movement in a precarious position should his predictions about Bryan's chances for success prove false. In the short run, the appeal to Filipinos to hold out, at least until the American election in November, gave the revolutionaries a period of several months in which to strengthen their movement and organize themselves for the continuation of the guerrilla war against the Americans.

Propaganda could not hold all of the inhabitants of the Philippines to the revolution. As the year 1900 progressed the guerrillas observed the growing number of Filipinos willing to accept offices under the Americans and cooperate in their municipal governments. Revolutionary leaders also noticed a decline in the morale of their own troops, and the effect of the surrender of many officers and men in 1900 was "disastrous."[22] In some locations the revolutionaries found the people unwilling to supply guerrilla units with money and supplies. Inhabitants of towns and villages refused to purchase insurgent *cédulas* or to enlist voluntarily in guerrilla bands. Some Filipino commanders were convinced that whole towns were *Americanista*, and evidence of increasing popular support of the Americans precipitated a crisis in the revolutionary ranks.[23] Guerrilla commanders knew that interaction between Americans and Filipinos was harming their movement, and, as one guerrilla leader stated, "continuous contact with our enemies may cause the gravest damage to our sacred cause," the damage coming as a direct consequence of the American "policy of attraction."[24] The revolutionaries attempted to prevent Filipinos from returning to their homes in towns occupied by American troops, and Aguinaldo urged his men to use every effort to combat American propaganda. The revolutionaries tried to prevent Filipinos from serving the Americans, particularly as municipal officials, and they also attempted to force those Filipinos already having accepted offices under the Americans to resign. They viewed the continuing spread of the American military government with its humane and benevolent policies as a major threat.[25]

When exhortations to patriotism and other propaganda techniques failed to prevent Filipinos from cooperating with the Americans or from refusing to support guerrilla units, the revolutionaries resorted to terrorism. As early as March, 1900, guerrilla leaders began to threaten townspeople with dire consequences should they accept American rule or otherwise show signs of abandoning the revolution. General Arcadio Maxilom threatened to destroy any town recognizing the Americans and kill all the male inhabitants. Another revolutionary commander threatened Filipinos with death if they failed to report information on American movements to the guerrillas and aided the Americans with information or as guides. By the middle of 1900 a full-scale campaign of terrorism had begun, and terror became a primary weapon of the revolutionaries. They used it against those actively engaged in aiding the Americans as spies, guides, or scouts, and against those accepting offices under the military government. It was used to prevent further surrenders of Filipino soldiers and to keep guerrillas from taking advantage of the American amnesty offer. The revolutionaries even terrorized Filipinos who paid taxes to the Americans or accepted American *cédulas*. In short, terror was a weapon against anyone who might, in any conceivable way, be contributing to an American victory.[26]

Probably the most widespread terror was against officials of the American-sponsored municipal governments. The revolutionaries decreed that any officeholder was, by the fact of his holding such a position, a traitor to the Philippine Republic and was to be treated as such. Terrorists murdered municipal officials as an example to others who might be contemplating the acceptance of an office under the Americans. The only sure way for one to escape such a fate was either to resign, if the Americans would permit it, or to collaborate with the local revolutionary committees organized within each village. Guerrilla leaders recommended to their superiors the taking of "four or five lives" in each village to strengthen the power of the committees, and officials or any other Filipino who might have shown signs of friendship to the Americans lived in fear of punishment.

The methods the revolutionaries used to carry out their policy of terror varied widely. The penalties invoked ranged from a fine to decapitation or burial alive. Aguinaldo wanted the punishment of traitors done by summary courts martial convened by the commanders of guerrilla units, but as the terror campaign increased in intensity its methods became less discriminating. Judgments and executions took place on the spot; recourse to official trials or a set code of laws and penalties was the exception rather than the rule. The revolutionaries applied terror in many forms to prevent Filipinos from giving support to the Americans. They paid rewards for the assassination of important local officials collaborating with the Americans. Specific crimes of collaboration such as acting as spies or guides and surrendering firearms were punished summarily by death. Filipinos committing minor offenses were beaten, fined, deprived of their personal property, or burned out of their homes. When the revolutionaries could not punish the guilty party inside the town, they kidnapped their victim and took him to an area where it was safe to administer whatever penalty seemed called for by the situation. When even this was too much of a risk, the revolutionaries attempted to turn the Americans against the collaborators by any subterfuge that might succeed in getting the Americans to cease protecting the intended victim. Even in towns garrisoned by the army, Filipinos could not feel safe or secure from the revolution's terror.[27]

Throughout the towns and villages, terrorists carried out the work of summarily punishing any act that could be interpreted as treason. By the middle of November 1900, instructions had been issued throughout the Philippines that guerrillas, down to the lowest subordinate, familiarize themselves with the verb *dukutar* so that they would be able to put the abduction process into immediate practice whenever ordered to deal with any enemy of the republic. By the end of the year the Americans had recorded 350 known assassinations and 442 assaults, and, in view of the fear that prevented many Filipinos from reporting acts of terrorism, probably many more acts went unnoticed by the American authorities.[28]

Filipino terrorism was highly successful. The Americans soon realized that the progress made in organizing the military government and the evidence of popular support for the American cause were both superficial. The majority of Filipinos were unwilling, in 1900, to attach themselves completely to the Americans no matter how humanely or benevolently they were treated. The risk was too great, and Filipinos who could preferred to remain "on the fence." As one American observed, municipal officials were "between 'the devil and the deep sea.' If they were known to aid the insurgents, an American prison awaited them and if they sided with the Americans they stood a very good chance of getting their throats cut."[29] When they could, Filipinos refused to serve in the American governments, and, if they could not avoid it, they acted in a dual capacity, serving both the Americans and the revolutionaires. At the beginning of October, General MacArthur summed up the unusual situation that had developed in the towns.

> The presidentes and town officials acted openly in behalf of the Americans and secretly in behalf of the insurgents, and, paradoxical as it may seem, with considerable apparent solicitude for the interests of both. In all matters touching the peace of the town, the regulation of markets, the primitive work possible on roads, streets, and bridges, and the institution of schools, their open activity was commendable; at the same time they were exacting and collecting contributions and supplies and recruiting men for the Filipino forces, and sending all obtainable military information to the Filipino leaders.[30]

Thus, Filipinos tried to avoid the terror and, at the same time, keep at peace with the American army of occupation and take advantage of what progress could be achieved through cooperation with the Americans.

The revolution's system of hidden governments in the municipalities frustrated American efforts to bring the countryside under the army's control. In each town the local Katipunan committee operated as a branch of the revolutionary government, and in many cases officers of the committee also held offices in the American municipal government. Actions taken on behalf of the Americans were often sanctioned by the local guerrilla commander before being implemented. American authority was a sham, and the villages served as bases of supply for the guerrillas. They also afforded a secure place of refuge for guerrillas hard pressed by American units. General MacArthur recognized that "the most important maxim of Filipino tactics was to disband when closely pressed and seek safety in the nearest barrio, a maneuver quickly accomplished by reason of the assistance of the people."[31]

American officers seeing the situation close at hand found it difficult to understand how such conditions could continue in the face of revolutionary terror and American benevolence. Even Filipinos singled out for assassination usually did not appeal to the United States garrison for protection, and one officer believed that the people viewed terror as "a legitimate expression of governmental authority" on the part of the revolutionaries.[32] When the Americans tried to protect the municipalities and bring terrorists to trial, they found it almost impossible to obtain witnesses, even though most crimes were committed by one Filipino against another. Townspeople, acting in what appeared to be their own interests, withheld their wholehearted support from either the revolutionaries or the Americans. Instead, they sought to placate both. Avoiding the terror seemed more important than a possible American reaction to their duplicity. The American benevolent policy insured that the revolutionaries would be feared more than the Americans. Terror effectively blocked American work in the towns and prevented the Army from carrying out President McKinley's policy of "benevolent assimilation" until the question of sovereignty was settled.[33]

The inability of the Americans to give municipalities complete protection from guerrilla reprisals accounted, in part, for the effectiveness of the terror. Without protection, Filipinos refused to give their support to the army. The Americans, although their troop strength had increased to over 60,000, found it impossible to garrison all of the towns, and even in those towns that did have garrisons the troops were not sufficient to keep constant watch over the adjacent barrios. Often Americans would occupy a town, establish a municipal government, initiate school and public health programs, and then move on to another town, leaving those who had collaborated with them in the first municipal center to the mercy of the revolutionaries. Although the number of American garrisons increased steadily, the troops were spread very thinly. In July, the shipment of approximately 5,000 American soldiers to China to help put down the Boxer Rebellion strained American troop resources in the Philippines further. American officers recognized the problem, but they could do little about it. The report of the officer in charge of the provinces north of Manila effectively summed up the American dilemma.

> Success depended entirely on the preponderating influence in the respective localities of our troops or of the remnants of the insurgent forces still at large. In the more important towns of Pangasinan and

Tarlac, early and strongly held by considerable garrisons, the local governments were succeeding pretty
well, and charges of disloyalty were infrequent, while
in towns not occupied by troops or occupied with
small detachments and close to the scene of insurgent
operations they failed utterly.[34]

This officer perceived the direct connection between the collaboration of municipal officials with the guerrillas and the
American inability to cope with the problem because of the
shortage of troops.

In the northernmost portions of Luzon the geography of
the area—rugged, wooded mountains—combined with the lack
of men to make effective garrisoning impossible. The commander of the Americans in that region, like commanders elsewhere in the Philippines, traced his major problem to the
manpower shortage, reporting that "the longer the matter is
delayed the more troops it will take and the greater the expense, as the new conspiracy is gaining in numbers, courage
and efficiency every day."[35] For example, the provinces of
Ilocos Norte and Ilocos Sur, once thought pacified, were slowly
reverting to revolutionary control. All over the Philippines, the
Americans could not convince the inhabitants that they would
be protected from revolutionary terror for the simple reason
that the army could not, in fact, give such protection. Villagers
were, in most cases, at the mercy of the revolutionaries, and
they knew it. As Colonel Arthur Murray observed on Leyte,
"they would gladly take their oaths of allegiance if assured that
our troops would remain to protect them, but that if the troops
were to be taken away, they were afraid that they would be
murdered for being Americanistas."[36]

Revolutionary propaganda stressing the coming election
in the United States and the chance that the Philippines might
be given independence as a result of a Democratic victory increased the doubt among the inhabitants of the towns and
villages. Judge Taft, head of the second Philippine commission,
summed up the problem presented to those already having
chosen to support the Americans. Living in fear because of
"the uncertainty . . . as to whether the policy of retaining the

Islands is to be maintained," they knew "that should that policy be abandoned and independence be granted they should suffer the tortures of the damned for their present attitude."[37] Filipinos that had not already committed themselves, the majority of the inhabitants in most places, could not logically, in view of the circumstances, make any final decision concerning the question of support for the Americans until the result of the election was known. Even on Negros, the most thoroughly pro-American area, General Smith reported that the islanders were afraid to come over completely to the Americans for fear that the United States might abandon the islands and leave them to an independent government under revolutionary control.[38] Benevolence and humane treatment had shown many Filipinos the advantages of American rule, and the revolutionaries themselves had observed the effectiveness of the American campaign of pacification. Circumstances favorable to the commencement of a campaign of terrorism and the uncertainty that accompanied the coming election in the United States effectively prevented the Americans from taking advantage of the good will they had accumulated as a result of their beneficent work in the islands in 1899 and 1900. Furthermore, the Americans needed time to adjust to the changed conditions of a guerrilla war.

The American army had not understood the significance of the Filipino change to guerrilla warfare at the end of 1899, and, as a result, the increasing elusiveness of pacification in 1900 came as a surprise. The Americans expected that little remained in 1900 but a mop-up campaign, and they had proceeded accordingly. They emphasized the establishment of facilities for the institution of a colonial government. Prisoners were released after being disarmed, and the Americans exhibited complete confidence that their program of humanitarian pacification would succeed as soon as the Filipinos became aware of the benevolent intentions of the United States. Military operations seemed secondary; the Americans had no visible enemy to fight.

A growing frustration on the part of the Americans came, in part, from the realization that pacification was no closer in 1900 than it had been throughout 1899. Filipino surrenders virtually stopped after Aguinaldo and his subordinates called for renewed efforts on the part of their followers in an attempt to influence the American election.[39] The casualties among American troops patrolling and scouting from their garrisons in 1900 were greater than those sustained in the 1899 offensive against the regular Filipino army. Between June and November 1899, a period of active warfare, the Army lost 481 men, 104 through battle deaths. In the next six months, December 1899 to May 1900, a period of supposed quiet, it lost 674, of which 150 were battle deaths.[40] American garrisons found that, contrary to their expectations, they spent as much or more time searching for and fighting guerrillas in 1900 as they had in 1899 when the revolutionaries had maintained an army in the field.[41] The difference was that in 1900 the campaign was more difficult and the enemy more elusive.

The guerrilla war of 1900 was an extremely frustrating experience for the American troops charged with the task of pacifying the Philippines. The guerrillas only fought when victory seemed a certainty, and most engagements took place between small, isolated American units and well-informed guerrillas occupying ambush positions in situations calculated to place the Americans at a disadvantage. The guerrilla system of espionage, the shadow governments operating behind the scenes in the municipalities, and the reign of terror in the towns and villages all worked to the advantage of the guerrillas and kept the American garrisons completely in the dark concerning guerrilla plans, movements, and strength. Americans found themselves besieged in their own garrisons, and in some regions it was considered unsafe to go forth in units of less than forty or fifty men.[42] After an attack, the revolutionary forces assumed civilian garb and concealed themselves among the peaceful inhabitants of the towns and barrios. American soldiers could never be sure just who was an active revolutionary and who might be a potential friend. One officer, writing home to his mother, spoke of the frustrations of this facet of the guerrilla war.

It has occurred several times when a small force stops in a village to rest the people all greet you with

> kindly expressions while the same men slip away go
> out into bushes, get their rifles and waylay you fur-
> ther down the road. You rout them and scatter them
> they hide their guns and take back to their houses
> and claims to be amigos.[43]

Under such circumstances the pacification campaign seemed a
never-ending process, and the topography, flora, and climate of
the Philippines was such that even the most routine operations
were difficult.

Supply of the numerous, often isolated, garrisons was a
major task, and communications presented equally difficult
problems. All work had to be done with insufficient troops over
long distances with inaccurate maps. The hostility and fear of
the population prevented the formation of an adequate system
for the accumulation of intelligence data, while the language
barrier prevented proper interrogation of suspects. Despite the
steady increase in medical personnel, over 117 small garrisons
were without medical officers, and the problem of furnishing
proper medical care to the men working under such hardships
was tremendous. Fatigue, sickness, and a sense of futility all
combined to make the American soldier's work extremely de-
pressing. One officer described the condition of his unit as
follows:

> about one half of the men are fast becoming unfit for
> guard duty through "nervousness." I have tried every
> means to quiet them but many are very young, mere
> boys, in fact, and are so unstrung that they are
> unreliable for night duty, and the least thing in the
> daytime causes them to jump for guns.[44]

The problems of guerrilla warfare were such that in mid-1900
it appeared that the revolutionaries might succeed, given sufficient time, in completely demoralizing the American army
before the latter could achieve anything approaching effective
pacfication of the islands.[45]

The political debate taking place in the United States had
an adverse effect on the morale of the army in the islands. To

say, as one correspondent did, that "soldiers were wrathy at the discovery of anti-expansionist pamphlets in captured insurrecto headquarters" was an understatement.[46] Members of the army were convinced that anti-imperialist activities in America cost both American lives and dollars. Anti-imperialists, for their part, went so far as to send propaganda to American soldiers in an attempt to undermine the war effort. In the United States, the debate between the anti-imperialists and their critics was intense, and their opponents voiced sentiments substantially in agreement with those of soldiers in the Philippines. The *New York Tribune*, in a partisan blast, stated that the war "would have ended long ago were it not for Bryan. He is more the leader of these people now than Aguinaldo, and every American soldier that is killed during these months can be laid directly to his door."[47] Although the mass of people in America seemed to support McKinley and his Philippine policy, the soldiers in the islands could not overlook the effect of the anti-imperialist opposition on the conduct of the war.

In the United States, opinion seemed divided into three groups. A minority of "super-patriots" thought the anti-imperialists partly responsible for the war and wanted to deal with them as traitors, while the "anti's," for their part, contended that the Filipinos were only battling for their rights. Moderates, by far the great majority, found the war distasteful and wanted it brought to a close as speedily as possible. All groups criticized the President and accused him of failure to exhaust the possibilities of conciliation, dilatory prosecution of the war, suppression of news from the Philippines, and a lack of aggressiveness and overoptimism on the part of the army there. As a result, the administration put increasing pressure on the army to end the war while avoiding any acts that might be used as political capital by the opposition.[48]

With mounting political pressures at home and the increasing frustrations of the unsuccessful campaign against the guerrillas, American officers viewed the refusal of Filipinos to respond to American benevolence and deny support to the revolutionaries with great suspicion. Americans complained of the Filipinos' lack of gratitude, noting that "when captured and

again set free they have shown their lack of appreciation of the
policy of magnanimity by again appearing in arms against us at
the first opportunity."⁴⁹ Some Americans refused to trust any
Filipino and began to assume that the whole population was actively in league against them. As one officer observed, "it is the
same old story—if U. S. troops are strong, it is 'mucho amigo';
if weak, it is cruel death."⁵⁰ By the time this observation was
made, "gugu" had replaced "nigger" as the soldier's universal
term of reference for the Filipinos, and in the eyes of many soldiers all "gugus" looked and acted alike.⁵¹ General James F.
Smith probably came as close as any observer to a successful
analysis of the problem that had developed. Speaking of the
people of Negros, Smith noted that

> they have a certain amount of sympathy for a true in-
> surgent. . . . Although they realize that the insurrec-
> tion is a mistake, they have the human sympathy
> which all have for their own blood battling in a
> wrong cause. That was the thing which many military
> officers in charge of stations could not understand or
> did not appreciate. They expected that these men,
> with these sympathies (probably having brothers or
> relatives in the field), would not only openly but ag-
> gressively espouse the American cause.⁵²

When support for the Americans was lacking, when
benevolence and humanity seemingly went unrewarded, some
Americans decided to take matters into their own hands and
break away from the official policy of benevolent pacification.

In August 1900, Colonel Robert L. Bullard wrote in his
diary, "It seems that ultimately we shall be driven to the
Spanish method of dreadful general punishments on a whole
community for the acts of its outlaws which the community
systematically shields and hides."⁵³ By that time other
American officers had passed this conjectural stage, and they
were already initiating their own programs of terror calculated
to elicit information from Filipino villagers and to end the support of the guerillas by civilians. The Macabebe scouts that the
Americans had enlisted used torture as a means of obtaining in-

formation, but the American command deplored such acts and prevented them whenever possible. By the middle of 1900, however, Americans as well as Macabebes resorted to the "water cure" and other forms of terror. They seized people and forcibly filled their stomachs with water until they revealed the hiding place of guerrillas, supplies, or arms. The Americans forced Filipinos to act as guides. They burned to the ground barrios adjacent to spots where revolutionaries committed ambushes, sabotage, or acts of terror. In short, for some American soldiers, benevolent pacification and humanitarian treatment of revolutionaries or any other Filipinos was a thing of the past. In the thinking of these Americans, the policy had failed, and counter-terror seemed the only answer to the conditions prevalent in 1900.[54]

The official policy of the Army remained that of benevolent pacification, and commanders issued orders in an attempt to reinforce it and prevent the abuses that seemed to come with increasing frequency as the frustrations of the guerrilla war mounted. In southern Luzon officers were cautioned that "no end can be so desirable or important to justify a departure from the recognized laws of war or a resort to any deliberate measures of cruelty." In Leyte they were told that natives were to be treated "with the utmost kindness and consideration unless it is positively known that they are insurgents."[55] Elsewhere instructions were similar, but abuses continued.

Some American commanders had either never seen the value of benevolence or were tired of seeing humanely treated Filipinos ambush and mutilate the men of their commands. An American surgeon in the islands placed part of the blame for the increasing brutality on fatigue, the hardships of garrison duty, homesickness, and frustration caused by the guerrilla war.[56] In any case, by the middle of 1900 the army's official policy of benevolent pacification was carried out wholeheartedly only in garrisons where individual commanders were personally committed to it. In other areas, commanders were either apathetic or even opposed to it.[57]

General MacArthur faced an extremely difficult set of problems during the first few months of his command in the

Philippines. As military governor, he was presented with two pressing problems over and above those of the guerrilla war and the breakdown of the American policy of benevolent pacification. His relations with both the civil commission headed by Taft and with the press correspondents in Manila were, at best, strained. At a time when he should have been devoting all of his available time to the problems of pacfication, he was forced to devote energy to these problems ancillary to those of a regular military command.

The American campaign was going badly in 1900. The correspondents knew it, and the result was an increasing number of clashes between the press and the army censors in Manila. Correspondents charged, probably with some justification, that much of the censorship was political rather than military. They were prevented, they said, from sending any news that could be used by McKinley's political opposition, that might alarm the folks back home, or that spoke of American reverses in the field. For example, censors prohibited the use of the word "ambush" in press dispatches. Incoming messages, in particular those reporting anti-imperialist activities, were also censored, and editors of local newspapers in Manila complained of restrictions placed upon them by the military command. As a result of the complaints, General MacArthur took virtually the same position that General Otis had taken at an earlier date. He acknowledged his willingness "to dispense with censorship" if the War Department so desired. Both McKinley and Root, however, did not seem anxious to end restrictions on the news completely. Too much was at stake politically to allow uncensored messages to flow freely from the islands, but too much was also at stake to appear to be unreasonable in restricting legitimate news coverage of events there. The solution, as in 1899, was to decrease censorship without official recognition that any problem existed.[58]

When the President sent the Taft Commission to the Philippines he assumed that the war was almost at an end. The time seemed perfect to begin the change from military to civil government. Upon the arrival of Taft and the commissioners, however, the situation was such that the immediate initiation of civil rule was impossible. Unfortunately, General MacArthur viewed the appointment of the commission as an indication of a lack of confidence in his ability to deal with conditions in the islands. Taft reported that the General regarded the office of military governor as "mediatized" and himself personally humiliated as a result of the transfer of legislative authority to the commission in September. To MacArthur's credit, he did not openly complain about the presence of the commissioners. In his dealings with them he was formal and reserved, but not obstructive. Still, the conflict between the military governor and the commission was bound to influence the conduct of the campaign of pacification. The lack of complete cooperation between civil and military authorities in Manila was soon transferred to the provinces and complicated the pacification effort. Taft, unlike MacArthur, complained constantly to Secretary Root and others in the United States and the Philippines about the conduct and attitude of the General. He referred to the General's extreme formality in dealing with the requests and acts of the commission as "military etiquette gone mad," and he implied to Root that perhaps a change of commanders might be in order after the election.[59] This failure of the chief civil and military authorities to work harmoniously only added to the problems facing the army in 1900.

The Americans in the Philippines had been highly optimistic after their successful offensive at the end of 1899. Most of them thought that the war would soon be over and that it was time to begin the construction of a humane and benevolent government. By the middle of 1900, these dreams were completely shattered. What the Americans had viewed as the break up of the revolutionary movement was in reality only a shift from regular to guerrilla warfare. The army's progress in the organization of municipal governments, schools, and other institutions proved to be superficial when Filipino terror insured the continuing support of guerrilla units by the villages. Municipal officials served both American and insurgent masters, and by mid-year the war was, at best, stalemated. The revolutionaries, at first depressed by the apparent swing in popular support to the Americans, became more optimistic as the possibility of a Democratic victory in the American presidential election gave them renewed hope of independence.

The result was an aggressive guerrilla offensive beginning near the end of the rainy season.[60] The efforts of the American army to win the guerrilla war only ended in frustration. Many Americans became dissatisfied with benevolence and the humanitarian approach to pacification, and almost all of them recognized that some change was needed if the army was to achieve the elusive goal of pacifying the Philippines. Benevolence alone was not sufficient. A new policy was needed, and the time was right for a change as the middle of 1900 passed.

NOTES

1. Mariano Cabrebo, circular, Jan. 14, 1900, Philippine Insurgent Records (PIR) 936.7; Vlease to Esprindión Borgia, Oct. 17, 1899, PIR 57.3.

2. Reprinted in *Annual Reports of the War Department for the Fiscal Year Ended June 30, 1900*, HD 2, 56th Cong., 2d sess., VI, 72. See also Pantaleon García, "Instructions for Guerrillas and Flying Columns," Nov. 25, 1899, Taylor, "Compilation," 37GV; Taylor's summary of Filipino guerrilla technique, 47 HS.

3. Taylor, "Compilation," 47HS.

4. Ibid., 51HS; E. Riego to Torres, Mar. 3, 1900, PIR 530.7. For some idea of the isolation and wanderings of Aguinaldo see Simeon A. Villa's diary printed in *Affairs in the Philippine Islands, Hearings before the Committee on the Philippines*—of the United States Senate, SD 331, 57th Cong., 1st sess., pt. 3, 1987-2060. Villa was Aguinaldo's physician and later his chief of staff. The diary covers the period from Nov. 13, 1899 to Mar. 22, 1901.

5. Robert Lee Bullard, MS Diary, Book I, Mar. 8, 1900, Robert Lee Bullard Papers.

6. García to Secretary of War, Oct. 6, 1899, PIR 51.1.

7. Casimiro Tinio, Circular No. 42, Mar. 17, 1900, PIR 51.9; Engracio Orense, letter, Jan. 30, 1900, PIR 1198.6; Edo Chincilla to Ambrosio Moxica, 1900, Robert H. Noble, "Compilation," VI, 771; Vicente Lukban to Local Presidents, Mar. 29, 1900, PIR 882.1; Frederick L. Sawyer, *Sons of Gunboats* (Annapolis, 1946), 53.

8. For reports and instructions pertaining to Filipino guerrilla operations in 1900 see Aguinaldo to Artemio Ricarte, June 27, 1900, PIR 638.3; Aguinaldo to Local Presidents of Gerona, Victoria, Paniqui, and Moncada, Nov. 1, 1899, PIR 638.10; General Order of the General Staff, Feb. 12, 1900,

PIR 980.1; Lukban, "Obligations of Guerrillas," Apr. 26,
1900, PIR 1241.2; Francisco Salandoni, "Guerrilla Warfare,"
June 10, 1900, PIR 1042.6; "Instruction for Guerrillas," Oct.
11, 1900, PIR 646.2. In Taylor, "Compilation," see Paula
Parado to Moxica, Mar. 2, 1900, 81HK; San Miguel, orders,
Dec. 19, 1899, 39GV; Soliman, "Orders to Detachments,"
Nov. 16, 1899, 36-37GV. In Noble, "Compilation," see F.
Malandacon's plan to attack towns in Negros, Sept. 15, 1900,
XIV, 2364-65; Quintin Salas, "Instructions for Guerrillas,"
Apr. 30, 1900, XIV, 2293-96.
    9. Juan Villamor, *Unpublished Chronicle of the Filipino-
American War in Northern Luzon, 1899-1901*, 3 vols., (Manila,
1924), I, 68-74. On the revival of the Katipunan see in Taylor,
"Compilation," García to Torres, Dec. 14, 1899, 40GV; cer-
tificate issued to Torres, Jan. 1, 1900, 41GV; Aguinaldo to
to Trías, Aug. 15, 1900, 33GV; Teodoro Gonzalez's commis-
sion to Tomás Alup Remigio, Jan. 7, 1900, 43GV; San Miguel
to Acting Military Chiefs from Iba to Lubao, Dec. 6, 1899,
37GV.
    10. On the duties of the committees see in Taylor, San-
dico, instructions, July 15, 1900, 55GV; Ambrosio Flores,
"Instructions for the Organization of the Corps of Guerrilla
Militia," Jan. 5, 1900, 43GV; José Cavestany, instructions,
May 15, 1900, 50GV. In Noble, "Compilation," see
"Memorandum of General in Chief in Visayas," Oct. 5, 1900,
XVIII, 2944-49; Padre Praxedes Magalona, "Memorandum
for Setting up Dictatorship of the Katipunan," Oct. 3, 1900,
XXXII, 4925-30. Also see Cavestany to President of
Dagupan, May 15, 1900, PIR 883.6.
    11. In Taylor, "Compilation," see Aguinaldo, "Notice of
Justice," Aug. 3, 1900, 31-32GV; Emilio Zurbano, proclamation, Sept. 25, 1900, 61GV. Also see Salvador Manuel to Manuel Abarca, Oct. 2, 1900, PIR 884.3, and Paula Pardo to Mateo Zopete, Sept. 2, 1899, PIR 483.10. Petitions in U.S., Congress, Senate, *Protests Against American Civil Government in
the Island of Cebu, Philippine Islands*, SD 234, 56th Cong., 2d
sess., 1901. For insight into the dilemma of black soldiers in
the Philippines, see Willard B. Gatewood, Jr., *"Smoked
Yankees" and the Struggle for Empire: Letters from Negro Soldiers, 1898-1902* (Urbana, 1971), 237-316.
    12. Maria C. Lanzar, "The Anti-Imperialist League", in
Philippine Social Science Review 3-4 (1930-1933). In particular, see chap. 3, "The American Anti-Imperialist League,"

and chap. 4, "The Anti-Imperialists and the Election of 1900," 3 (1930): 24-41. See also Harrington, "The Anti-Imperialist Movement in the United States, 1898-1900," *Mississippi Valley Historical Review* 36 (1967): 211-30; Rufino Deloso to U.S. Commander at Oroquieta, Oct. 25, 1900, "Diary of Events, 1-14 Nov. 1900," AGO 353532; Mascardo to North American People, July 1, 1900, Taylor, "Compilation," 17KK.

A recent interest in the anti-imperialists has generated much new material. See Robert L. Beisner, *Twelve Against Empire: The Anti-Imperialists, 1898-1900* (New York, 1968); E. Berkeley Tomkins, "Scylla and Charybdis: The Anti-Imperialist Dilemma in the Election of 1900," *Pacific Historical Review* 136 (1967): 143-61, his "The Old Guard: A Study of Anti-Imperialist Leadership," *Historian* 33 (1968): 366-88, and his *Anti-Imperialism in the United States: The Great Debate, 1890-1920* (Philadelphia, 1970); Richard E. Welch, Jr., "Motives and Policy Objectives of Anti-Imperialists, 1898," *Mid-America* 51 (1969): 119-29; William George Whittaker, "Samuel Gompers, Anti-Imperialist," *Pacific Historical Review* 38 (1969): 429-45.

13. Taft to Root, Sept. 13, 1900, Root Papers.

14. Letter of John T. McCutcheon, Apr. 19, 1900 quoted in Philippine Information Society, "A Period of Guerrilla Warfare," *Facts about the Filipinos*, I (No. 9, 1901), 18-19. In Taylor, "Compilation," see Order No. 301, Aug. 8, 1900, 32GV; Lukban to President and Inhabitants of Samar, Mar. 17, 1900, 59-60HK.

15. Lukban to Local Presidents, Feb. 4, 1900, PIR 1241.9; letters of Paula Pardo in PIR 2035; Sandico to Local Chief in Licab, Sept. 28, 1900, PIR 567.1.

16. In Taylor, "Compilation," see unsigned, undated proclamation, 25GV; unsigned proclamation, Feb. 1900, 25GV; circular, May 4, 1900, 26GV. In Noble, "Compilation," see Nationalist Army of Iloilo, proclamation, Oct. 1, 1900, I, 32; Delgado, proclamation, June 13, 1900, III, 327; Moxica to Zone Commanders of Guerrillas, June 8, 1900, V, 705. See also P. H. Poblete, editorial in *El Grito del Pueblo*, July 24, 1900, PIR 425.3; Aguinaldo to Torres, Aug. 2, 1900, PIR 527.7.

17. "News from Our Representative in America," PIR 610.4.

18. Sandico to True Filipino Patriots, June 1900, PIR 1119.4.

19. Aguinaldo to Ricarte, June 27, 1900, Taylor, "Compilation," 26GV.

20. Aguinaldo to Macabulos, June 27, 1900, Taylor, "Compilation," 27GV. For copies of many of Aguinaldo's orders for the pre-election offensive see 26-29GV.

21. Aguinaldo to Filipino Generals, Field and Line Officers and Soldiers, Oct. 29, 1900, PIR 1037.2.

22. National Army of Operation in Iloilo, proclamation, Oct. 1, 1900, PIR 1054.4.

23. In Taylor, "Compilation," see the summary taken from PIR 1084, 49HS; Vito Belarmino to Commander of Southern Luzon, Feb. 28, 1900, 46GV. See also Maxima to Roque and Hernandez, 1900, PIR 1198.2; Mateo Luga to Cueva de Guadalupe, Feb. 2, 1900, PIR 1219.5; Bonifacio Morales to Torres, Aug. 8, 1900, PIR 555.3; Climaco to "Cousin," 1900, PIR 1204.5; Dom. Gellada to Local President of Tigbauan, Sept. 20, 1900, PIR 1054.1.

24. R. F. Santos, Circular No. 21, Aug. 24, 1900, Taylor, "Compilation," 58GV.

25. Eustasio Malolos to Mateo Almosara, Mar. 24, 1900, PIR 1219.7; Aguinaldo to Julian Pilar, Aug. 2, 1900, Aguinaldo Collection, Minnesota. In Taylor, "Compilation," see García to Torres, Feb. 10, 1900, 45-46GV; José Alejandrino, unnumbered general order, Sept. 1900, 58GV; Torres, Circular No. 633, Sept. 11, 1900, 59GV; 42-43HS. In Noble, "Compilation," see Pio Claveria to Local President of Tigbauan, Nov. 21, 1900, I, 12; Fullón, order, July 11, 1900, IX, 1454; Maxilom, proclamation, Mar. 14, 1900, XXXII, 5077-79.

26. Maxilom, proclamation, Mar. 14, 1900, Noble, "Compilation," XXXII, 5077-79; Manuel Tinio, proclamation, Mar. 20, 1900, Taylor, "Compilation," 47GV. In Taylor, "Compilation," see also Mariano Trías, proclamation, Nov. 24, 1900, 70GV; Pecho Caballes, proclamation, July 15, 1900, 55GV; Alejandrino, proclamation, July 1900, 53GV; 42-43HS, 53HS.

27. An excellent overall description of the terror is Taylor, "Compilation," 53HS. Also in Taylor see Alejandrino, order, Sept. 1900, 58GV; Manuel Tinio, proclamation, Mar. 20, 1900, 47GV; Trías, proclamation, Nov. 24, 1900, 70GV; Juan M. Gutierrez to Inocencio Peralta, Nov. 4, 1900, 66GV; Villa to Chiefs of the Philippine Guerrillas, Nov. 15, 1900,

92FZ. See also Aguinaldo to Trías, Aug. 8, 1900, PIR 638.5; Cailles to Presidents of Nagcarlan, Rizal, Saluyan, St. Rosario, San Pablo, and Alaminos, May 6, 1900, PIR 220.4; Dionicio Papa to Rufo Uyos, May 19, 1900, PIR 970.4; Maxilom, "Instructions for the Magdudukuts," June 22, 1900, PIR 981.1.

28. Robert Bacon and James Brown Scott, eds., *The Military and Colonial Policy of the United States: Addresses and Reports by Elihu Root,* 90. On abduction or *dukutar* see Maxilom, "Instructions for the Magdudukuts," June 22, 1900, PIR 981.1; M. Pacheco to Local Chiefs of Sogod, Kabalian, Anajauan, Hinundayan, and Hinunangan, Oct. 4, 1900, PIR 981.5; Villa to Chiefs of the Philippine Guerrillas, Nov. 15, 1900, Taylor, "Compilation," 92FZ.

29. Comment of Phelps Whitmarsh included in Taft to Root, Oct. 10, 1900, Root Papers.

30. *War Department, 1900,* HD 2, 56th Cong., 2d sess., VI, 61.

31. Ibid.

32. Taylor, "Compilation," 18HS.

33. Ulysses G. McAlexander, *History of the 13th Regiment United States Infantry* (n.p., 1905), 188-91; Declaration of R. Paulilio, May 28, 1900, PIR 1101.10; unsigned to Nicolas Ruces, Sept. 16, 1900, PIR 1042.2; G. R. to Moxica, Apr. 7, 1900, Noble, "Compilation," VI, 717; Fred R. Brown, *History of the Ninth U.S. Infantry, 1799-1909,* 364-65; James Parker, *The Old Army,* 315; Daniel R. Williams, *The Odyssey of the Philippine Commission* (Chicago, 1913), 60.

34. *Annual Reports of the War Department for the Fiscal Year Ended June 30, 1901,* HD 2, 57th Cong., 1st sess., VI, 110.

35. Entry of Sept. 7, "Diary of Events, 23 Aug.-21 Sep., 1900," AGO 344290.

36. "Reports of the 43rd," II, Oct. 31, 1900, Allen Papers.

37. Taft to William R. Day, Aug. 16, 1900, Taft Papers.

38. *War Department, 1900,* HD 2, 56th Cong., 2d sess., XI, 254-55.

39. *War Department, 1901,* HD 2, 57th Cong., 1st sess., V, 125-31.

40. U.S., Congress, Senate, *Number of Deaths of Soldiers in the Philippines,* SD 426, 56th Cong., 1st sess. (1900), 4.

41. McAlexander, *History,* 114-32; Brown, *History,* 390.

Brown indicated that the 9th Infantry scouted an average of 400 miles a month.

42. *War Department, 1900*, HD 2, 56th Cong., 2d sess., V, 330.

43. John L. Jordan to Mother, Feb. 18, 1900, Jordan Papers.

44. H. A. Thayer, "Reports of the 43rd," I, Apr. 4, 1900, Allen Papers.

45. On the problems of the guerrilla war see *War Department, 1901*, HD 2, 56th Cong., 2d sess., V, 330-31, VI, 226-27; Cushman Kellogg Davis to Henry F. Hoyt, Feb. 9, 1900, Cushman Kellogg Davis Papers; Schwan to Corbin, Feb. 16, 1900, Corbin Papers; MacArthur to AG, July 26, 1900, *Correspondence Relating to the War with Spain, April 15, 1898-July 30, 1902*, II, 1192; Clarence Lininger, *The Best War at the Time* (New York, 1964), 130-36; testimony of Taft, *Affairs in the Philippine Islands*, SD 331, 57th Cong., 1st sess., pt. 1, 70; Bullard, MS Diary, in particular Aug., Sept. 1900, Bullard Papers; John L. Jordan's letters to his mother in Jordan Papers, in particular those of Feb. 5 and 18, 1900.

46. Frederick Palmer, *With My Own Eyes*, 160.

47. Oct. 22, 1900, 1. Charles J. Crane, *The Experiences of a Colonel of Infantry*, 361; Luther B. Grandy to Cousin, Apr. 2, Dec. 8, 1900, Willis Grandy Briggs Papers; Taft to Root, July 14, Aug. 23, 1900, Root Papers; Joseph Wheeler to Otis, Jan. 3, 1900, PIR 1168.2.

48. Lynn, "The Genesis of America's Philippine Policy," (Ph.D. diss., Univ. of Kentucky, 1936), 134-39.

49. *War Department, 1900*, HD 2, 56th Cong., 2d sess., VI, 227.

50. Bullard, MS Diary, Feb. 3, 1900, Bullard Papers.

51. Palmer, *Own Eyes*, 156.

52. *Lands Held for Ecclesiastical or Religious Uses in the Philippine Islands, Etc.*, SD 190, 56th Cong., 2d sess., 232-33.

53. Bullard, MS Diary, Aug. 17, 1900, Bullard Papers.

54. Vivid evidence of changing attitudes and the actions following such changes can be found in William Carey Brown, diary, entry for June 1, 1900, and William Eggenberger to mother, May 4, 1900, both in U.S. Military History Research Collection. Congressional investigations uncovered other evidence of American terror. See *Charges of Cruelty, Etc., to the Natives of the Philippines*, SD 205, 57th Cong., 1st sess., 3-

43 and *Affairs in the Philippine Islands*, SD 331, 57th Cong.,
1st sess., pt. 2, 988.
    55. General Order No. 24, Headquarters, Department of
Southern Luzon, June 5, 1900, and Circular No. 3, Headquarters, First District, Department of the Visayas, June 26, 1900,
Affairs in the Philippine Islands, SD 331, 57th Cong., 1st sess.,
pt. 2, 988-89.
    56. H. C. Rowland, "Fighting Life in the Philippines,"
McClure's Magazine 19 (1902) : 241-47.
    57. Taft to Root, July 14, 1900, Root Papers; William
Howard Taft and Theodore Roosevelt, *The Philippines* (New
York, 1902), 84. It is difficult to assess the effect of either
Filipino terrorism or that of the Americans on the attitude of
the great majority of Filipino villagers. The revolutionaries succeeded in forcing villagers to outwardly behave in a manner
favorable to the revolution. American terror could, and did, do
the same. However, most American commanders and some
revolutionaries were convinced that, in general, terror drove
people away from rather than toward the cause of the terrorists. The official American attitude toward terror has
already been demonstrated. For evidence of the reaction
against terrorism by Filipino revolutionaries see Honeste Ruiz
to Moxica, Aug. 11, 1900, PIR 1204.3; Agustin Banes Bello
to Superior Military Commander, Leyte, Aug. 21, 1900, PIR
879.3; B. Dimaguila to Trías, Nov. 30, 1900, Taylor, "Compilation," 71GV. The whole question of the effect of terrorism
needs further study. Students of guerrilla warfare have been
willing to generalize concerning the effects of terror by government forces, assuming that it is generally counterproductive.
These same experts, however, are reluctant to make definite
statements concerning the use of terror by guerrillas. It is possible that, in a situation such as the military stalemate in the
Philippines in 1900, guerrilla terror is equally counterproductive in terms of its ability to positively influence the attitudes and thoughts of the people concerning the guerrillas and
their revolutionary movement.
    58. MacArthur to AG, Oct. 21, 1900, *Correspondence*,
II, 1221; Harold Martin, "The Manila Censorship," *Forum* 31
(1901): 462-71; *New York Tribune*, May 20, 1900, II, 2;
Harold Martin to unknown, Oct. 1900 in Corbin to MacArthur, Oct. 19, 1900, *Correspondence*, II, 1220; Rafael Palma,
My Autobiography (Manila, 1953), 27-28.

59. Taft to Root, Oct. 10, also Sept. 18, Oct. 13 and 16, 1900, Root Papers; Taft to J. B. Bishop, Horace H. Lurton, John C. Spooner, and others, Nov. 30, 1900, Taft Papers; Dean C. Worcester to Mrs. Henry W. Lawton, Oct. 10, 1900, Henry W. Lawton Papers; Williams, *Odyssey*, 63, 153; Ralph Eldin Minger, "William Howard Taft: The Development of His Concepts of American Foreign Policy, 1900-1908" (Ph.D. diss., University of Southern California, 1958), 49-78; Rowland Tappan Bertoff, "Taft and MacArthur, 1900: A Study in Civil-Military Relations," *World Politics* 5 (1953): 196-213.

60. In the 1950s and 1960s, as air power began to play an increasingly important role in counterguerrilla operations, there has been much anxiety about guerrilla offensives during the rainy season, a time when the air arm could not be used effectively. On the basis of the army's experience in the Philippines, such fears may be groundless. The Philippine revolutionaries were no more disposed to fight during the rainy season than were the Americans. Both in 1899 and 1900 the guerrillas were no more active in the rainy season than any other time during the year and, judging from American casualty figures, probably a little less active. When, in October 1900, the Japanese consul in Manila inquired of the revolutionaries how many rifles they could put into the field against the Americans, the answer was 10,000 in the wet season but 20,000 "in dry weather." (See Oct. 11, 1900 report of conference between Mr. Hojo and Mariano Trías, PIR 446.11.) Since guerrilla supply facilities were irregular at best, it was more than probable that they did not have any real offensive capability except in the areas close to their homes or base camps during the rainy season. On the other hand, the more regular supply facilities of the Americans enabled them to patrol constantly in both wet and dry weather. In fact, one might even assume that the advantage lies with the counterguerrilla forces during the wet season. The "monsoon offensive" that became such a well publicized threat of the guerrilla wars of the period after World War II probably represents the fears of modern armies, which depend on air power. The ability of regular forces to supply themselves in the field, even without airborne supplies, has increased tremendously since 1900. On the other hand, guerrilla forces still depend primarily on the same sources of motive power that were being used by both sides during the Philippine campaign.

6

A REEVALUATION OF POLICY

In 1900, members of the American force in the Philippines recognized that benevolence alone could not achieve pacification. The frustrations of guerrilla warfare and the mounting evidence that the islands were no closer to peace in mid-1900 than they had been in 1899 prompted many suggestions for a modification of the whole approach to the problem of pacification. Almost all the participants in the campaign recognized the need for some form of change in American policy. The ensuing debate was concerned with the magnitude and direction of those changes.

The discussion over the proper pacification policy came at the point in 1900 when Americans began to realize that benevolence, although it had won adherents for the Americans, had not brought about the end of the revolution. The Americans were greatly divided in their opinions. For some of the officers and men in the islands, the answer to the problem of pacification seemed to be a harsher, more repressive policy calculated to make the Filipinos more afraid of the American army than they were of the revolutionaries. This group argued that fear of the Americans would force Filipinos to end their conspiracy against the United States and aid the Americans against the more irreconcilable nationalists. Colonel Arthur Murray of the 43rd Infantry, long an advocate of benevolence, had changed his opinions by December 1900, and he, for one,

believed that the time had arrived for "more severe measures."
He was certain that, at least within his command on Leyte, the
kindness and consideration shown to the inhabitants was
"largely if not wholly unappreciated" and that the Filipinos
were inclined to regard lenient and humane treatment "as an
evidence of weakness."[1] Other soldiers who at one time had
been firmly committed to the policy of benevolence voiced
similar sentiments. One, who in August 1900 saw education as
"the first necessity" for the Filipinos and seemed certain that
humanitarian pacification would work in favor of the
Americans in the long run, completely changed his mind by October. At that time he was happy to hear rumors of a planned
offensive where there would be, in his words, "none of our
'friendly policy' business but some straight shooting." He was
convinced, as were some of his fellow officers, that "this
business of fighting and civilizing and educating at the same
time doesn't mix very well."[2] Enlisted members of the
American force had evolved a ditty that portrayed their feelings
even more succinctly. Referring to the Filipino, they took the
position that "he may be a brother of Big Bill Taft, but he ain't
no brother of mine!"[3] Their answer to the problem posed by
the Filipino revolutionaries was to "civilize 'em with a Krag."

Many acts of violence and brutality committed by
Americans in 1900 were calculated measures in keeping with
the concept of harsh pacification advocated by some officers.
One officer who recommended more forceful techniques of
pacification noted with pleasure that some commanders were
becoming bolder in carrying out reprisals that were not in keeping with the policy of the authorities in Washington and
Manila.[4] In the Visayas, General Hughes observed that
operations had become more severe as the war continued. In
1900, some officers sanctioned the destruction of towns, barrios, and individual buildings used by the guerrillas; similar un-
dertakings by American troops in 1899 would have been
severely punished. The General believed that such actions
depended almost entirely on the officer in command on the
scene and that commanders fresh from the United States were
less inclined toward harsh reprisals than those who had been
stationed in the islands for some time.[5]

Both the Filipino revolutionaries and American civilians noted the unofficial change toward a harsher campaign. Reports of representatives of the civil commission to Taft tended to confirm the observations of General Hughes.[6] A Filipino communication observed that the Americans were changing their tactics and "setting fire to the hamlets situated in the vicinity of places where attacks are made." It also reported that the Americans were moving the occupants of the barrios into the garrisoned towns. The Filipino observer feared this latter policy because it removed the people from the influence of the guerrillas. He looked upon the American reprisals in a different light, however, telling his guerrilla chief that he thought American repression "increases the hate of the people and redounds to the benefit of our ideal."[7] Still, regardless of the possibility that terror might drive people away from the American cause and the fact that such a policy was counter to that officially sanctioned, some American commanders continued to advocate the adoption of greater severity in dealing with the Filipinos.

General Loyd Wheaton was one of the principal advocates of increased repression in the pacification effort. Taft, in a letter to Secretary Root, observed that Wheaton had "not the slightest patience with a policy which looks towards forgiveness and conciliation of the natives."[8] Wheaton was convinced that the "Tagalo delights in all forms of treachery; deceit and chicane. . . . Without a redeeming feature of character he is only fit for a government of force untrammelled by any of the figments and fictions of government based upon the consent of the governed." The General advocated "swift methods of destruction" to bring "a speedy termination to all resistance," and he believed that it was "no use going with a sword in one hand, a pacifist pamphlet in the other hand and trailing the model of a schoolhouse after."[9] As he reportedly observed, "You can't put down a rebellion by throwing confetti and sprinkling perfumery."[10]

The most radical suggestions made by any officer were those of Brigadier General S. B. M. Young, one of Wheaton's subordinates in the Department of Northern Luzon. General Young advocated what he termed "methods of European nations" to deal with rebellious "Asiatics." He desired, for example, that military commanders be given "supreme authority" in the islands with full right of press censorship and the right to deport any reporter whose presence was "deemed harmful." He thought the army should be forced to recognize that "Asiatics have no idea of gratitude, honor or the sanctity of an oath" and to treat them accordingly.[11]

General Young had many specific recommendations. He wanted to deny the Filipinos the benefits of the laws of war as practiced by the Americans, inspiring them, instead, "with a greater fear of the reigning government than they had of the rebels" and retaliating in kind for acts of assassination and murder. He recommended a summary death penalty for spies, assassins, and those taking up arms after having taken the American oath of allegiance. All whose presence was "deemed prejudicial to the permanent sovereignty of the reigning power" were to be deported. Young advocated the confiscation of all real and personal property of known revolutionaries and their "aiders and abettors." Filipinos would be concentrated into zones under absolute military control, and areas used as guerrilla bases and rendezvous would be devastated. Young would have only Americans appointed to high office in the islands, and he wanted preference for such appointments for discharged soldiers. The final establishment of civil government would come only at the request of the military commander in the Philippines. Although General Wheaton favored these suggestions made by Young, he recognized that, as desirable as he thought they were from a military point of view, they were impractical in view of the reaction they would bring from the American public.[12]

Officers proposing a more severe policy usually referred to General Order No. 100, 1863 series, the American guide on the rules of land war that had been drafted during the Civil War. Captain John H. Parker set forth the typical argument for a more strict adherence to the provisions of General Order 100 in a letter to Vice-President Theodore Roosevelt. Parker, like Young and other fellow officers, thought that "the fundamental obstruction to complete pacification" was "the attempt to meet a half civilized foe . . . with the same methods devised for civilized warfare against people of our own race, country and blood." He called particular attention to the provisions of paragraphs 82-85 of the general order. Those paragraphs authorized the death penalty against murderers, highway robbers, persons destroying property, spies, conspirators, and the part-time guerrilla. Such people were not entitled to the privileges of prisoners of war when captured, but could be summarily executed. Captain Parker complained that the United States, instead of utilizing these provisions of General Order 100, had "applied the methods of the kindergarten where other nations habitually, and successfully, use the most stringent measures." Parker thought that officers who had shown restraint and discipline in 1899 and the first half of 1900 were completely capable "to make the few punitive examples that will be needed."[13]

General Order 100, to which Captain Parker and many of his brother officers often referred, was an established principle of United States military law. It was taught at the United States Military Academy, and it had gained acceptance internationally, being used in 1870 by the Prussian army in France and by the Hague conference in 1899. The order, taken as a whole, was not nearly as severe or harsh a code as those officers advocating its complete application in the Philippines portrayed it. Paragraph 4, for example, stated that officers administering the order were to be guided at all times by the principles of "justice, honor, and humanity," and paragraph 15 maintained that men in war never ceased to be "moral beings, responsible to one another and to God."[14] Humanitarian in its general tone, the order distinguished military necessity and martial law from cruelty and oppression.

In 1900, however, several paragraphs of the order that seemed to apply directly to the situation in the Philippines were not being utilized in the pacification effort. General Order 100 officially recognized the right of retaliation, the classification of intermittent guerrillas as "highway robbers or pirates," and the classification of those who rise up in arms against an occupying or conquering army as "war rebels" who were not entitled to the privileges of prisoners of war. Any person having communication with the enemy or giving them information while living in an area under martial law was considered a "war traitor" and subject to severe penalty, up to and including deaths.[15] The officers of the army had been taught to regard General Order 100 as the last word on questions concerning the laws of war. In the situation of stress and frustration accompanying the guerrilla war they naturally turned to General Order 100 in their efforts to repress guerrilla terror and prevent Filipinos from aiding or tolerating the guerrillas and the revolutionary committees in the villages.

By the middle of 1900, even an officer as firmly committed to the concept of benevolent pacification as General MacArthur was becoming depressed and seeking a way to end the guerrilla war as quickly as possible. William Howard Taft, the leader of the Philippine Commission, observing MacArthur's mood, wrote Secretary Root that the General seemed to be coming to the conclusion that all of the Philippine people were opposed to the Americans and that he looked upon his task as one of "conquering eight millions of recalcitrant, treacherous and sullen people."[16] The General had very little hope that the establishment of civil government under the commission would do any good, and he viewed pacification as a strictly military problem.[17] General MacArthur was under great pressure from Washington to end the war as quickly as possible; the campaign against the guerrillas was going badly; pacification seemed an elusive goal; and the General was certainly ready to institute a change in policy. The question, of course, was what changes to make. In mid-1900, General MacArthur was still uncertain as to what policy he should pursue in the future.

Taft's advice did little to clarify matters. Some of Taft's recommendations seemed to support those of officers calling for more severity; others implied that he considered the military government too harsh and arbitrary to achieve pacification. He favored the proclamation of a second amnesty after the American presidential election, at which time Filipinos who did not lay down their arms would "be treated as outlaws and subject to the severest penalties." He thought that deportation of revolutionary leaders to Guam, a technique used previously by the Spaniards, and judiciously administered hanging would "have a most useful effect." In October, he wrote to Root that after the election "the time will have come to change our lenient policy," and by the end of the month he wrote that he thought General MacArthur "much too merciful in commuting death sentences against *ladrones*," or thieves, as many Americans had begun to refer to the Filipino guerrillas. Taft seemed convinced that a change of policy would encourage Filipinos friendly to the Americans and reduce the number aiding the revolutionaries. At the same time, however, he advocated such severe measures as making ex-revolutionaries ineligible for public office, confiscating all property of revolutionaries, and enforcing a strict sedition law aimed at the news media in the islands.[18]

While many of Taft's suggestions called for a harsher policy of pacification, he also made statements calling for a continuance of the benevolent policy. On one occasion he complained to General MacArthur that the lack of a conciliatory policy by an officer in the Ilocano territory of northern Luzon had caused a resurgence of the revolution in that area.[19] He also criticized the military government for its arbitrary nature. He thought it incapable of cultivating good will among the people or convincing them of America's beneficent goals in the islands. Taken together, Taft's recommendations were, to say the least, confusing. Although he seemed committed to a benevolent policy, as a representative of the McKinley administration he obviously desired to end the war quickly. To achieve that goal, he was willing to advocate measures more severe than those contemplated by General MacArthur and similar to those recommended by officers no longer committed to a humane policy of pacification.

Everything pointed to the need for a change in American policy. There were recommendations enough from officers in the field. The actions of many soldiers had shown that, in any case, complete benevolence could no longer be retained as the actual pacification policy. Still, General MacArthur and his superiors in Washington were responsible for developing whatever new doctrine would be used in the attempt to end the war at the earliest opportunity, and they were firmly committed to the idea of benevolence. The General was acutely aware of

194   SCHOOLBOOKS AND KRAGS

his responsibility, and after the failure of his amnesty bid in
July 1900, he carefully assessed conditions in the Philippines
before formulating a new plan of action.

In making his assessment the General relied heavily upon
captured Filipino records and documents that came into
American headquarters from all over the archipelago. Captain
Robert H. Noble, given the task of compiling captured records
in the Visayas, commented that "the insurgents were very prone
to put in writing all their official acts,"[20] understandably
so, since the great majority of the revolution's leaders were
literate and familiar with the methods of the Spanish
bureaucracy. They failed, however, to take proper precautions
to prevent their documents from falling into American hands.
Consequently, General MacArthur and other commanders had
a ready supply of data concerning the revolutionaries' aspirations, methods, and intentions. From these sources, they knew,
for example, of Aguinaldo's campaign to increase guerrilla
operations in the hope of influencing the election in the United
States. They knew also that the revolutionaries were making
strenuous efforts to hold the Filipinos to their cause, and
General MacArthur interpreted their use of terrorism to accomplish that goal as an encouraging sign. The Philippine Insurgent Records, as the mass of captured material came to be
called, represented an important source of American
knowledge about conditions in the islands and, in particular,
about the revolutionary movement. The army used them as an
aid in making plans for its new pacification policy.[21]

At the time that General MacArthur was giving considerable thought to the problems facing the army, one particularly significant document came into his hands. It was a
study by First Lieutenant W. T. Johnston on "The Methods
Adopted by the Insurgents for Organizing and Maintaining a
Guerrilla Force." Completed in May, the report reached the
General at the end of June. It contained insights into the process by which the revolutionaries used the towns garrisoned by
the Americans as bases for their own guerrillas. Although
Lieutenant Johnston had studied only the towns in La Union
Province, General MacArthur was convinced that the condi-
tions portrayed in the report, with modifications for specific

localities, could be applied to any part of the islands, and more particularly to all of Luzon.[22]

Johnston's report only confirmed what had been apparent to many officers throughout 1900. The revolutionaries, not the Americans, controlled the towns and villages. In the town of San Fernando, for example, not only were local officials collecting contributions for the revolution, but they had given the town treasury to the guerrillas. They were also communicating with other towns and planning ways in which to resist the Americans. All of this happened in a municipality garrisoned by American troops. In San Juan, the president falsely translated information given by a young boy and prevented the capture of guerrillas close to an American patrol. In another town, money given the guerrillas from the town treasury was hidden under the entry of "public improvements." General MacArthur called Johnston's report "the best description which has reached these headquarters of the insurgent method of organizing and maintaining a guerrilla force."[23]

In addition to the numerous recommendations for increasing severity, the captured Filipino documents, and Johnston's report, General MacArthur had the usual flood of advice from subordinates, Filipinos, and civil authorities. General Wheaton, although favoring repressive measures, also thought that a key factor in pacification was the protection of the mass of Filipinos from the terror and coercion of the revolutionaries. He was certain that the majority of the inhabitants in his department would accept the authority of the United States if they could be protected and convinced of the American intention to remain in the islands. General Hughes had come to a similar conclusion in his command. He was attempting to protect as many towns as he could while continuing the civil affairs efforts that he thought could best obtain the goodwill of the population.[24] In addition to urging the deportation of revolutionary leaders and stiffer penalties for those aiding the guerrillas, Taft thought that the Army was in need of a better system for obtaining and assessing military intelligence data, and Colonel Enoch Crowder, MacArthur's military secretary, concurred.[25]

Many officers and the civil commissioners advocated

more utilization of Filipinos as scouts and police. The lack of knowledge of local languages, customs, and terrain on the part of American troops placed them at a great disadvantage in their attempts to locate and destroy the guerrillas. The use of some scouts in 1899 and the early part of 1900 had convinced many American officers that natives could be relied upon to give excellent and loyal service. Though many officers suggested that the number of Filipinos in arms be increased, General MacArthur was not completely convinced that Filipinos thus enlisted could be trusted. The question of whether or not a native force would come under the control of the military or civil authorities also presented a problem. There were many recommendations for a large force of native troops, however, when the General was giving his greatest thought to the development of a new pacification policy.[26]

Filipinos friendly to the United States also gave General MacArthur considerable advice. Their general ideas were summed up by Felipe Buencamino, a former cabinet officer of Aguinaldo who had taken up the American cause after his capture. Buencamino communicated with General MacArthur in mid-1900 and presented his idea for what he termed a political and military "counterrevolution" by Filipinos convinced of the futility of the revolutionary movement.[27] This union of Filipinos favorable to American sovereignty would, according to Buencamino, physically aid the American cause and destroy revolutionary morale. The movement was to be organized and conducted through the press in Manila and committees in the provinces and towns. Filipinos would be encouraged to enter into the pacification process by helping to defend themselves against terror and guerrilla action. "The object of this organization," wrote Buencamino, "would be to direct public opinion toward peace and submission to American Sovereignty, and at the same time to place in the hands of the American authorities information concerning the personnel, correspondence, arms, and resources of the insurgents."[28] Militarily, Buencamino wanted to starve out the enemy by separating them from their sources of supply in the towns and villages.

General MacArthur carefully analyzed the recommendations and data that he received from his own officers, friendly

Filipinos, the Taft commission, and captured documents. He also devoted much of his time to a study of the Far East and, in particular, the colonial administrations of the European powers there.[29] From this accumulated knowledge he was able to develop his own assessment of the problems facing the army on the eve of the American election.

The General concluded that revolutionary control over the towns and villages was the major problem. Their civilian inhabitants furnished the guerrillas with supplies, information, and refuge. Without this support, guerrilla warfare could not continue. Pacification would result when the Americans were able to isolate the guerrilla from his civilian base. Like many of his officers, General MacArthur had grown to distrust most Filipinos. He was convinced that fear of terror and intimidation was not the only reason for what he viewed as "the united and apparently spontaneous action of several millions of people" in resisting the American occupation. Since a single traitor in each town would be sufficient to destroy the complex revolutionary organization, the fact that such traitors were rare was proof to him that adhesion to the revolutionary cause stemmed primarily from "ethnological homogeneity."[30] Aguinaldo would no doubt have used the term "patriotism."

General MacArthur's analysis of the situation in the Philippines was not completely pessimistic, for he did believe that the attitude of the inhabitants toward the revolutionaries was changing. Data gained from a study of captured documents made him certain that they were tiring of the revolutionary collections and terror tactics. He hoped that, given time, the loyalty of the people might be transferred to the Americans. In a report to Washington, he noted with pleasure an incident where the president of San Pablo had openly criticized the revolutionaries for terrorizing innocent Filipinos. Writing to his barrio chiefs, the president commented that it was no longer possible to consider the guerrillas as defenders of the Philippine nation since they were incapable of resisting or effectively fighting the Americans and could only bring harm to their own countrymen. He urged his people to repudiate the guerrilla war and take a position of neutrality in which they would offer aid to neither the Americans nor the guerrillas. In response to threats of terrorism by the local guerrilla chief, the president wrote an even stronger letter to his barrio chiefs in which he stated that "the Americans are here solely for the purpose of protecting and defending us from attack and injury by those who are evil disposed, and in order that we may become enlightened as are they and other free nations."[31] General MacArthur interpreted this and other captured documents as evidence of a counterrevolutionary movement beginning to manifest itself in the towns and villages, and he saw the need to use this reaction in a way that would aid the army in its pacification efforts.

In the past, Filipinos had misinterpreted the benevolent policy of the Americans. In its field operations the army had rarely taken action against villagers even when it had suspected them of giving aid and assistance to the guerrillas. Prisoners taken in battle had been disarmed and released, and the Americans had treated the part-time guerrilla like any other combatant. All of this had been done in the hope that the Filipinos would recognize the beneficent intentions of the United States in the islands and end the war of their own volition. General MacArthur recognized, however, that this policy had not achieved the desired result. Personally, he was inclined, as were many of his subordinates, to adhere more closely to the provisions of General Order 100. In analyzing the situation, he concluded that "centuries of monarchical colonial administration" had made the Filipinos "suspicious of, rather than grateful for, any declared or even practiced governmental beneficence," and he was certain that they "looked upon the lenient attitude of the United States as indicating conscious weakness."[32] He thought that the Americans had neither made an adequate statement of their determination to hold the islands nor done enough to protect those Filipinos showing their friendship toward them. All of this would have to change if pacification was to be achieved.

A revolutionary, writing to General Manuel Tinio, had referred to General MacArthur as "the most able American General in politics and in diplomacy." He had added, "I greatly fear his astuteness."[33] Perhaps nowhere was this as evident as in General MacArthur's continuous effort to insure that the basic elements of the benevolent policy were retained in the new policy of pacification that he was formulating. Convinced that benevolent and humane conduct of operations was the best course of action over the long run, he would not relinquish his belief that resistance to American sovereignty would end only when the Filipinos were "thoroughly informed of American institutions and purposes."[34]

General MacArthur had great faith in what he termed "the imperishable ideas of Americanism," and he refused to undertake any program not in keeping with "beneficent republican American institutions."[35] He sought, instead, to continue a policy calculated to attach the Filipinos to the American cause through an appeal to their self-interest and gratitude. For MacArthur, as for his predecessor, General Otis, education was an extremely important factor in the pacification process. In response to commission legislation concerning school expenditures, the General wrote: "I know of nothing in the department of administration that can contribute more in behalf of pacification than the immediate institution of a comprehensive system of education." He viewed the extension of school facilities as "an adjunct to military operations, calculated to pacify the people and procure and expedite the restoration of tranquility throughout the archipelago."[36] Convinced that time and patience would act in favor of the Americans, General MacArthur consistently rejected the recommendations of his subordinates for a highly repressive policy. On the question of continued benevolence, the General even found himself in disagreement with the civil commissioners who advocated a harsher policy than he was willing to undertake. Although Taft complained to Secretary Root that the General continually delayed measures calculated to increase the severity of the American campaign against the guerrillas, the General stubbornly held to the policy of benevolence that had characterized American operations in the islands since 1898.[37]

The basic policy that the General finally adopted resembled closely the campaign undertaken by Captain Henry T. Allen and the 43d Infantry on the islands of Samar and Leyte. Although Captain Allen was committed to the concept of benevolent pacification, he recognized that benevolence alone was not enough to accomplish the goal of bringing peace to the islands. He therefore sought a middle course calculated to appeal to the mass of Filipinos by kind and humane treatment, while making guerrilla warfare as costly as possible to its practitioners. Colonel Murray, Allen's immediate superior, soon recognized the value of the Captain's technique.[38]

Knowledge of Allen's work spread throughout the Philippines. One of his fellow officers on Panay wrote him that

> your methods have been watched from here and I find that . . . you handle the enemy without gloves and that the result is very satisfactory. I have informed all hands that things are in pretty good shape on Leyte and that it is due to your policy of treating the good man very well indeed and the bad man very harshly, that it was the curacha [dance] or the carcel [jail] with us and no middle ground.[39]

Others officers such as Generals Kobbé and J. Franklin Bell were also familiar and in sympathy with Allen's technique of pacification.[40] General MacArthur may have been influenced by any one of them. The final policy developed at the headquarters in Manila closely resembled that of Captain Allen in its stress on benevolence for the many and severe penalties for the minority who refused to submit peacefully to the Americans.

NOTES

1. "Reports of the 43d," III, Dec. 3, 1900, Allen Papers.
2. John L. Jordan to Mother, Aug. 29, Oct. 19, and Oct. 29, 1900, Jordan Papers; See also Charles J. Crane, *The Experiences of a Colonel of Infantry*, 321; R. K. Evans to AG "Diary of Events, 22-30 Sep., 1900," Records of the Adjutant General's Office (AGO) 349353; John H. Parker to Roosevelt, Oct. 13, 1900 quoted in Roosevelt to Root, Nov. 24, 1900, Root Papers; Frank B. McKenna to Acting AG, Department of Southern Luzon, Oct. 10, 1900, "Diary of Events, 15-31 Oct., 1900," AGO 352496.
3. Robert F. Morrison in Manila *Sunday Sun* quoted in Ralph Eldin Minger, "William Howard Taft: The Development of His Conception of American Foreign Policy, 1900-1908," 61.
4. Crane, *Experiences*, 361-62.
5. Testimony of Hughes, *Affairs in the Philippine Islands, Hearings before the Committee on the Philippines of the United States Senate*, SD 331, 57th Cong., 1st sess., pt. 1, 558-62.
6. George K. Hunter to Taft, May 16, 1900, Phelps Whitmarsh to Taft, Sept. 14, 1900, Taft Papers.
7. Sixto Reyes to General and Politico-military Commander of Cebu, June 2, 1900, Taylor, "Compilation," 51GV.
8. Taft to Root, Oct. 21, 1900, Root Papers.
9. Wheaton's endorsement, Jan. 11, 1901, on J. M.

Thompson to AG, Jan. 4, 1901, "Diary of Events, 12-30 Jan., 1901," AGO 369140.

10. Frederick Palmer, *With My Own Eyes*, 151. See also Worcester to Mrs. Lawton, Dec. 5, 1900, Lawton Papers; "Minutes of the Philippine Commission, Nov. 10, 1900, Forenoon Session," Root Papers.

11. Young to AG, Department of Northern Luzon, Jan. 17, 1901, "Diary of Events, 12-30 Jan., 1901," AGO 369140.

12. Young's suggestions and Wheaton's comments are both in ibid.

13. Parker to Roosevelt, Oct. 13, 1900, forwarded in Roosevelt to Root, Nov. 24, 1900, Root Papers. See also, for similar thinking, Crane, *Experiences*, 361-62; R. K. Evans to AG, Department of Northern Luzon, Aug. 23, 1900, "Diary of Events, 22-30 Sep., 1900," AGO 349353.

14. *Affairs in the Philippine Islands*, SD 331, 57th Cong., 1st sess., pt. 2, 971-72.

15. Paragraphs 27, 28, 82, 85, 90, 91, ibid., 973-78. For a general treatment of General Order 100 see Richard C. Brown, "Social Attitudes of American Generals, 1898-1940," (Ph.D. diss., University of Wisconsin, 1951), 41-46.

16. Taft to Root, Aug. 18, 1900, Root Papers.

17. Taft to Root, July 26, Aug. 18, 1900, Root Papers.

18. Taft to Root, Sept. 21, Oct. 10, 31, Nov. 14, 1900, Root Papers; Taft to Horace H. Lurton, Sept. 22, 1900, to Lodge, Oct. 17, 1900, to William R. Day, Dec. 10, 1900, to Henry M. Hoyt, Jan. 7, 1901, Taft Papers.

19. Taft to Root, Nov. 14, 1900, Root Papers.

20. Noble, "Compilation," preface.

21. For examples of the use of the Philippine Insurgent Records (PIR), see MacArthur to AG, Aug. 31, 1900, *Correspondence Relating to the War with Spain, April 15, 1898-July 30, 1902*, II, 1203-1204; MacArthur to AG, Aug. 29, Sept. 21, 1900, AGO 344307, Incls. A and B; J. Fernando to Torres, Sept. 12, 1900 with note by an American, A. B. H., to arrest the author, PIR 559.3; J. Dayrit to Alejandrino, Dec. 7, 1900 with notes on use of document by F. D. Grant, PIR 625.1; Wheaton to AG, Division of the Philippines, Nov. 5, 1900, "Diary of Events, 1-14 Nov., 1900," AGO 353532.

22. The report is published in *Annual Reports of the War Department for the Fiscal Year Ended June 30, 1900*, HD 2, 56th Cong., 2d sess., VIII, 257-64.

23. Ibid., 265.

24. Ibid., VI, 197, 230-54.

25. Taft to Root, Nov. 14, 1900, Root Papers.

26. A. S. Burt to Taft, Aug. 14 and 24, 1900, Edwin F. Glenn to Taft, Aug. 22, 1900, George Curry to Taft, Sept. 3, 1900, all in Taft Papers; James Parker, "Some Random Notes on the Fighting in the Philippines," *Journal of the Military Service Institution of the United States* 27 (1900): 337-38; Louis Livingston Seaman, "Native Troops for Our Colonial Possessions," *North American Review* 171 (1900): 847-60; testimony of James F. Smith, *Lands Held for Ecclesiastical or Religious Uses in the Philippine Islands, Etc.*, SD 190, 56th Cong., 2d sess., 229-31; MacArthur to AG, Aug. 7, 1900, *Correspondence*, II, 1197.

27. *Annual Reports of the War Department for the Fiscal Year Ended June 30, 1901*, HD 2, 57th Cong., 1st sess., V, 119.

28. Felipe Buencamino, "Memorandum Concerning the Philippine Problem," Nov. 1, 1900, Taft Papers.

29. Edward M. Coffman, *The Hilt of the Sword: The Career of Peyton C. March* (Madison, 1966), 18.

30. *War Department, 1900*, HD 2, 56th Cong., 2d sess., VI, 62. See also MacArthur to Taft, Sept. 14, 1900, Taft Papers.

31. Innocente Martinez to Barrio Chiefs, Sept. 20, 1900, "Diary of Events, 1-14 Nov., 1900," AGO 353532.

32. *War Department, 1901*, HD 2, 57th Cong., 1st sess., V, 90.

33. Sandico to Manuel Tinio, July 26, 1900, Taylor, "Compilation," 89LY.

34. *War Department, 1900*, HD 2, 56th Cong., 2d sess., VI, 71.

35. Testimony of MacArthur, *Affairs in the Philippine Islands*, SD 331, 57th Cong., 1st sess., pt. 2, 869.

36. *War Department, 1901*, HD 2, 57th Cong., 1st sess., V, 257-58.

37. Taft to Root, Nov. 30, Dec. 27, 1900, Root Papers. See also Rowland Tappan Berthoff, "Taft and MacArthur, 1900: A Study in Civil-Military Relations," *World Politics* 5 (1953): 205.

38. Murray to Allen, Oct. 22, 1900, Allen Papers.

39. Frank C. Prescott to Allen, Nov. 15, 1900, Allen Papers.

40. Allen to Kobbé, Mar. 24, 1900, Bell to Allen, Mar. 14, 1901, Allen Papers; Kobbé, "Diary," 160-64.

7

STRUCTURING A SUCCESSFUL
PROGRAM OF PACIFICATION

Timing was an important factor in the implementation of a revised policy of pacification. Until the results of the election in the United States became known in the Philippines little could be done to counter the effect of guerrilla propaganda stressing the need for continued resistance to influence the election. As early as August 1900, General MacArthur realistically reported to Washington that "little or nothing is to be expected in the way of practical pacification before next December," by which date he assumed the impact of the election would have had time to weaken the Filipino will to resist. The General was confident that the guerrilla bands were being held together with great difficulty and that many revolutionary leaders were thoroughly sick of living in the mountains. He noted with pleasure the statement of Teodoro Sandico in a captured document that, if McKinley was elected, the people of the islands would probably accept United States sovereignty in the hope of realizing more of their aspirations through American benevolence than they had been able to secure through continued warfare.[1]

General MacArthur selected the period after the election as the perfect time to begin a vigorous campaign, and the army went on the offensive after the receipt of the news of McKinley's reelection in November 1900. These operations in November actually started before General MacArthur had completed the plans for a new approach to the problem of pacification, and they represented an effort to bring a speedy end to the guerrilla war that would make changes in the pacification program unnecessary. Although this heightened military pressure on the guerrillas in November and December achieved some success, both General MacArthur and commission president Taft were not satisfied with the rate of progress. MacArthur feared that the guerrilla war would become a chronic problem if pacification were not forthcoming, and Taft, in his correspondence home, admitted that guerrilla victories in the preelection campaign enabled the movement to continue much longer than he had anticipated. Victory, if it were to come at all, would not be gained through a collapse of the revolutionary force. The Americans would have to win it. Fortunately, they were better prepared than at any previous period in the Philippine campaign to deal with the problems posed by the guerrilla. By the middle of December 1900, they had a new plan of action and sufficient resources to carry it through to a successful conclusion.[2]

Conditions in the Philippines were excellent for a major offensive against the revolutionaries. The number of American troops approached 70,000, the largest number available for service there at any time during the hostilities. Many of these troops were veterans of the previous campaigns and were acclimated to the adversities of tropical warfare. The rainy season had ended, and the American units would be undertaking their field operations during a period of relatively dry weather. From the point of view of men, material, and climate, the situation in the Philippines was auspicious for the operations that were beginning to unfold as a part of General MacArthur's plan for pacification.

General MacArthur outlined the objective of his campaign in a message to his department commanders on December 19. He stated that the new pacification effort was based on his strong opinion "that one of the most effective means of prolonging the struggle now left in the hands of the insurgent leaders is the organized system by which supplies and information are sent to them from occupied towns." The objective of the campaign was "to interrupt and, if possible, completely

destroy this system." The army was to use a strict enforcement
of the provisions of General Order 100 in its operations to
isolate the guerrilla from his civilian base. General MacArthur
instructed his department commanders that whenever action
under the order was necessary "the more drastic the application
the better, provided, only, that unnecessary hardships and personal indignities shall not be imposed upon persons arrested
and that the laws of war are not violated in any respect
touching the treatment of prisoners."[3] To insure that the
American actions would not be misunderstood by the Filipinos
and to clarify for them the changes that were taking place in
American policy, MacArthur issued a proclamation, dated
December 20, in which he outlined some of the more important
provisions of the laws of war affecting the Filipino guerrillas.

General MacArthur's proclamation of December 20 contained the guidelines for the policy that the Americans would
follow throughout 1901. He acknowledged the American obliga-
tion to give protection to all people residing within occupied
places who were performing with fidelity the duties imposed
upon them, the foremost of these duties being strict obedience
to the commanding general of the occupying force. From the
time of the proclamation forward, all seeking to prevent this
reciprocal relationship through the use of intimidation and terror were to be answerable collectively and individually to the
military authorities of the American colonial government for
violation of the laws of war. Offenders were to be tried for murder or any other crime resulting from their actions. The proclamation explained that "persons residing within an occupied
place who do things inimical to the interests of the occupying
army are known as war rebels, or war traitors, according to the
nature of their overt acts, and are punishable at the discretion
of the tribunals of the occupying army." The General further
stated that "in such a case a plea of intimidation can rarely be
accepted." The newspapers and other periodicals of Manila
were especially warned to take care against the publication of
any article that might be considered seditious or harmful to the
occupying army. A special section of the proclamation was
directed to the part-time guerrilla. It noted that "men who participate in hostilities without being part of a regularly-organized

force, and without sharing continuously in its operations, but who do so with intermittent returns to their homes and avocations, divest themselves of the character of soldiers, and if captured are not entitled to the privileges of prisoners of war."[4] After December 20 General MacArthur hoped that Filipinos would no longer interpret American benevolence as weakness.

The new pacification program differed from the unqualified benevolence characteristic of American policy in the first two years of the war. When General MacArthur issued special instructions to department commanders on implementing the program implied in his December proclamation, he told them to keep close surveillance on anyone suspected of aiding the revolutionaries. They were to assume that all prominent families that had not committed themselves to the Americans by some public action or declaration were, either willingly or under compulsion, engaged in or knew those who were providing the guerrillas with supplies and information. These Filipinos were to be considered accessories to the system organized to continue the guerrilla war.[5] Garrison commanders were instructed that if no "convincing proof" could be found, "suspicion amounting to moral certainty" would be acceptable for the arrest of suspects. Compulsion, intimidation, or fear would not be accepted as excuses for any deed done in support of the revolution. The new American policy was to make the Filipinos think that "compliance with insurgent demands will be as dangerous as a refusal."[6] Commissioner Taft summed up this aspect of the new program in one of his letters to Secretary Root, writing that "there are many arrests made every day now of insurrecto emissaries, sympathisers and officers hiding in Manila, and suspected characters and identified insurgents are sent here from all parts of the Islands." As Taft observed, "it has ceased to be a good joke to be an insurrecto."[7]

The Americans also stopped releasing disarmed prisoners of war. Instead, they began a system to inter prisoners and to keep careful records of those detained. Filipinos suspected of supplying guerrillas were to be sent to Manila. In keeping with the course of action suggested by the Taft Commission, the more important revolutionary leaders were to be deported to

Guam and held there until the restoration of peaceful conditions in the Philippines. The first of the deportations took place in January, 1901. It included both military and civil officers of the Filipino government, foremost among them being Apolinario Mabini. Imprisonment and deportation of numerous other Filipinos followed as the Americans made known their new policy of detaining prisoners for the duration of hostilities.[8]

The Americans made a special effort to erradicate terrorism, the weapon that had effectively defeated their attempts at benevolent pacification in 1900. The Army applied the provisions of General Order 100 to seemingly good effect. Evidence of American success in the discovery, location, trial, and conviction of Filipino terrorists filled the general orders published by the Division of the Philippines throughout 1901.[9] In many cases the death penalty followed. Executions increased as part of a program calculated to convince the Filipinos that they had little to gain and a great deal to lose by continued resistance.

General MacArthur placed special emphasis on the creation of better facilities for the collection and examination of intelligence data to aid in the surveillance of Filipinos suspected of helping the guerrillas and to improve the army's knowledge of the organization and methods of the revolutionaries. Throughout 1899 and 1900 the army in the Philippines had had no adequate system for the analysis of military intelligence. The only agencies remotely acting in this capacity were the Department of Secret Service, whose operations were confined to Manila, and the custodians of the captured Filipino records. Functioning on a low budget and with little manpower, it kept a record of Manila newspaper items that could be considered seditious and attempted to suppress the city's revolutionary organizations that were involved in recruiting men, securing supplies, and forwarding funds, information, and propaganda to the guerrillas and the Hong Kong junta. The success of the Secret Service prior to November 1900 had been limited. Officially, similar organizations did not exist in other American garrisons, and the numerous valuable documents captured from the revolutionaries were not handled in any systematic manner. The army's attempt in 1900 to send an agent to Hong Kong for surveillance of the revolutionary junta had been a complete failure, and further attempts of that nature had not been made.[10] With the revision of the program for pacification at the end of 1900, however, a change came in the army's attitude on the problems of collecting and analyzing military intelligence.

On December 13, 1900 the army organized a Division of Military Information as a part of the Adjutant General's Office in Manila. Its primary function was the collection and dissemination of military intelligence data. The captured Filipino records and documents that were continuously being sent to Manila from the outlying commands were its speical concern. Similar organizations were established in subordinate military commands, and at each station commanding officers were instructed to make as full a use as possible of a secret service. They were to pay agents "liberally" and give them as much protection as possible.[11] In Manila, the Secret Service made an extra effort beginning in November to break up revolutionary organizations in and about the city, and between November 1, 1900 and February 1, 1901 its agents arrested about 600 persons, of whom 250 were insurgent officers. By the beginning of 1901 the army had developed the basis for an efficient system of collection and dissemination of military intelligence data, although why such action had not been initiated before was a question that remained unanswered.[12]

The rapid increase in the number of American garrisons throughout the islands was another part of General MacArthur's plan to isolate the guerrillas from the villages. The number rose from about 400 at the beginning of the campaign to 502 within a few months.[13] The Americans occupied every important municipality and strategic point; military districts were reorganized to improve the effectiveness of the garrisons; and American units held positions blocking trails used by the guerrillas. In one case, on the island of Marinduque, the American commander lacked troops to occupy all of the inhabited places on the island and issued orders that the populace was to concentrate in those towns that could be held. People passing in and out of the occupied towns were required to report to the commanding officer of each garrison. According to Major Fred A. Smith, the commander on the island, the measure worked

> to break up the heretofore rapid means of communication which the insurgents used to keep fully informed of the movements of our troops as well as intercommunication between their own. It has also removed the fears of those who were afraid to come in and created a feeling of confidence in our good intentions.[14]

Population concentration was also used successfully by units of the 20th Infantry in Ilocos Sur.[15] In general, American garrisons served the dual purpose of protecting people from terror while preventing the aid and supply of the guerrillas by the villagers.

Offensive action against the guerrillas by American units in the field complemented the spread of American garrisons throughout the islands. Units scouted and patrolled constantly and allowed the guerrillas no rest or sanctuary. General Young reported that his men in northern Luzon were scouting mountain trails "hitherto considered inaccessible to American troops" and that they had, as a consequence, discovered and destroyed numerous hidden cuarteles and magazines.[16] Guerrilla units, hard pressed by the Americans, could not maintain themselves as fighting forces. Short of food and continually harassed by American troops, the revolutionaries were forced to break into small bands or return to their homes. In most of the Philippine Islands, by the middle of 1901, guerrilla operations were confined mainly to terrorism against their own people and to firing at night into towns garrisoned by the Americans. Their effectiveness as a military force ceased as a result of the continuous pressure exerted by the Americans. At the same time, the American garrison system denied the guerrillas the rest, supplies, and information that had been furnished in the past by the villages.[17]

General MacArthur wanted to augment his plan to isolate the guerrilla and harass him in the mountains by a tight blockade of the islands and a widespread program of road building. The blockade, to be performed by the navy, would serve the same function on an island wide scale as the garrisons served on land. The guerrillas, prevented from obtaining supplies from their local surroundings, were to be prevented from getting the needed items from other islands. The sale of hemp either by guerrilla agents or by Filipinos and foreign companies paying taxes to the guerrillas had provided a source of ready cash. The closing of the hemp ports was one way to stop this flow of money to the revolutionaries. Washington, however, would not approve the General's request to close all the ports in southern Luzon and the Visayas because it feared the effects such a move might have on the world hemp market. Nevertheless, the navy continued the patrolling begun in 1899, and, combined with a rigid system for licensing commercial craft, it did much to prevent the revolutionaries on one island from supplying those on another.[18]

The General's road building program, instituted in cooperation with the Taft Commission, sought to increase the rapidity and mobility with which American units could operate against the Filipino troops in the field. MacArthur's goal was to make the roads in the archipelago passable in all seasons. Looking forward to the time when the islands would be pacified, the General wanted to develop a system whereby mounted American units could be garrisoned at central points connected by telegraph. Mobile troops operating on all-weather roads would eventually allow a reduction in the number of American units needed to maintain peace. At the same time, any work done toward developing such a system in 1900 and 1901 contributed directly to the immediate goal of pacification. The blockade and road building, like the garrisons and aggressive action of American units in the field, were calculated to make the new campaign of pacification swift, rigorous, and decisive. The focus of this military action was the isolation of the guerrilla from his source of supply and his pursuit and destruction in the field.[19]

On December 11 the War Department had sent an order to General MacArthur which had seriously upset his plans for a new campaign of pacification. It directed him to prepare to return the volunteer units, then approximately 28,000 men, to the United States.[20] This force, raised by Secretary Root in 1899, made up an important part of the General's experienced troops. Their withdrawal during 1901 would mean another dangerous period of readjustment and troop shortage similar to that experienced by General Otis at the end of 1899. General MacArthur had known that sooner or later the volunteers would have to return to the United States, but the War Department order came at a most inopportune time.

From the moment he assumed command in the islands, General MacArthur had hoped to involve Filipinos actively in their own defense against the revolutionaries. With the contemplated withdrawal of the volunteers and his plans for a large offensive campaign, it became even more imperative that Filipinos be armed and enlisted in the American service to offset the loss of American troops. The General instructed his department commanders to regard all matters touching upon the organization of local police forces "as emergency work," and authorized them to increase the number of scouts in their districts "to the limit of safety."[21] In the past, General MacArthur and other American officers had voiced suspicions that the great mass of Filipinos could not be trusted, and they had been reluctant to arm local police or make large increases in the number of scouts enlisted. In December 1900, however, no alternative seemed available if offensive actions were to be continued after the withdrawal of the volunteers. Consequently, officers were urged to put every possible energy into work that would spell disaster for the pacification program if the Filipinos enlisted proved disloyal.

Up to the end of 1900, the army's experience with Filipino scouts had been good. Macabebes, in service since 1899, had been of great value when properly supervised by American officers. They were, however, cruel and brutal in their treatment of other Filipinos, and the Americans knew that any force of scouts would need to be closely supervised. Inhabitants of the provinces of Ilocos Norte and Ilocos Sur had served courageously and loyally as scouts since the American occupation of northern Luzon near the end of 1899. The experience of the army with these two groups had been so good that throughout 1900 the number of scouts authorized in the Philippines was constantly increased. By January 1, 1901 a force of 1,402 scouts existed, and further increases were authorized for the offensive campaign underway. The power to authorize the enlistment of scouts was transferred from the headquarters in Manila to the department commanders. By the middle of June 1901, over 5,400 scouts were in service and plans were underway to systematize the organization of the scout units as a regular part of the American force garrisoning the islands. The army, however, was very reluctant to enlist Tagalogs as scouts, and in both 1901 and 1902 the great majority of Filipinos enlisted were Macabebes, Ilocanos, and Visayans.[22] Filipino troops became an important element in MacArthur's overall plan of operations.

Encouraged by the work of the scouts, General MacArthur had attempted to organize a system of municipal police in the towns in June 1900, but, like his amnesty bid at the same time, the outcome did not live up to his expectations. Thinking that the Filipinos could be organized to protect themselves from terror, he authorized local commanders to establish and arm police to act both within the municipalities and also as constabulary in the area surrounding their towns. Police proved useful in Manila, parts of northern Luzon, and on Negros, but elsewhere the results were disappointing. The municipalities lacked sufficient funds to maintain an adequate police force, and revolutionary influence was so great in most villages that the police could not be relied upon in any case. In some localities revolutionaries gained control of the police. As the guerrilla war increased in intensity, American officers were reluctant to arm Filipinos, and in general their feelings toward the organization of armed municipal police were in agreement with those expressed by Major General John C. Bates in command of the Department of Southern Luzon. Bates thought that the organization of the police was "a grave error," and he was convinced that, in view of past experience with the Filipinos, "these people are not to be trusted."[23] General MacArthur, however, was not to be deterred. Certain that the situation following the election of McKinley was more favorable than it had been in June, he again urged his subordinates to organize local police units. He authorized increased pay for police to be taken from insular rather than local funds. As with the organization of scouts, he regarded such work as an emergency task to be expedited immediately, and by June 1901, the number of police in the archipelago numbered over 6,000, of whom approximately 40 percent had firearms.[24]

The question of Filipino troops and police brought General MacArthur and the army into conflict with Taft and the civil commission. Although the General recognized the need to organize Filipinos in their own defense, he was unwilling to allow the civil authorities to control any group of armed natives. He wanted a system of scouts attached to regular army units, with constabulary and local police operating in the municipalities under the direct supervision of his garrison commanders. The General was unalterably opposed to raising native units of regimental size. Taft and the commission, thinking primarily of the development of civil government in the Philippines, desired a constabulary completely divorced from the army and under the control of the commission. The commission used the opinions of numerous military officers to bolster its arguments for such a force; although many officers probably gave more thought to the advancement of their careers in such an organization than to its merits.[25] As a result of the difference of opinion between the military and civil authorities in the islands, the forming of a native constabulary was postponed, but the numbers of scouts and municipal police increased greatly as the new program of pacification was implemented.

On the surface, most of the changes taking place in the American pacification campaign appeared to increase its severity and to abandon the policy of benevolent pacification, but this was not the case. Provost-Marshal-General Bell's comments to the officers serving under him placed the policy changes in their proper perspective. Bell began by stating that he had "frequently heard the opinion expressed that no good has been accomplished" by the old policy. He continued:

> I cannot concur in that opinion, for I feel convinced that this policy has had a good effect. Had we been building for a day only or solely in order to put an

end to hostilities, a different policy might have been indicated, but . . . we have got to continue to live among these people. We have got to govern them. Government by force alone cannot be satisfactory to Americans. It is desirable that a Government be established in time which is based upon the will of the governed. This can be accomplished satisfactorily only by obtaining and retaining the good will of the people. . . . Our policy heretofore was calculated to prevent the birth of undying resentment and hatred. This policy has earned for us the respect and approval of a large majority of the more intelligent and influential portion of the community. We cannot lose their support by now adopting such measures as may be necessary to suppress the irreconcilable and disorderly.[26]

General Bell thought that the increased severity accompanying the new pacification policy was selective enough to make things more difficult for the revolutionaries without alienating Filipinos who had already been convinced of American good intentions. Fear and anxiety were to be created not among those friendly to the Americans, but among those who were reluctant to accept them after more than two years of benevolence. Bell recognized that the severity envisioned by General MacArthur would require many American officers to subordinate their personal views and friendships that they had made with Filipinos. They were to be sustained by the conviction that by following the new policy they were doing "the greatest good for the greatest number." General Bell told his subordinates to remember that the new policy was not one of "harsh and indiscriminate persecution," but of "considerate firmness."[27] Although more severe than that followed in 1899 and most of 1900, the new approach to pacification was still based on the idea that benevolent and humanitarian action was needed to win the enduring friendship of the great mass of Filipinos. It was not aimed at the Filipinos as a people, but at a selected group who by their actions prevented the pacification of the islands.

Unfortunately, some Americans did not have as good an

understanding of the new policy as General Bell, and for them it represented the inauguration of a campaign of severity. Consequently, some enlisted men could interpret the new policy as one of "taking *no* prisoners" with MacArthur "sweeping everything as he goes," and officers could write of substituting "the effective noose for the futile school-book."[28] The cruelties and abuses that appeared in increasing numbers during 1900 continued, and those men who so desired could interpret the new pacification policy as a sanction for such action.

Although crimes against Filipinos continued throughout 1901, the men who committed or tolerated cruelty and uncalled for severity represented only a fraction of those in responsible positions in the Philippines. The official policy of the army, as General Bell had rightly discerned, was one of benevolence. Conduct contrary to the official policy, violations of the articles of war, or conduct contrary to the spirit of General Order 100 was not tolerated by most responsible commanders in the islands. They punished men guilty of offenses immediately.[29]

Under the new policy of pacification the army was still involved continually in work to improve the level of living of the Philippine villagers and win acceptance of American sovereignty through benevolent acts, just as it had been under the old policy. The organization of municipal governments, sanitation and public health efforts, school work, fiscal reform, and public works all continued throughout 1901. In that respect absolutely no change had taken place.[30]

The major emphasis of military civil affairs work changed slightly in 1901 as the army transferred more and more power and responsibility to the civil commission. For example, in January the commission passed a municipal code that superceded the orders of the military government. By that date the army had already established some 500 governments. The focus of army activity in the towns turned away from the organization of municipal governments to specific aspects of the operation of those governments. Civil affairs reports indicated a concern for sanitation, education, the collection and disbursing of municipal revenue and taxes, the organization of native police units, and the economic development of the municipalities, with emphasis on the inhabitants resuming their normal routines as soon as possible.[31]

The Chief Surgeon of the Division of the Philippines, who also acted as the head of the insular board of health, coordinated public health work in the provinces. Medical officers of military units continued to act as health officers in the towns, and the whole procedure was based on methods followed in Manila since 1898. The extensive program of vaccination begun in 1899 continued. Because of a lack of ice plants to keep the virus fresh, the Americans resorted to the arm-to-arm method of vaccination that the Spaniards had employed and with which Filipino vaccinators were thoroughly familiar. By the end of 1901, over a million people had been vaccinated. In other areas of public health work the army's progress was similar.[32]

The army transferred overall direction of school affairs to the Taft Commission on September 1, 1900, but work continued to follow the recommendations submitted by Captain Todd. Although the supervision of education was in the hands of civilians, the military continued their active role as school organizers, builders, and teachers at the local level.[33]

Under the new pacification policy, the Americans not only continued their benevolence toward the townspeople and villagers, but also continued it toward revolutionaries who surrendered voluntarily. Although the new policy provided for the detention of prisoners captured by American troops and the arrest and retention of those suspected of aiding the guerrillas, American propaganda made a special appeal to Filipinos to surrender. Those who did and took the oath of allegiance to the United States were released immediately. Payments of $30 Mex. for each weapon surrendered continued and were advertised widely by proclamation. This policy was based upon General MacArthur's very accurate assessment that arms were one resource that could not be replaced. The $30 Mex. was a powerful incentive to Filipino soldiers to defect from the guerrillas with their weapons. It was enough money to give them a chance to return to their former peaceful existence in the community. MacArthur had initiated the money-for-guns policy in northern Luzon in late 1899. He increased its scope as a part of

218   SCHOOLBOOKS AND KRAGS

the new policy of pacification at the end of 1900. By March
1901, Filipinos voluntarily bringing in firearms could obtain
the release of prisoners of war in numbers equal to the number
of arms surrendered. Wives, relatives, or sweethearts of revolutionaries might, by surrendering weapons, free their loved ones.
General MacArthur termed the system evolved for the purchase of weapons one of his "most important" policies.[34]

Filipinos supported the American campaign in a new way
at the end of 1900. General MacArthur and the commission
had both been approached by Filipinos advocating a popular
"counterrevolution" in favor of American sovereignty in the
Philippines. The result of this movement was the formation of
the Filipino Federal party pledged to work toward peace and
having as its immediate goal the pacification of the islands.
Prominent Filipino conservatives like Dr. T. H. Pardo de
Tavera and Florentino Torres, who had previously aided the
American government in Manila, helped organize the party.
Dr. Frank S. Bourns, having returned to the islands after a
short stay in America, worked to assure the party members of
the American determination to remain in the Philippines. The
party platform included a firm commitment to individual
rights, the separation of Church and state, and the furtherance
of the benevolent work already begun by the army. The public
announcement of the formation of the party followed General
MacArthur's December 20 proclamation of major changes in
the American pacification policy.[35]

Organized to offer Filipinos an alternative to Aguinaldo's
independence movement, the Federal party directed Philippine
political activism toward American ends. Pro-American in its
orientation, its political strength came from the upper- and
middle-class Filipinos to whom further war offered little appeal
and possible economic ruin. In positions of traditional leadership in Philippine society, these men could exert a powerful
influence on the mass of Filipinos who were only indirectly
associated with the revolutionary movement.[36]

In towns throughout the Philippines, party members
began organizing committees to combat the influence of the
revolutionaries and to work energetically for pacification. In
some cases they found committees organized and waiting for

them when they went into towns. They also made an effort through direct contact and letters to bring about the surrender of revolutionary leaders and their guerrilla bands. When surrenders were obtained, Federal party members then attempted to enlist the guerrilla leaders in their cause. As Buencamino had promised, the efforts of the party were directed to organizing the Filipinos against the revolutionaries and in support of the Americans. The party became a powerful force for molding public opinion, exerting pressure on the revolutionaries to end the war, and preparing the way for the inauguration of civil government under the auspices of the Taft Commission. The members undertook these tasks with vigor, and the work of the Federal party was an important adjunct to that of the army and the commission in the attempt to convince Filipinos of the sincerity of the American promises of local government, material progress, and continuing benevolence.[37]

With the formation of the Federal party near the end of December 1900, General MacArthur's program of pacification was complete. A comprehensive approach to the problems of guerrilla warfare, it embodied the experience gained by the Americans throughout 1899 and 1900. Commanders such as MacArthur and Bell had recognized the value of benevolence. They had rejected recommendations for extreme repression and purposeless severity. Instead, not only was the army continuing its efforts in areas such as public health and education, but its actions were augmented by the work of the Taft Commission. This work and the inducements given to the revolutionaries to surrender had been successful enough in 1900 to force the guerrillas to adopt a policy of terror and intimidation. The new program not only retained the inducements and propaganda appeals of the past, but enlisted the support of Filipinos in attempts to explain America's beneficent intentions and encourage guerrillas to surrender. As an added incentive to surrender and to end the activities of the part-time guerrilla and those aiding the revolution from the towns, General MacArthur invoked the provisions of General Order 100. In 1899 and 1900 the Americans had given the Filipinos inducements for supporting them, but there had been little penalty for supporting the revolution. With the initiation of the new pacification policy, both positive and negative incentives existed for accepting American sovereignty.

Militarily, the primary aims of the revised pacification program were the isolation of the guerrillas from their bases of supply in the towns and the protection of civilians from revolutionary terrorism. Filipinos, acting as scouts, police, guides, and agents, were utilized to a greater extent than ever before. The Americans placed great emphasis on involving Filipinos in their own defense against the revolutionaries. At the same time, American troops were reorganized to garrison as many towns as possible. Other units were equipped to maintain continuous pressure on the guerrillas in the field. Recognizing the importance of intelligence data in a campaign against guerrillas, General MacArthur had not only reorganized the existing facilities for that purpose, but also created new agencies for the collection and dissemination of military information. By 1901, the army had embarked on a broad spectrum of actions calculated to win Filipinos to the American cause and to deal effectively with those who refused to accept American rule.

The year 1901 would be the test of whether or not the Americans had structured a successful program of pacification. The defeat of Bryan in the American election had lowered the morale of the revolutionaries but had not brought the mass surrenders and collapse which Americans in the Philippines had expected. Aguinaldo urged his guerrillas to continue their resistance. Propaganda from the Hong Kong junta sustained the hope that political events in the United States might still be influenced by their actions. Disappointed but not defeated, the revolutionaries would have to be beaten decisively. By January 1901, pacification had not been achieved. The events of the next few months would indicate whether the army's new policy would be more successful than that of complete benevolence which had failed in 1900 after its apparent success in 1899.

NOTES

1. MacArthur to AG, Aug. 25, 1900, Records of the Adjutant General's Office (AGO) 344307; MacArthur to AG, Aug. 31, 1900, *Correspondence Relating to the War with Spain, April 15, 1898-July 30, 1902*, II, 1203-1204.

2. MacArthur to AG, Dec. 3 and 25, 1900, *Correspondence*, II, 1232, 1237-38; Taft to William R. Day, Dec. 10, 1900, Taft Papers.

3. *Annual Reports of the War Department for the Fiscal Year Ended June 30, 1901*, HD 2, 57th Cong., 1st sess., V, 93.

4. Ibid., 91-92.

5. Ibid., 93.

6. Arthur L. Wagner to Commanding General, 4th District, Department of Southern Luzon, Dec. 26, 1900, "Diary of Events, 14-29 Dec., 1900," AGO 360651.

7. Taft to Root, Dec. 27, 1900, Root Papers.

8. *War Department, 1901*, HD 2, 57th Cong., 1st sess., V, 94-95; Taft to Root, Dec. 27, 1900, Root Papers; U.S., Congress, Senate, *Deportation of A. Mabini and Others*, SD 135, 56th Cong., 2d sess., 1901, 3; Wheaton to Commanding General, 1st District, Department of Northern Luzon, Dec. 30, 1900, "Diary of Events, 29 Dec., 1900-12 Jan., 1901," AGO 365565.

9. Compare the orders in *General Orders and Circulars Issued from Department of the Pacific and 8th Army Corps and Division of the Philippines, 1900* with those in *General Orders, U. S. Army, Philippine Islands, 1901*.

10. *Annual Reports of the War Department for the Fiscal Year Ended June 30, 1900*, HD 2, 56th Cong., 2d sess., XI, 310-11; *War Department, 1901*, HD 2, 57th Cong., 1st sess., V,, 467; MacArthur to AG, Dec. 2, 1900, *Correspondence*,

II, 1232. Reports of Captain John S. Mallory from China are in AGO 357352.

11. Arthur L. Wagner to Commanding General, 4th District, Department of Southern Luzon, Dec. 26, 1900, "Diary of Events, 14-29 Dec., 1900," AGO 360651.

12. *War Department, 1901*, HD 2, 57th Cong., 1st sess., V, 132, 467; VIII, 88. Reports from the Secret Service for the period from December 1900 to January 1902, can be found in Corbin Papers under "C" for Chaffee. Initially the American conviction that the war would be short and the assumption at the beginning of 1900 that the war was ended might account for the lack of attention to the development of facilities for the collection and analysis of intelligence data. Also, the Filipino terror campaign made the organization of a corps of native agents and spies almost impossible during most of 1900.

13. *Annual Reports of the War Department for the Fiscal Year Ended June 30, 1901*, HD 2, 57th Cong., 2d sess., II, 31. For an excellent example of the use of garrisons by General Bell see VI, 30-41.

14. *Affairs in the Philippine Islands, Hearings before the Committee on the Philippines of the United States Senate*, SD 331, 57th Cong., 1st sess., pt. 3, 2443-45.

15. *Historical Sketch of the Twentieth United States Infantry* (n.p., n.d.), 41-43.

16. Young to AG, Department of Northern Luzon, Dec. 28, 1900, "Diary of Events, 29 Dec., 1900-12 Jan., 1901," AGO 365565.

17. On the use of mobile units as part of the pacification program see MacArthur to AG, Oct. 26, 1900, *Correspondence*, II, 1222. Good examples of the American pacification program at work are *War Department, 1901*, HD 2, 57th Cong., 1st sess., VI, *passim*.

18. MacArthur to AG, Dec. 25, 1900, Corbin to MacArthur, Dec. 26, 1900, *Correspondence*, II, 1237-38. On the Navy see Frederick L. Sawyer, *Sons of Gunboats*.

19. Testimony of MacArthur, *Affairs in the Philippine Islands*, SD 331, 57th Cong., 1st sess., pt. 2, 878; Ulysses G. McAlexander, *History of the 13th Regiment United States Infantry*, 156-64.

20. *War Department, 1901*, HD 2, 57th Cong., 1st sess., V, 131.

21. Thomas H. Barry to Commanding General, Department of Northern Luzon, Dec. 22, 1900, BIA 1184, incl. 9.

22. *War Department, 1901*, HD 2, 57th Cong., 1st sess., V, 131, 86-87; MacArthur to AG, June 7, 1901, *Correspondence*, II, 1284. A history of the enlistment of Filipino scouts is in "Diary of Events, 30 Jan.-15 Feb., 1901," AGO 369141. See also *War Department, 1900*, HD 2, 56th Cong., 2d sess., V, 209-10; Frederick Funston, *Memories of Two Wars: Cuban and Philippine Experiences*, 319; *War Department, 1902*, HD 2, 57th Cong., 2d sess., IV, 481.

23. Bates to Secretary, U. S. Military Governor, Nov. 11, 1900, AGO 386153, incl. 1.

24. *War Department, 1901*, HD 2, 57th Cong., 1st sess., V, 244; Thomas H. Barry to Commanding General, Department of Northern Luzon, Dec. 22, 1900, BIA 1184, incl. 9; *War Department, 1900*, HD 2, 56th Cong., 2d sess., VI, 64-65.

25. MacArthur to AG, Nov. 15, 1900, AGO 386153; A. S. Burt to Taft, Aug. 14 and 24, 1900; Edwin F. Glenn to Taft, Aug. 22, 1900; and George Curry to Taft, Sept. 3, 1900, all in Taft Papers; Taft to Root, June 15, July 26, Aug. 21, Sept. 13, 1900, Root Papers; Worcester to Mrs. Lawton, Dec. 5, 1900, Lawton Papers.

26. Bell to AG, Dec. 31, 1900, "Diary of Events, 29 Dec., 1900-12 Jan. 1901," AGO 365565.

27. Ibid.

28. Jim Nisbet to Tibbie Nisbet, Jan. 11, 1901, Nisbet Papers; McAlexander, *History*, 171.

29. See testimony of Taft, *Affairs in the Philippine Islands*, SD 331, 57th Cong., 1st sess., pt. 1, 75-78; Hughes, pt. 1, 643; MacArthur, pt. 2, 870-71; Clarence Lininger, *The Best War at the Time*, 162-63.

30. *War Department, 1901,* HD 2, 57th Cong., 1st sess., VI, 142-43, 162-66, 201-202; *Affairs in the Philippine Islands*, SD 331, 57th Cong., 1st sess., pt. 2, 1799-1853, pt. 3, 2461-2543; U.S., Congress, Senate, *The Philippine Situation* [Jun. 3, 1902 speech of Senator Albert J. Beveridge], SD 422, 57th Cong., 1st sess., 1902.

31. *War Department, 1901*, HD 2, 57th Cong., 1st sess., V, 241; VI, 116, 160-62, 201-207.

32. Charles R. Greenleaf, "A Brief Statement of the Sanitary Work so far Accomplished in the Philippine Islands, and of the Present Shape of the Sanitary Administration," *Reports and Papers of the American Public Health Association, 1901* 27 (1902): 158; *War Department, 1901*, HD 2,

57th Cong., 1st sess., III, 676-79; "Annual Report of Chief
Surgeon, Department of Northern Luzon," June 30, 1901,
AGO 399549, incl. 22. For an example of health work in the
municipalities see James Parker, *The Old Army*, 351-52.
      33.   U.S., Department of the Interior, *Report of the Com-
missioner of Education, 1900-1901* (Washington, 1902),
1323-24; "Report of Gilbert N. Brink, Division Superintendent
of Schools for Pampanga, Bulacan, & Bataan Provinces,
1901," BIA 2074, incl. 11; *Affairs in the Philippine Islands*,
SD 331, 57th Cong., 1st sess., pt. 1, 432; Kennon, "Civil Affairs Report for Dec. 1900," Jan. 10, 1901, U.S. Military
History Research Collection; Kennon, "Civil Affairs Report
for Jan. 1901," Feb. 10, 1901, Kennon Papers.
      34.   MacArthur to AG, Mar. 25, 1901, *Correspondence*,
II, 1262. See also *War Department, 1901*, HD 2, 57th Cong.,
1st sess., V, 102-103. According to Taft the policy of allowing
guns to be traded for prisoners was the idea of Brigadier
General George W. Davis and not MacArthur; Taft to Root,
Mar. 17, 1901, Root Papers.
      35.   *War Department, 1901*, HD 2, 57th Cong., 1st sess.,
V, 96, 122; Taylor, "Compilation," 20-22 HS; Worcester to
Mrs. Lawton, Dec. 5, 1900, Lawton Papers; Taft to Root, Dec.
27, 1900, Root Papers.
      36.   Onofre Corpus, "Western Colonization and the
Filipino Response," *Journal of South East Asian History*
3 (1962): 18.
      37.   Pardo de Tavera to MacArthur, Mar. 14, 1901, *War De-
partment, 1901*, HD 2, 57th Cong., 1st sess., V, 115-16, also
96; C. A. Conant, "American Work in the Philippines," *International Monthly* 5 (1902): 360-61. For specific examples of Federal party work see Bourns to Taft, Apr. 4, 1901, Taft Papers;
Buencamino to anon., Mar. 1901, U.S., Congress, Senate, *Political Affairs in the Philippine Islands*, SD 259, 57th Cong., 1st
sess., 1902, 7: Wheaton to AG, Feb. 4, 1901, "Diary of Events,
30 Jan.-15 Feb., 1901," AGO 369141.

8

YEAR OF VICTORY, 1901

General MacArthur's comprehensive plan for pacification, set in motion at the end of 1900, continued without pause in 1901, and for many Americans the new year promised to be a victorious one. Aggressive action by army units in the field, an increasing number of municipal garrisons to provide security, the judicious use of General Order 100 against Filipino terrorists and supporters, the persistent efforts of the Federal party, the acceptance by Filipinos of a role in their own defense, active American propaganda, and American benevolence all combined to make continued guerrilla warfare difficult. In the early months of 1901 the elusive goal of pacification seemed near. In almost every portion of the Philippine archipelago the Americans were successful. Rapidly accumulating evidence showed a complete breakdown of the revolutionary movement and a widespread swing of popular support away from the guerrillas. After a frustrating year of guerrilla warfare, a year of victory was finally at hand for the United States Army.

The revolutionaries reacted immediately to the new American pacification policy. One revolutionary, certain that General MacArthur's December proclamation was seriously affecting the Filipino cause, wanted steps taken at once to send men into the towns to combat its influence.[1] Aguinaldo, in a statement issued on January 17, 1901, accused the Americans of "shameless violations of the most elementary laws" by their policy of deportation, imprisonment, and execution aimed at revolutionary leaders, terrorists, and supporters. He charged the Americans with "sowing the seeds of a civil war" through their use of Filipinos as municipal police and army scouts. To contend with the new American policy, Aguinaldo proposed that guerrilla units capture more American prisoners to force exchanges for those Filipinos held by the army. Another of his suggestions, aimed specifically at the Federal party, called for the trial of party members as traitors, and he recommended that those joining it be "punished with special rigor."[2] Aguinaldo was determined that the defeat of Bryan in November and the new American pacification policy would not bring an end to Filipino resistance.

Revolutionary propaganda in 1901 differed little from that of 1900, except that the election was no longer an issue. The revolutionary junta in Hong Kong maintained a steady stream of material calculated to buoy up Filipino morale. Immediately after news of Bryan's defeat, the president of the junta issued a communiqué to the guerrilla chiefs stating that they could still influence the American Congress by continued war. He said that two more years of fighting would be sufficient to bring about a popular repudiation of McKinley's imperialist policy, and he reminded the guerrillas that other nations, no doubt referring to Cuba, had struggled longer. Clippings from American and other foreign newspapers were dispatched regularly to the islands to keep the guerrillas apprised of the work of the anti-imperialists in the United States.[3]

Propaganda generated by revolutionary leaders in the Philippines stressed Filipino victories while masking those of the Americans and magnifying American cruelty. Guerrilla chiefs exhorted the Filipinos to ignore the counter revolutionary movement of the Federal party, and stressed the long hoped for victory through the triumph of the Democratic party in the United States or from foreign intervention against the Americans by a power such as Germany. American soldiers were reminded of the advantages that would accrue to them if they surrendered themselves and their weapons to the guerrillas. But, on the whole, the Filipino revolutionaries could alter their propaganda very little to meet the changed American pacification policy.[4]

Propaganda was not, however, the primary weapon of the revolutionaries. Terror continued to be their principal means of combating the growing American influence in the towns. The widespread terrorism evident in 1901 indicated, as it had in 1900, that if left alone and unthreatened the great mass of Filipinos would not voluntarily support the revolution.

The techniques of terrorism employed in 1901 remained substantially the same as those used in 1900. Filipino terrorists that the army was fortunate enough to capture were found guilty of such crimes as arson, kidnapping, assault, and murder. A hardened soldier like Brigadier General Frederick Funston remarked that descriptions of the acts committed were enough to give one "cold chills."[5] General Hughes, reporting from the island of Panay, vividly summarized the revolutionary terror campaign in his area.

> The situation of the island is simply hell. The insur-
> rectos have given play to their rage and a native
> messenger caught in Antique is prepared for Ham-
> burger steak, while a native in Iloilo with a certificate
> of allegiance about him is made into hash. There
> were four of them caught near Pototan the other day
> and that was their condition.[6]

Hughes also recorded that the insurgents had attempted widespread burning of towns and barrios.

Captain John R. M. Taylor, head of the Division of Military Information in Manila and chief translator of the captured revolutionary documents, maintained after the war's end that the severity of the measures used by the guerrillas to prevent popular support of the Americans was an indication of the extent of that support.[7] Revolutionary activities in 1901 gave credence to Taylor's thesis. Terrorism was often aimed specifically at the new American policy of pacification. For example, the revolutionaries went to great efforts to prevent the spread of the Federal party. General Juan Cailles informed his men that all persons who attempted to persuade townspeople to

sign any documents of a political nature were to be shot
without trial and that captured members of the Federal party
were to be executed immediately as traitors. Other guerrilla
commanders issued similar orders. The revolutionaries also
branded as traitors and marked for terror attacks those who
surrendered their weapons, those using arms to obtain the
release of prisoners, and those who tried to induce others to
surrender their persons or weapons. To prevent Filipinos from
joining the police and scouts organized by the Americans, one
guerrilla commander attempted to forbid all males from entering the garrisoned towns in his region. The revolutionaries were
also worried by the increasing number of Filipinos acting as
American spies.[8] Terror tactics, useful in 1900, proved insufficient in 1901 to stop a swing of Filipino support to the
Americans.

In 1901, for the first time since the American occupation
of the Philippines began, large numbers of Filipinos defied
warnings and terror to work for peace and the acceptance of
American sovereignty. Groups of Filipinos throughout the
islands embarked on an active campaign of letter writing calculated to convince the guerrillas remaining in the mountains
that the time had come to admit defeat and to surrender.[9]
American officers had less difficulty obtaining guides, agents,
and informants in the villages than in previous years.
Townspeople organized against the revolutionaries. In Zam-
bales Province, for example, three towns met jointly and passed
a resolution notifying the leaders of the guerrillas in their
region that they would cease furnishing them assistance and
that, if they did not surrender their weapons, the citizens of the
towns would lead the Americans to their hiding places.[10] Elsewhere, a revolutionary chief complained that the townspeople in his area were preventing his men from obtaining supplies
while the town president was bombarding his guerrillas with
propaganda comparing the great hardships of guerrilla campaigning to the easy life of the people under American protection.[11] To the revolutionaries in the field the collapse of
their hold over the municipalities was readily apparent. The
constant propaganda and increasing support given by
townspeople to the Americans made continuation of the war
more and more difficult.

The Federal party was successful in its work of organizing the provinces. The party leaders, proud of their efforts, cabled the United States Senate in January that people were joining the party "by thousands."[12] They urged that civil government be initiated at the earliest opportunity to take advantage of the increasing support given the Americans. Taft wrote a month later that the Federal party was "spreading like wild-fire throughout the Islands," and he took that as proof that the great majority of Filipinos were truly "anxious for peace under the sovereignty of the United States."[13] In the first three months of 1901 over 250 Federal party committees were organized, and the membership of the party stood at about 150,000 by mid-year. When the civil commissioners journeyed on a tour of the provinces of Pampanga, Tarlac, and Pangasinan to gather data and organize local governments, they observed great public manifestations of confidence and adhesion to the American cause, organized by the party. General José Alejandrino, writing long after the war had ended, claimed that the campaign of the Federal party subtracted men and resources almost daily from the revolutionary cause.[14] General MacArthur viewed the growth of the party as evidence of a changing attitude on the part of the Filipinos, and he noted that it was accompanied by "the immediate and almost complete discontinuance of the service of information and supply between the towns and the field guerrillas."[15]

Evidence of the collapse of the revolution was unmistakable. Surrenders of revolutionary soldiers and leaders took place with increasing frequency after the American offensive began in November 1900, and continued throughout 1901. Those who surrendered and took the oath of allegiance usually brought in their weapons. The number of firearms surrendered increased steadily as the year progressed. Insurgent surrenders in November and December 1900 were over 1,300 a month, compared to a total of less than 500 for the previous three months combined. After a slight drop to approximately 900 and 750 respectively, in January and February 1901, they again increased to almost 7,000 in March, over 6,000 in April, and between 1,000 and 2,000 each month in May, June, and July. Statistics on the surrender of weapons showed a similar pattern. From August to December 1900, a total of less than

200 firearms were surrendered. In January and February 1901, however, over 900 were given up each month. From March to May a total of over 7,500 were relinquished.[16]

While surrenders of men and equipment were taking place, captures of men and arms by American units in the field also reached new highs. The largest number of revolutionaries captured was in December 1900 and January 1901, about 700 and 1,300 respectively. The record for the capture of weapons came during the first three months of 1901. The rate of casualties suffered by the American troops steadily diminished. Taken as a whole, statistics on surrenders, captures, and losses were striking evidence of the rapid collapse of the revolutionary guerrilla force and its diminished effectiveness. By April, the number of engagements between American units and the scattered bands of guerrillas had fallen to a third of what it had been during the peak of American activity at the beginning of the year.[17]

Americans in the Philippines became increasingly optimistic as evidence of the revolution's collapse accumulated. As early as January 9, 1901, Taft wrote that "the march of events is all towards us" and that the remaining guerrillas were rapidly degenerating to the status of bandits.[18] General MacArthur thought that the surrender of General Martin Delgado on Panay was of great importance because it signified the end of organized resistance in Iloilo Province. General Wheaton reported the administration of the oath of allegiance to over 1,000 Filipinos on a single day in a town in northern Luzon. One American officer could only look upon such an event in his area with suspicion and disbelief, certain that such widespread oath taking must have been ordered by Aguinaldo or some other revolutionary leader. The surrender of Simon Tecson represented the end of well-organized resistance in northern Luzon and led General MacArthur to report to Washington on February 12 that he hoped for the suspension of hostilities in all the islands at an early date. The surrender of Mariano Trías in southern Luzon and the capture of Ananais Diocno on Panay in March both added to American optimism. General Hughes thought that Diocno was the "most troublesome insurgent general" on Panay. MacArthur referred to the surrender of Trías as a "most auspicious event" that indicated the "final stage [of] armed insurrection."[19]

A highly encouraging sign for the prospects of long-term pacification of the islands was the willingness of Filipinos to finally accept a role in their own self-defense. The growth and increased efficiency of the Filipino scouts and municipal police were evidence that many Filipinos had chosen to cast their lot with the Americans. The work of the scouts was praised highly by many American officers who came in contact with them.[20]

Developments in municipal police units were indicative of the growing concern of Filipinos for their own defense. As late as January 1901, American commanders in northern Luzon considered municipal police completely unreliable. The pressure accompanying the return of the second American volunteer army to the United States made the development of native police units imperative, however, and their organization proceeded throughout 1901. In February, the Americans made great strides in the formation of police units, and General Wheaton, who had complained about the police in his department in January, wrote in March that they were "improving in efficiency and loyalty . . . and are now in many instances furnishing information and are aiding in the capture of murderers and assassins to whose control they have long been subjected."[21] Wheaton thought that improved conditions would even allow further extension of the police system. The improved situation that he noticed was similar to that on other islands.

By May, Filipino townspeople, in the face of pressures of revolutionary terror, had accepted the burden of defending themselves with American aid from bandits, terrorists, and guerrillas. Prior to 1901, protection of the municipalities had been a task almost solely for the American army. By the end of the year, however, American commanders reported cases, such as that in the town of Carmona in Cavite Province, where poorly armed and underpaid municipal police, unaided by American troops, repulsed guerrilla attacks.[22]

One sign of the growing number of Filipinos supporting the Americans was the outward display by many people of their desire to obtain the protection and other advantages of an American garrison and municipal government, even though such actions made the town a target for guerrilla reprisals. In towns like Bangued in northern Luzon, citizens met to offer resolutions of fidelity and allegiance to the Americans and made appeals to their neighbors to cease resisting and do likewise. When townspeople heard that the American garrison in their town was to be moved, they would petition for its retention. In these signed documents, people made no secret of their deep regret at seeing the American units leave. Often the petitioners asked that specific officers be retained in their midst, usually praising highly the work that this or that man had done to bring order, progress, and happiness to their towns.[23] Even revolutionaries recognized the excellent work done by Americans in the municipalities, and General Villamor noted that the "meritorious and prudent conduct" of one officer of the 5th Infantry "brought the capitulation of the guerrilla soldiers of Abra." That officer was later made the first civil governor of the province "upon petition of the inhabitants."[24] Colonels C. C. Hood and Cornelius Gardener were the choice of the Filipino municipal leaders of Cagayan and Tayabas provinces for similar posts.[25]

Captured revolutionary documents also contained evidence of the growing support for the Americans in the municipalities. General Cailles in Laguna Province received a summary of the problems developing for the guerrillas and their supporters. The president of Majayjay, a revolutionary, complained to him that the American policy of attraction was having its full effect not only upon the wealthy people of the town, but upon the common people as well. He could, in fact, not even rely upon the fidelity of his own police whose hearts, he feared, belonged to the Americans. General Trías, on the occasion of his surrender, also commented on the unmistakable shift of popular support away from the guerrillas.[26]

Final evidence of the declining power and effectiveness of the revolutionaries was the widespread growth of the influence of the American colonial government. As early as January 1901, Secretary Root became optimistic enough about developments in the Philippines to consider the complete transfer of all governmental functions from the military to the

Taft Commission. Root wrote Taft that he wanted a military commander over American forces in the islands "who will administer them with the predominant purpose of getting the Government out of military hands and into civil hands at the earliest practicable moment."[27] He was glad that Taft agreed that the time was near to appoint a civil governor.

In the next few months the civil commissioners journeyed throughout the Philippines organizing provincial governments to support the municipal governments already established or in the process of development. They visited thirty-three provinces. These journeys were gestures of good will contributing to the overall program of pacification, and they provided the initial impetus for the formation of provincial civil governments in all of the provinces visited.[28]

Other evidence of greater American governmental control in the islands was the increasing revenue collected by the insular authorities. The rather steady growth of tax receipts could be interpreted as signifying more willingness on the part of Filipinos to pay American taxes in defiance of the revolutionaries. This diversion of funds also affected Filipino attempts to collect taxes. American internal revenue receipts rose each year after 1899, although American fiscal policy had been one of tax reduction. Starting at $240,754 in 1899, revenue grew to $561,993 in 1900, and to over $966,400 in 1901. The following year, 1902, the annual receipts were over $3,000,000.[29]

Many Americans viewed an event that occurred in March 1901 as the most important of the guerrilla war. General Funston—accompanied by four American officers posing as prisoners and a force of eighty-one Macabebe scouts, four ex-revolutionary officers, and a guerrilla messenger—successfully deceived the revolutionaries, gained access to Aguinaldo's camp in northern Luzon, and captured the Filipino leader. The whole operation, conducted in a single month, was a masterpiece of deceptive stratagem. The *Vicksburg* had transported Funston's men to the northern coast of Luzon and landed them on March 14. They captured Aguinaldo on March 23, and the whole group embarked on the *Vicksburg* again on the twenty-fifth. Aguinaldo was brought to Manila.[30]

The fortuitous acquisition of a set of letters from Aguinaldo to his subordinates had prompted Funston's feat. A municipal president had convinced the bearer of the dispatches to surrender himself and the letters to the Americans. The messenger knew the whereabouts of Aguinaldo. A letter requesting reinforcements for Aguinaldo's camp presented the perfect cover for the movement of Funston's Macabebe force inside enemy territory. The Americans had long sought the capture or surrender of Aguinaldo, and General MacArthur viewed the perfect execution of Funston's plan and the seizure of Aguinaldo alive as the "most momentous single event of the year."[31] The General wanted to make as much of the opportunity that had presented itself as he could and to use Aguinaldo's capture to bring about, if possible, the complete and immediate collapse of the revolution. Washington, however, told him to proceed cautiously in his plan to use Aguinaldo as a part of his pacification campaign, and warned him to make no promises to the revolutionary leader that were not specifically contained in the amnesty proclamation of the previous June.[32]

Shortly after his arrival in Manila, Aguinaldo showed a disposition to cooperate with the Americans. He might have arrived at that state as a consequence of conferences with Chief Justice Cayetano Arellano, but in any case he could not have failed to note the growing support given the Americans by the Filipino townspeople or overlooked the other evidence that the revolutionary movement was already disintegrating. He agreed to issue a proclamation on behalf of the Americans, urging the surrender of the revolutionaries remaining in the field. General MacArthur wanted to issue a new amnesty proclamation at the same moment. Fearing that Aguinaldo's presence in the Philippines might act as a stimulus to continued revolt, the General also recommended that Aguinaldo be taken to the United States with a few prominent Filipinos to observe and study American institutions. Although the government in Washington thought that a proclamation by Aguinaldo calling for peace would be excellent, it declined to extend the amnesty or to allow Aguinaldo to come to the United States lest his visit provide anti-imperialist propaganda. No reasons were given for the decision not to extend the amnesty.[33]

Aguinaldo issued his proclamation near the end of April. In it, he acknowledged that as far as he could discern the country had "declared unmistakably for peace." He urged those Filipinos still in arms to surrender. For his own part, he publicly accepted the sovereignty of the United States and called attention to the evidence of American liberty and generosity already visible in the islands.[34] Aguinaldo, like so many Filipinos before him, accepted peaceful existence under American rule in place of continued guerrilla war.

The importance of Aguinaldo's capture and the publication of his proclamation was difficult to assess. General MacArthur was convinced of their great significance. Most Americans then and since have viewed the capture as the turning point that marked the end of the Philippine revolt. Numerous revolutionaries surrendered in the two months following the event, but the collapse of the revolution had really begun with the American offensive following McKinley's reelection in November 1900. Increasing surrenders of men and arms, the development of the concept of self-defense among the Filipino townspeople, the marked decrease of effectiveness of the guerrillas, and the more general evidence of a swing in popular support toward the Americans dated from the beginning of 1901, not from the end of March. Although this was never recognized by any great number of individuals, some American observers in the islands did see that the end had begun some months before Aguinaldo's capture. Dr. Bourns, writing to Taft on April 4, was convinced that the surrender of Trias was an event of much greater significance, and he noted that the military authorities had greatly magnified the importance of the capture of Aguinaldo. Taft accepted Bourns' view of the situation, writing that the revolutionaries had, as evidenced by the surrender of Trias, already recognized that the people of the Philippines "longed for peace under a government by the United States." James A. LeRoy, secretary to Commissioner Worcester, wrote in retrospect that the capture of Aguinaldo was "merely a spectacular incident in the general movement toward peace at the time."[35] This view should certainly have been accorded more attention than it received at the time. Although the capture represented an important step toward pacification, it was by no means the key event in the campaign initiated months earlier.

The insurrection had started to collapse before the capture of Aguinaldo, and it continued to survive after the loss of its leader. Some guerrilla chiefs refused to surrender and vowed to continue fighting. The Hong Kong junta urged the continuation of the war with a stronger hand, complaining that Aguinaldo had been too lenient.[36] Malvar assumed leadership over the remaining revolutionary forces. Operating in Batangas Province, he refused to recognize the development of a popular movement to end the war. He maintained that the laboring classes, the people who, according to him, "act with greater honesty of intentions and are more sincere in their aspiration," had not given up hope in the eventual success of the Philippine revolt.[37] Consequently, he refused to terminate the guerrilla war until convinced that a true change in attitude had taken place among the common people of the islands. Although the war was nearing its end, resistance continued despite mounting evidence of growing support for the Americans. The Americans continued to be optimistic.

Following the capture of Aguinaldo, the movement to place complete control of the insular government in the hands of the civil commission came to fruition. In accordance with a presidential directive, Secretary Root issued instructions in June that on July 4, 1901 the Philippine Commission would begin to exercise full executive as well as legislative authority in the islands. Taft was appointed civil governor of the Philippines, and all civil power previously exercised by the military governor passed to him. The instructions issued to the commissioners in April 1900 were to continue to guide them in their actions, but the transition to civil government was not an easy task.[38]

An undercurrent of civil-military friction had been present in the Philippines since the arrival of the first commission in 1899, and the relations between General MacArthur and Taft had been somewhat strained throughout the operation of the second commission. Taft filled his letters to the United States with references to the friction. Although he wrote that he thought the history of their difficulties would never be written, he did his best to insure that adequate mention of them would be recorded for posterity in his own correspondence.[39] Taft portrayed General MacArthur as a man "who spends too much time in defending his own jurisdiction, . . . and preserving his dignity, to give all the time that is needed to the prosecution of military matters."[40] Taft had made his ideas concerning the General known to Secretary Root, and the Secretary provided that when the power of the military in civil affairs was transferred to the commission, General MacArthur would be replaced as the military commander in the islands.

As early as February 1901, Root had written Brigadier General Adna R. Chaffee telling him of the decision to place him in command of the Philippine force upon the appointment of a civil governor. In that letter, Root outlined his plans for the future relationship between the army and the civil government. It was to be substantially the same as that in the United States, with complete subordination of the military to the civil authority. Root wrote that in Washington the government was convinced that the establishment of civil government would hasten pacification. Chaffee's task would be "to get the Army out of the governing business and get its officers back to the performance of their proper functions as soldiers. . . . the sooner . . . the better." Although admitting that the transfer of power would proceed gradually, Root left no doubt that General Chaffee's primary task would be to insure that the transfer would take place in an atmosphere of "harmony and perfect cooperation." He told Chaffee candidly that a change of command would accompany the transfer of power because the subordination of the military to the civil authority would be easier with a commander who had not previously held any civil power in the Philippines. Chaffee, unlike MacArthur, would not be in the position to look with disfavor on what appeared to be a loss of authority. Instead, Chaffee was "free from any such predisposition . . . [assuming command] purely as a soldier to discharge difficult and delicate but well-defined duties."[41] Root hoped to end the civil military friction that had been so apparent during the previous two years.

Taft, for his part, evidenced a certain prejudice against military men in general. He commented to a friend that, although he did not know Chaffee, he doubted whether the new commander would be "any easier to get along with than MacArthur." But Taft observed that, "as the relation of the civil authority to the military will be changed with his taking command, we can probably *compel* a different situation."[42] The relations between the civil authority and the new commander could hardly have begun less in the spirit that Root contemplated.

Although civil and military leaders did not always agree on the relationship of the military force in the Philippines to the civil government being formed there, they usually agreed that civil government played an important role in the pacification process. At the beginning of 1901, Taft wrote Root that the civil governmental organization represented an effective means of mobilizing "active native support in ferreting out those who are responsible for a continuance of ladronism and guerrillaism." He thought that the development of civil government in pacified areas would be "an object lesson to the people of the disturbed provinces of the rewards which they might reap by securing peace."[43] Martial law and military government would be the penalty for continued resistance. General MacArthur, in commenting on the organization of provincial governments taking place early in the year, wrote that he thought they would be "useful agencies in the work of pacification," and he told his department commanders to regard them as of great enough value to be instituted prior to the complete pacification of any given province. The organization of civil government in Albay and the promise of it in Marinduque were both followed by a surrender of the revolutionary forces in those provinces.[44] While civil and military officials disagreed on the question of supremacy of authority, both were willing to admit that civil government was an inducement that they could use to achieve the goals of the pacification campaign. Given all of their differences of opinion, Taft was still able to commend General MacArthur for "doing everything in his power" to aid the commission in the establishment of municipal and provincial governments.[45]

Although the government in Washington and the commission wanted the civil authority in absolute control of the insular government, the realities of the situation in the islands gave the army a large role in its development. In 1901, soldiers continued to be the only representatives of the United States government spread throughout the Philippines. The army contained almost all of the personnel experienced in insular civil affairs. Taft was quick to realize that military personnel would have to play a large role in any plan for the extension of the civil government. He wrote MacArthur as early as February 1901 for assistance in selecting provincial officials, stating that he thought it best, "if possible, to select American volunteer officers who have been on duty in the province in which they are to be appointed."[46] The army had almost a monopoly of those men in the islands whom Taft thought were qualified to serve in the key positions of provincial supervisors, engineers, and treasurers. He recognized that the experience gained by officers having served in positions such as provincial governors and internal revenue collectors was much too valuable to be wasted. He also asked the help of military governors and garrison commanders in finding Filipinos who might be qualified to hold offices in the civil government.[47]

Even after the insular government was transferred to the commission and Taft was appointed civil governor, the military continued to play a key role in the development of civil government at the local level. An order issued on July 20, 1901, gave the army the specific mission of organizing governments in areas still in rebellion and therefore still under military control. Officers charged with the administration of civil affairs in those provinces were considered to be discharging their duties as officers of the insular government, reporting directly to the civil authority, and performing their functions under the direction of the civil governor. In both school and public health work the army continued to carry out the programs of the civil government at the municipal level, and major public works projects were planned and executed by the Corps of Engineers.[48]

Taking advantage of the growing willingness of Filipinos to organize for their own self-defense and looking forward to the time when the islands would be pacified and the army replaced by an insular police force, in July 1901 the commission organized a constabulary for the maintenance of peace,

law, and order in the provinces. The constabulary, separate
from both the army and the municipal police, consisted of units
of no more than 150 men in each province. Enlisted members
were drawn from the provinces in which the units were formed,
but officers or inspectors were drawn chiefly, but not exclusively, from the ranks of the American army. Captain Henry
T. Allen was detailed as chief of the constabulary. The commission had sought the development of such a force since 1900,
and it had been both impressed with the effectiveness of the army's Filipino scouts and the limited ability of municipal police
forces to deal with problems of lawlessness outside of their immediate village surroundings. The advantages of Filipino
troops, with their ability to distinguish between members of the
native population, their knowledge of Filipino languages and
customs, their familiarity with local terrain features, and their
access to intelligence data had already been demonstrated.
From its beginning the Philippine Constabulary was a success.[49]

By November 1901 the Philippine Constabulary had
enlisted almost 1,000 men, and by January 1902 it had a force
of about 3,000 actively working to keep peace and to aid the
army in those areas still unpacified. Captain Allen maintained
a policy of appointing, for the most part, natives recommended
by the military, and he was pleased with the support given the
constabulary by the majority of army officers.[50]

The constabulary was particularly adept at dealing with
the problem of brigandage that had plagued the Philippines for
centuries. Although poorly armed with shotguns and .45
caliber revolvers because of the fear that members of the force
might desert to the revolutionaries with their weapons, the constabulary tracked and brought to bay numerous bands of ladrones. As a police force its effectiveness was unquestioned. It
also contributed to the more pressing problem of ending the
guerrilla war and achieving a state of complete pacification in
the islands.[51]

The contribution of the constabulary to the army's program of pacification was extremely important. The formation
of the force, coinciding with the pacification and transfer to the
civil government of many provinces in northern Luzon and the

Visayas, enabled the Americans to concentrate their troops more effectively in areas still plagued by guerrilla bands. It eased, in part, the strain provoked by the return of the volunteer units to the United States, as had the increases in both army scouts and municipal police. As a consequence, whereas in July 1901 the army garrisoned 491 posts with 49,937 men, by December 1 it held only 372 posts with 37,340 troops. Because the constabulary maintained its own bureau of information, it contributed directly to the army's pool of intelligence data. As the revolution collapsed, whole provinces were held by the constabulary without the aid of the army.[52]

The constabulary and civil authorities were able to keep peace in a large number of provinces because of the success of the army's program of pacification in the first half of 1901. The effective area of revolutionary control and military operations had been narrowed until by the middle of the year Taft could write that "only four or five provinces remain afflicted with the guerilla warfare." By the beginning of July only the province of Batangas and adjacent areas in southern Luzon and the islands of Cebu, Bohol, and Samar in the Visayas remained unpacified. From the Department of Northern Luzon, General Wheaton reported the "absolute termination" of armed resistance.[53]

General MacArthur, in a move to speed pacification, had begun a policy of publicizing the surrender of large revolutionary forces or important guerrilla commanders by the release of prisoners held by the Americans since the beginning of the new policy. With the publication of Aguinaldo's proclamation in April, 1,000 Filipinos were released. Another 1,000 were freed in early May with the surrender of General Manuel Tinio and other revolutionary leaders in the provinces of Abra and Ilocos Norte. Later in May another 500 were released under similar circumstances, and 1,000 more followed in June.[54] The Federal party's work to induce revolutionaries to surrender had been most effective, and by June its members had been instrumental in obtaining the surrender of sixteen important officers. Felipe Buencamino, speaking for the party, wrote that the revolution was "morally and materially dead."[55]

In the face of overwhelming evidence that the revolutionary movement was collapsing, the army did not make the mistake that it had in 1899 by assuming that the decreased effectiveness of the guerrillas could be equated with complete pacification. The more severe pacification measures instituted at the end of 1900 were continued after the capture of Aguinaldo. The threat of deportation remained. At the same time that ports in pacified provinces were being opened, the blockade of the islands was sustained, and ports on the island of Samar, for example, were closed. Arrests, trials, and convictions under the provisions of General Order 100 and the instructions issued by General MacArthur in December 1900 also continued.[56] The aggressive campaign of pacification made Filipino resistance more and more difficult.

By the latter half of 1901 the guerrillas remaining in the field resorted, in desperation, to widespread terror, but to little avail. The growing support given the Americans by the Filipinos and the increasing pressures of the American campaign of pacification were proving too much for the revolutionaries. Guerrilla leader Pedro Caballes summarized the problems facing him in a letter to General Malvar concerning the work of the ex-revolutionary Juan Cailles and the Americans in Laguna province.

> General, I cannot regulate the towns in my jurisdiction, because the traitor Cailles is always hunting for me with a force of American soldiers. . . . there are one hundred towns which do not want more war, and will tranquilly recognize the supreme authority of the United States. For the rest, the traitor Cailles, who is trying to catch me, is putting municipal officers in the towns of this province in order to establish a civil government.[57]

Caballes asked permission to resort to widespread arson in an attempt to prevent the withdrawal of popular support. On Samar one of Lukban's subordinates reported that burning was the only weapon left to him, and by the end of the year General Wheaton reported from southern Luzon that the guerrillas found it necessary to impress recruits by force.[58] All of the evidence available to the Americans at the end of 1901 showed that the campaign was a complete success. As far as the majority of provinces in the Philippines were concerned, pacification was at hand.

NOTES

1. Pedro Lardizabal to Maximo Abad, quoted in A. W. Corliss to AG, Department of Southern Luzon, Jan. 7, 1901, "Diary of Events, 12-30 Jan., 1901," Records of the Adjutant General's Office (AGO) 369140.

2. Aguinaldo, "In Self-Defense," Jan. 17, 1901, Taylor, "Compilation," 35GV.

3. E. Riego to Our Brave Generals and Heroic Partisans, Nov. 10, 1900, Philippine Insurgent Records (PIR) 507.3; "Recortes y traducciones de la prensa extranja," Noble, "Compilation," XXI, 3564; Arthur Lee, "Carta de America," Jan. 17, 1901, Noble, "Compilation," XXI, 3565.

4. Taylor, "Compilation," 55HS; Lukban, proclamation, Feb. 25, 1901, PIR 968.10; Lukban to Local Chiefs, Mar. 8, 1901, PIR 1144.10; Villa to Jeciel, Jan. 13, 1901, PIR 1282.

5. Frederick Funston, *Memories of Two Wars: Cuban and Philippine Experiences*, 374. See also *General Orders, U.S. Army, Philippine Islands, 1901, passim.*

6. Hughes to AG, Manila, Dec. 19, 1900, "Diary of Events, 14-29 Dec. 1900," AGO 360651. Examples of terrorism in addition to those in general orders for 1901 are unsigned letter to General in Chief [at Nagcarlan], Apr. 6, 1901, PIR 1142.8; Pedro Caballes to Cailles, Mar. 29, 1901, PIR 1205.1; Manuel Quiroque to Cailles, Mar. 21, 1901, PIR 1205.2.

7. Taylor to Chief of Bureau of Insular Affairs (BIA), Jan. 23, 1903, PIR 1048.1.

8. Taylor, "Compilation," 54HS; Emilio Zurbano, proclamation, Mar. 22, 1901; Pedro Caballes to Cailles, Mar. 1901, Taylor, "Compilation," 78-80GV; E. S. Wright to AG, 2d District, Department of Southern Luzon, AGO 421607, incl. 12: Mariano Noriel, proclamation, June 25, 1901, PIR 568.3; R. F. Santos to Esteban Nieves, Dec. 4, 1900, Taylor, "Compilation," 73GV; E. Villareal to Ramón Santos, Feb. 13, 1901, PIR 1014.7; P. E. del Rosario, circular, May 27, 1901, PIR 1218.5.

9. An excellent summary of the arguments used to try to induce the revolutionaries to surrender is that presented in unsigned letter to General Diocno and the Chiefs and Officers under His Orders, Feb. 1901, PIR 878.5. The Iloilo Peace Committee was particularly active in corresponding with revolutionaries on Panay. See Iloilo Peace Committee to Martin Delgado, Nov. 27, Dec. 27, 1900, to Quintin Salas, Jan. 21, 1901, Noble, "Compilation," XXXI, 4839-43, 4845-50, XI, 1823-25.

10. Taft to Root, Jan. 13, 1901, Root Papers.

11. Antonio Guevara to Vito Belarmino, Mar. 15, 1901, Taylor, "Compilation," 80GV. On swing of popular support to Americans see also Jordan to Mother, Feb. 13, Apr. 5, 1901, Jordan Papers; testimony of Hughes, *Affairs in the Philippine Islands, Hearings before the Committee on the Philippines of the United States Senate*, SD 331, 57th Cong., 1st sess., pt. 1, 668-69.

12. U.S., Congress, Senate, *Civil Government in the Philippine Islands*, SD 119, 56th Cong., 2d sess. 1901.

13. Taft to John Coffey, Feb. 22, 1901, Taft Papers.

14. *Annual Reports of the War Department for the Fiscal Year Ended June 30, 1901*, HD 2, 57th Cong., 1st sess., IX, 165, V, 115-16; José Alejandrino, *The Price of Freedom* (Manila, 1949), 172.

15. *War Department, 1901*, HD 2, 57th Cong., 1st sess., V, 97.

16. Statistics taken from a chart prepared by AG, Manila, in Taft Papers, container 67.

17. Ibid.

18. Taft to Root, Jan. 9, 1901, Root Papers.

19. MacArthur to AG, Jan. 12, and Feb. 12, 1901, *Cor-*

respondence Relating to the War with Spain, April 15, 1898-
July 30, 1902, II, 1245, 1253; Wheaton to AG, Jan. 21, 1901,
"Diary of Events, 12-30 Jan., 1901," AGO 369140; Wheaton
to AG, Feb. 26, 1901, "Diary of Events, 15-27 Feb., 1901,"
AGO 371701; MacArthur to AG, Mar. 16 and 19, 1901, *Cor-*
respondence, II, 1259-60.

   20. Testimony of Hughes, *Affairs in the Philippine*
Islands, SD 331, 57th Cong., 1st sess., pt. 1, 571-73; James
Parker, "Some Random Notes on the Fighting in the Philip-
pines," *Journal of the Military Service Institution of the*
United States 27 (1900): 317-40; J. N. Munro, "The Philip-
pine Native Scouts," *Journal of the U. S. Infantry Associa-*
tion 2 (1905): 178-90; Charles D. Rhodes, "The Utilization of
Native Troops in Our Foreign Possessions," *Journal of the Military*
Service Institution of the United States 30 (1902): 1-22; John
W. Ward, "The Use of Native Troops in Our New Possessions,"
Journal of the Military Service Institution of the United
States 31 (1902): 793-805.

   21. Wheaton to Secretary to the Military Governor in the
Philippine Islands, Jan. 10, and Mar. 11, 1901, BIA 1184,
incl. 9 and 13.

   22. James F. Wade to AG, Manila, Sept. 21, 1901,
"Diary of Events, 21 Aug.-11 Oct., 1901," AGO 409151.

   23. Wheaton to AG, Feb. 11, 1901, "Diary of Events, 30
Jan.-15 Feb., 1901," AGO 369141. See also Wheaton to AG,
Mar. 31, 1901, "Diary of Events, 14 Mar.-17 Apr., 1901,"
AGO 382667; Estefano Salomon to Commander of the
Detachment of Gubigon, Aug. 13, 1901, PIR 1054.6. See the
petitions in *Affairs in the Philippine Islands*, SD 331, 57th
Cong., 1st sess., pt. 2, 1799-1853, pt. 3, 2461-2543.

   24. Juan Villamor, *Unpublished Chronicle of the Filipino:*
American War in Northern Luzon, 1899-1901, III, 11.

   25. Taft to Root, Aug. 25, Feb. 8, 1901, Root Papers.

   26. Taylor, "Compilation," 54HS; Trías to Malvar, Apr.
13, 1901, PIR 896.7.

   27. Root to Taft, Jan. 21, 1901, Root Papers.

   28. *War Department, 1901*, HD 2, 57th Cong., 1st sess.,
IX, 9-13.

   29. *Annual Reports of the War Department for the Fiscal*
Year Ended June 30, 1902, HD 2, 57th Cong., 2d sess., IV,
271. Collection of taxes, in addition to other administrative
tasks, depended on government control in the municipalities

and the absence of an effective revolutionary threat. This analysis of one non-military indicator of the extent of government control, i.e. tax receipts, was prompted by Bernard B. Fall's thesis that "when a country is being subverted . . . it is being outadministered." See "Insurgency Indicators," *Military Review* 46 (April, 1966): 8.

30. *War Department, 1901*, HD 2, 57th Cong., 1st sess., VI, 122-30; MacArthur to AG, Mar. 28, 1901, *Correspondence*, II, 1262-63.

31. *War Department, 1901*, HD 2, 57th Cong., 1st sess., V, 99.

32. Corbin to MacArthur, Mar. 29, 1901, *Correspondence*, II, 1263.

33. MacArthur to AG, Apr. 1 and 6, 1901, Corbin to MacArthur, Apr. 3 and 9, 1901, *Correspondence*, II, 1265-67.

34. MacArthur to AG, Apr. 10, 1901, ibid., 1267-68.

35. Bourns to Taft, Apr. 4, 1901, Taft Papers; Taft to Aaron A. Ferris, Apr. 25, 1901, Taft Papers; James A. LeRoy, "Mabini on the Failure of the Filipino Revolution," *American Historical Review* 11 (1906): 857n.

36. E. Riego to Generals of the Filipino Army, Apr. 8, 1901, PIR 1183.9.

37. Malvar to Trías, Apr. 19, 1901, Taylor, "Compilation," 82GV.

38. General Orders No. 87, Headquarters of the Army, June 22, 1901, *Correspondence*, II, 1287.

39. For examples see Taft to J. G. Schmidlapp, May 19, 1901, to William R. Day, May 22, 1901, Taft Papers.

40. Taft to Root, Jan. 13, 1901, Root Papers.

41. Root to Chaffee, Feb. 26, 1901, Taft Papers.

42. Taft to Howard C. Hollister, May 26, 1901, Taft Papers. For a general discussion of the civil-military friction in the Philippines see Rowland Tappan Bertoff, "Taft and MacArthur, 1900: A Study in Civil-Military Relations," *World Politics* 5 (1953): 196-213; Ralph Eldin Minger, "William Howard Taft: The Development of His Conception of American Foreign Policy, 1900-1908," 49-78.

43. Taft to Root, Jan. 9, 1901, Root Papers.

44. Crowder to Commanding General, Department of Southern Luzon, Feb. 5, 1901, BIA 2710, incl. 18; *War Department, 1901*, HD 2, 57th Cong., 1st sess., IX, 12.

45. Taft to Root, Mar. 17, 1901, Root Papers.

46. Taft to MacArthur, Feb. 5, 1901, BIA 2710, incl. 18.

47. Taft to John M. Harlan, May 19, 1901, Taft Papers.

48. *War Department, 1901*, HD 2, 57th Cong., 1st sess., VIII, 16-17; III, 676-79; VIII, 64-66, 381-85, X, 529-50.

49. Ibid., IX, 57-59; II, 65-66.

50. Ibid., II, 66; Allen to Charles G. Treat, Jan. 14, 1902, Allen Papers; Allen to John A. Johnston, Jan. 21, 1902, Allen Papers.

51. On the continuing work of the Philippine Constabulary see John R. White, *Bullets and Bolos* (New York, 1928); Harold H. Elarth, *The Story of the Philippine Constabulary, 1901-1948* (Los Angeles, 1949); Vic Hurley, *Jungle Patrol* (New York, 1938); Edgar G. Bellairs [Charles Ballentine], *As It Is in the Philippines* (New York, 1902), 228-38; George Yarrington Coats, "The Philippine Constabulary; 1901-1917" (Ph.D. diss., The Ohio State University, 1968).

52. *Affairs of the Philippine Islands*, SD 331, 57th Cong., 1st sess., pt. 1, 214-22.

53. Taft to Henry B. G. MacFarland, May 19, 1901, Taft Papers; Taft to Root, July 8, 1901, Root Papers; MacArthur to AG, May 19, 1901, *Correspondence*, II, 1280. See also Apr. 30, 1901, II, 1273.

54. *War Department, 1901*, HD 2, 57th Cong., 1st sess., V, 100-101.

55. *Political Affairs in the Philippine Islands*, SD 259, 57th Cong., 1st sess., 24.

56. Hughes to AG, Division of the Philippines, Apr. 26, 1901, "Diary of Events, 18 Apr.-16 May, 1901," AGO 383381; General Orders No. 40, May 15, 1901, No. 42, May 16, 1901, Office of the Military Governor in the Philippine Islands, *Philippine Islands Military Governor: General Orders and Circulars, Special Orders, 1901; General Orders, U. S. Army, Philippine Islands, 1901, passim.*

57. Caballes to Malvar, July 22, 1901, PIR 752.7.

58. T. Aceill to Lukban, July 21, 1901, PIR 940.7; Wheaton to AG, Division of the Philippines, Dec. 3, 1901, "Diary of Events, 15 Nov.-11 Dec., 1901," AGO 417338.

9

SAMAR AND BATANGAS, LAST STRONGHOLDS OF REBELLION

Near the end of September 1901 an event took place that triggered a reaction among the American military that almost succeeded in ruining the excellent groundwork already laid for the complete pacification of the Philippines. In the town of Balangiga on the island of Samar the inhabitants, in cooperation with guerrillas from the neighboring region, massacred C Company of the 9th Infantry. Of the three officers and seventy-one enlisted men of the company present in the town, only twenty-six survived. The company had only been in Balangiga a short while. They had with them a supply of approximately 28,000 rounds of ammunition, almost all of which fell into the hands of the revolutionaries.[1]

The attack at Balangiga shocked the Americans in the Philippines. After a vigorous campaign on Samar completed in August, General Hughes had assumed that the island was almost pacified.[2] The men of C Company had been caught completely unawares, and the plans of the plotters had been executed perfectly. Lukban, the revolutionary leader on Samar, publicized the victory widely.[3] American soldiers throughout the Philippines, upon hearing about the massacre and receiving the reports of the detail sent to burn Balangiga and bury the mutilated bodies of their comrades, thought of little but revenge. The Americans did not care that, preceding the massacre, C Company had forced the inhabitants of the municipality

248

to clean the town under guard, working all day in the sun, and that at night approximately ninety Filipinos had been confined in two army tents designed to house sixteen soldiers each. What mattered was that forty-eight Americans had been cruelly murdered and mutilated by Filipinos.[4]

That the deception had been planned before the soldiers came to the town made the act even more despicable to most Americans. A letter, captured prior to the occupation of Balangiga, told the whole story. The local president had written Lukban that the municipal leaders had agreed to pursue "a fictitious policy" with the Americans when they arrived and that when the occasion was right the people would "strategically rise up against them."[5] The letter had been captured in August. The massacre was on September 28. As Captain Taylor rather academically observed at a later date, "if it had been read in time in Iloilo, . . . [it] would have prevented the destruction of that company of the 9th Infantry."[6] This knowledge could only have infuriated the Americans even more. The number of captured documents had become so large that, even with the better facilities developed by the army for reviewing them, the Americans could not adequately assess all of the intelligence data available. Balangiga was one result. Ironically, a general order issued on the very day of the massacre had provided that each army post maintain its own intelligence office.[7]

General Chaffee's response was immediate, and it mirrored that of many American soldiers in the Philippines. "The condition of mind of officers and men in these islands is largely in error," he wrote to General Hughes after receiving news of the attack.

> Their opinion is that the people are far more friendly than they really are, and that they are satisfied with our presence among them. . . . as a rule I would not trust 50 percent of the male population, and they must not be trusted.

Suspicion was to be the duty of every American soldier. According to Chaffee, Filipinos could henceforth show their loyalty to the Americans only through acts that could not be misunderstood. Words were to mean nothing. Americans, wrote Chaffee, were to be "stern and inflexible," and he wanted the Filipinos to have a "wholesome fear" of the army. He wanted his officers to punish every hostile act of any inhabitant "quickly and severely." He ended his communiqué to Hughes with the statement that another hundred American lives would probably be lost retrieving the guns and ammunition lost at Balangiga.[8]

General Chaffee dispatched two battalions of infantry to Samar with what may be inferred as instructions to deal severely with anyone they found resisting American authority there. He wrote Adjutant General Corbin that if they carried out the idea that he had in mind, "they will start a few cemeteries for *hombres* in Southern Samar." As far as Chaffee was concerned, the Balangiga incident marked the end of the policy of benevolent pacification. He thought that in the past the army had been "entirely too lenient," and according to Taft, he was convinced that the only way to achieve peace was to pin down the Filipinos "with bayonets for ten years until they submit."[9]

Many members of the army reacted to the news of the Balangiga massacre with hostility toward all Filipinos, an attitude that promised to undo much of what had been accomplished by almost three years of benevolence. Governor Taft and a number of responsible men in American and Filipino circles were worried. The army had started to patrol heavily in areas previously pacified, including Manila, and in the provinces American sentries had accidentally shot and killed peaceful inhabitants. On the island of Leyte, the closest to Samar, the army began a series of arbitrary arrests and restrictions immediately following the Balangiga incident, although Leyte was completely under civil jurisdiction at the time.[10] Members of the Federal party feared that the increasing number of accusations and arrests were a serious threat to peace in regions where pacification had already been achieved,[11] and the Philippine Commission, in a report issued in October 1901, deplored the turn of events that had taken place following the massacre. "It will be a sad injustice," stated the commission, "if the Samar disaster shall induce on one side a rigor in the treatment of all Filipinos and on their part a consequent revulsion in those feelings of friendship toward the Americans which have been growing stronger each day with the spread and development of civil government."[12] Fortunately, at the end of 1901 the majority of the provinces in the islands were already under the complete control of the civil government.

General Chaffee and a number of American soldiers did not agree with the commission, the Federal party, and other observers that the revolt was in its final stages. Instead, as Taft observed, they had convinced themselves that they were "on a powder magazine and that an eruption of all the people may be expected at any time."[13] The Division of Military Information, in a report to the General, stated that an uprising would probably begin throughout the islands in January 1902. The document mentioned a "new movement" among the revolutionaries and rumors of meetings and plottings including attempts to reorganize the revolutionary militia. The report seemed more a mirror of army fears than of the realities apparent in most areas of the Philippines. Still, daily analyses submitted by the Division of Military Information continued throughout 1901 to be a blend of hearsay, rumor, and fear motivated undoubtedly by the disaster on Samar.[14]

The true situation in the Philippines as 1901 neared its end was very different from that imagined by General Chaffee and his agents in the Divsion of Military Information. Captain Allen, probably relying on more accurate data secured by his constabulary, wrote in December 1901 that "the general condition of the islands as regards pacification has never been so favorable as now."[15] On Cebu, where the problem had been a lack of American troops, General Hughes had begun an aggressive campaign in September 1901, and hostilities ended there in less than two months. Transferring his operations to Bohol, Hughes achieved the pacification of that island by the end of December. Approximately 75 percent of the archipelago's population were living in areas completely in the hands of the civil authorities, and the young but growing Philippine Constabulary seemed adequate to keep the peace in all but the still unpacified regions in and around Batangas Province

and on the island of Samar. Elsewhere, a rapid transfer of
authority from the military to the civil government had taken
place, and American troops had begun to collect themselves into larger garrisons as a prelude to the development of permanent army posts. Two mop-up operations were all that remained to achieve almost complete pacification.[16]

The two areas still unpacified had both successfully
resisted the army's offensive of 1901 and the new policy of
pacification. Batangas and the adjacent province of Laguna
were still under military rule, and the neighboring provinces of
Cavite and Tayabas, although under the civil government, were
not completely pacified. Malvar, Aguinaldo's successor, promised to make his last stand in this area south of Manila, and
the American commander of the region observed that the
revolution seemed destined to meet its death "in the place of its
birth and to die hard."[17] On the island of Samar Lukban's
guerrillas had successfully withstood the vigorous campaign of
General Hughes in August, and Lukban had been able to increase his strength after the victory at Balangiga. The great
desire in both Washington and the Philippines to bring the
revolt to a quick end insured that the final campaigns against
the revolutionaries would be vigorous.

From the beginning, many Americans recognized that the
mop-up campaigns initiated at the end of 1901 would be no or-
dinary ones. Emotional feeling was too high among the troops
sent to Samar in October for that campaign to be planned and
carried out dispassionately, and circumstances were not
favorable for humane or benevolent action on the part of
American troops who remembered vividly the stories of the
"treachery" at Balangiga. In and around Batangas the guerrilla
organization was so strong that most Americans thought that
equally harsh measures would probably be instituted there to
insure pacification. Even the leaders of the Federal party had
given up hopes that the American approach to pacification, so
humane and benevolent in the previous campaigns, would or
could continue against the recalcitrants that refused to end the
guerrilla war.[18]

The problems facing the Americans on Samar were
tremendous. The largest island in the Visayan group, 5,276

square miles, it had never been completely controlled by the Spaniards, and it was geographically well suited to prolonged guerrilla warfare. With one of the lowest population densities in the Philippine archipelago, Samar's more than 250,000 inhabitants were widely dispersed, 94 percent in numerous small coastal towns and villages with the remainder in scattered interior hamlets. The hinterlands were wild jungles crossed only by poorly marked trails. No roads penetrated the island's heartland, and its few rivers were unsuitable as avenues of advance. Because of the American shortage of troops during the Philippine campaign, the revolutionaries on Samar under the leadership of Lukban had roamed over the island at will. The Americans held only the major coastal towns and made infrequent sorties into the interior.[19]

The revolutionaries on Samar were well supplied. Hemp, the major crop of the island, was sold to foreign firms in exchange for cash or contraband. Only a narrow strait, eighteen miles long and no wider than a river, separated Samar from Leyte, and the revolution's supporters on Leyte could resupply their brethren on Samar almost without hindrance.[20] Lukban was an expert propagandist, and his proclamations were instrumental in keeping Samar's inhabitants loyal to the revolt and suspicious of the Americans. Although General Hughes thought he had concluded a successful campaign against Lukban in 1901, Balangiga proved that pacification was an illusion.[21]

The guerrillas followed the Balangiga massacre with attacks on other American garrisons, and the American command reacted immediately. Brigadier General Jacob H. Smith had already been selected for command of the Sixth Separate Brigade charged with pacifying the island, and he conferred with General Chaffee shortly after the affair at Balangiga. Chaffee's verbal orders were short and to the point. "We have lost 100 rifles at Balangiga and 25,000 rounds of ammunition. You must get them back. You can have $5,000 gold. Capture the arms if you can, buy them if you must; whichever course you adopt, get them back."[22]

From the very beginning of the campaign to pacify the island, Chaffee, Smith, and the troops sent to reinforce the 9th

Infantry on Samar were animated with a spirit of revenge, animosity, and suspicion. This made a rational approach to the problem of pacifying Samar difficult. The personality of the officer charged with the task made such an approach even more difficult. General Smith was a man given to strong talk and had been known in the past to emphasize a point in such a manner as to say more than he actually meant to imply.[23] In issuing instructions to his subordinates on Samar he outdid himself. To Major Littleton W. T. Waller, commander of a Marine battalion sent to help reinforce the troops on Samar, General Smith declared that he wanted "no prisoners." Evidently letting his emotions run away with him, Smith continued. "I wish you to kill and burn. The more you kill and burn, the better you will please me." He wanted, he said, to make the interior of the island "a howling wilderness."[24] Whether or not he really meant what he said, the very act of giving such orders gave the pacification campaign a tenor and direction that proved disastrous.

General Smith's campaign was poorly planned and faulty in its execution. Convinced that he could make Filipinos submit to American control by making "war hell," he sought to substitute "fire and sword" for the benevolent and humane policy that had preceded his campaign. The basic elements of his policy were few. All food and trade to Samar was to be ended to starve the revolutionaries into submission. He instructed his officers to regard all Filipinos as enemies and treat them accordingly until they showed conclusively that they were friendly by such specific actions as revealing information about the location of revolutionaries or arms, working successfully as guides or spies, or trying actively to obtain the surrender of the guerrillas in the field. He gave his subordinates carte blanche in the application of General Order 100.[25]

General Smith's "grand strategy" on Samar involved the use of widespread destruction in an attempt to force the inhabitants to cease supporting the guerrillas and turn to the Americans from fear and starvation if for no other reason. He used his troops in sweeps into the interior of the island in searches for guerrilla bands and attempts to capture Lukban, and he did almost nothing to prevent contact between the guerrillas and the townspeople. American columns marched over the island destroying habitations and draft animals and accomplishing little toward pacification. Major Waller, for example, reported that in an eleven-day span his men had burned 255 dwellings, slaughtered 13 carabao, and killed 39 people. Other officers reported similar activity. The orders issued by the General and his emotional statements at the beginning of the campaign had encouraged such unproductive actions. As the Judge Advocate General of the army observed, only the good sense and restraint of the majority of Smith's subordinates prevented a complete reign of terror on Samar.[26] Still, the abuses were sufficient to cause widespread complaint in the United States when they became known there near the end of March 1902.

In his attempts to stop trade with Samar, General Smith interfered with the civil government operating on Leyte. Working outside of his jurisdiction, the General arrested suspects on that island and transferred them to Samar. His meddling raised a furor within the civil government that finally provoked a crisis between military and civilian authorities in Manila. Governor Taft had left the Philippines for a rest following an operation, but Commissioner Wright, serving as acting governor, was quick to complain to General Chaffee about Smith's actions on Leyte. After an investigation by Chaffee, Smith was forced to modify his restrictions on trade and relax his hold on the island. His requests that the government of Leyte be transferred to his command and that all the ports of it and Samar be closed were denied. The Leyte men that he had arrested were released and returned to their homes.[27]

After three months of operation General Smith had accomplished little. On Leyte he had so aroused the population that the Philippine Constabulary had to repacify the province in 1902. In that campaign, however, Captain Allen relied on the "policy of attraction" that General Smith had repudiated. Acting governor Wright was convinced that Smith was "wholly lacking in tact, judgement and administrative capacity" and probably caused more problems than he solved. Even General Chaffee recognized that Smith's campaign had had little effect.[28]

In response to pressure from Chaffee, General Smith modified his approach to pacification during January and early February 1902. As a result, the campaign on Samar began to resemble that being carried on in the Batangas region by General Bell. The major changes included more favorable treatment of those Filipinos taking no active or voluntary part in the revolt, the relaxation of restrictions on trade and fishing, and a greater emphasis on providing civilians with food and other necessities. The increasing benevolence, it was thought, would act, as it had elsewhere in the Philippines, to win popular support for the American force and aid in the isolation of the guerrilla from the townspeople. Significantly, these changes in General Smith's campaign and even the wording of the February 13 circular in which they were outlined were exact copies of the policy initiated by General Bell in Batangas on December 9, 1901.[29]

An American force captured Lukban on February 18, 1902, and as a result of the changed program of pacification Lukban's successor finally surrendered to the Americans at the end of April. Had General Smith begun a benevolent policy earlier, the war on Samar might have been ended in February rather than two months later. The actions of the army had done so little to win over the island's inhabitants before that date, that even after Lukban's capture many Filipinos saw little real choice but to continue to resist what promised to be a harsh American rule.

By the time Smith's campaign on Samar ended, irreparable damage had already been done. Smith had stirred the population of Leyte to revolt and precipitated a serious crisis in the relations between the civil and military authorities in the islands. At the beginning of April, he was relieved of his command and sent to Manila where an investigation of his conduct on Samar was beginning that eventually led to the end of his military career. Perhaps worst of all, General Smith had raised the issue of brutality at a time when the anti-imperialist forces in America were recovering from their defeat at the polls the previous year and seeking to revive the criticism of American Philippine policy.

General Bell's campaign in southern Luzon presented a

great contrast to General Smith's on Samar. Rapid and over-whelming success made it an example of what could be achieved by the army in a limited amount of time when suffi-cient thought and planning went into the preparation of opera-tions. Bell's Batangas campaign represented all that Smith's work on Samar should have been and was not. It embodied the lessons that had been drawn from the army's previous pacifica-tion experience in the islands.

Near the end of 1901 conditions in Batangas and the sur-rounding region were comparable to those on Samar. Although approximately half the area of Samar, the Batangas region had almost twice the population. Although the inhabitants of the area were better educated and not as dispersed as those of Samar, their numerous towns and villages were highly or-ganized by the guerrillas. The system operating there to fur-nish support for the guerrillas represented the achievement of many months work on the part of the revolutionaries. While the Americans had concentrated on the pacification of northern Luzon, understrength American forces in southern Luzon had been virtually besieged in their garrisons. American units were so small and so widely dispersed that effective field operations were impossible. Travel by Americans and the distribution of supplies had to take place under a guard of from thirty to forty soldiers. Garrisons were often as small as ten to twenty-five men and in some cases were commanded only by a non-commissioned officer. The majority of the population in the area was under the direct control of the revolutionaries. Refus-ing to meet American units in the open, when hard pressed the guerrillas reverted to the role of the amigo, hiding their weapons and assuming a friendly attitude. The policy of pacification evolved and in operation throughout 1901 had had little effect on the inhabitants of Batangas.[30]

The Batangas region had been in revolt since the original uprising against Spain in 1896. The leaders of the Philippine revolution had come primarily from the Tagalog region, and the majority of them were from the provinces of Cavite, Batangas, Laguna, and Tayabas. This accounted at least in part for the widespread popular support of Malvar. Fear of revolu-tionary terror insured the cooperation of the remainder of the populace. Geography favored the Batangas rebels as much as those on Samar. The area was covered with dense tropical vegetation and rough mountains. Its roads were in almost impassable condition. With popular support and the aid of the geography, Malvar was determined to prolong the war until he was either killed or captured, and in 1901 the Americans seemed incapable of achieving either.

In November 1901, a major change had been made in the American commands throughout the Philippines as a prelude to campaigns to complete their pacification. General Wheaton was placed in command of the whole of Luzon, and General Bell was given command of the Third Separate Brigade operating in the Batangas area. Generals Chaffee, Wheaton, and Bell were all convinced that a major problem was the cooperation of local leadership elements and members of the Filipino elite in the revolution. Although this class of well-educated and moneyed Filipinos often gave American policies great verbal support, they also supported the guerrillas. To end this duplicity and isolate the guerrillas of Batangas, the American commanders decided to bring great pressure to bear on the elite group and make their further aid of the revolutionaries an extremely dangerous and unpleasant job.[31]

General Bell was an excellent choice to command the Third Separate Brigade. He had been successful in the pacification of Pangasinan Province in northern Luzon, and he had served an equally successful tour in the difficult position of the Provost-Marshal-General of Manila. As shown by his comments on MacArthur's new pacification policy in December 1900, he had an excellent understanding of the role of benevolence in pacification and the importance of both adequate intelligence data and the protection of the Filipino population. He was also well liked by the civil authorities in the islands.[32]

General Bell took command in Batangas at the end of November, and he immediately called together his subordinates and outlined the policy that he planned to pursue in pacifying the region. The speech he gave was very similar to that delivered to his officers in Manila in 1900. Beginning with a statement on the virtues of a benevolent approach to pacification, Bell explained that in an area such as Batangas, where complete benevolence had failed, a more rigorous policy was needed. The policy to be followed would be, therefore, one of isolating the guerrilla from his popular support, protecting all Filipinos seeking freedom from the revolutionaries, and punishing swiftly those who participated or aided in prolonging the conflict. To accomplish these goals the General planned a strict enforcement of the provisions of General Order 100. He told his officers that action, not words, would be the key to their policy. They were to be "considerate and courteous in manner, but firm and relentless in action." Since he was asking his men to undertake a policy including some severity, General Bell made known that he was not advocating torture, burning, or other unauthorized severities. These things, he said, probably did more harm than good. His policy was to be one of firm and relentless action completely divorced from brutality or atrocities.[33]

General Bell's pacification campaign in the Batangas region was highly organized, and the General retained control of the overall direction of operations at all times. Determined that the Filipinos should not misunderstand the American policy, he impressed upon his officers the importance of warning the people before instituting any repressive measures. The application of General Order 100, to be effective, had to be understood by the inhabitants of the area. They also had to be shown that if cooperative they would be protected and unharmed by either the guerrillas or American troops.[34]

A basic feature of General Bell's pacification policy was his plan for isolating the guerrillas from those supporting them. On December 8, 1901, he issued the second of a series of telegraphic circulars that were his means of controlling the campaign. In it, he ordered each garrison commander to establish a plainly marked area that was small enough to be adequately protected by the garrison troops. People living near these protective zones were informed that it would be dangerous to remain outside of them. Unless they moved into them by December 25 their property would become liable to confiscation or destruction to prevent it from being used by the guerrillas.[35]

Within the zones of protection, the Americans encouraged the Filipinos to erect new homes, and garrison commanders regulated the cost of necessities to maintain a reasonable price level. Army physicians furnished medical care free of charge, and the public health measures undertaken in the zones resembled those in typical American garrison towns. Schools were also provided, and all of the benevolent and humane actions that had characterized American operations in the Philippines since 1898 were evident in the zones of reconcentration. Public works projects and work for the military kept the people occupied and provided them with provisions. Filipinos unable to work and without funds were given supplies free of charge.[36]

Believing that "a short and severe war creates in the aggregate less loss and suffering than benevolent war indefinitely prolonged," General Bell was determined to make his campaign swift and decisive. As on Samar, the only acceptable and convincing evidence of support for the Americans was to be deeds, not words. Arrest and imprisonment, especially of the elite leadership element, was used as an important weapon to stop municipal officials and others from aiding the revolutionaries. Filipinos were interred on the basis of suspicion rather than complete certainty. As both General Bell and General Smith had noted, once a suspect was confined, evidence was obtained easily. Unlike General Smith, however, Bell retained more direct control over the actions of his subordinates, and he constantly reminded them to use "sound discretion" in their implementation of a policy of pacification that could easily be abused by officers lacking in responsibility or understanding.[37]

In the field, outside of the garrisoned towns and zones of protection, the Americans carried on a vigorous campaign. American columns scouted and patrolled constantly, searching for guerrilla units and supplies. Food found outside the population concentrations was confiscated or destroyed. People found outside the zones were escorted back to the American garrisons. American units were in the field constantly, and their pursuit was so relentless that guerrilla units were unable to remain more than twenty-four hours in one place. As many as 4,000 American troops were in the field at one time. They camped at strategic points, each unit "sending three or four detachments, with five or six days' rations, to bivouac at points radiating several miles from its base."³⁸ These units in turn set up bases and scouted in the areas where they camped. The Americans operated both day and night, and continued to press home their attacks against the revolutionaries despite the difficult terrain, the climate, and their own problems of supply in the field.

In his campaign, General Bell sought to bring pressure to bear on the guerrillas and those supporting them in the towns. He did both. The application of General Order 100 and the arrest of members of the elite was calculated to keep the townspeople in such a state of anxiety and apprehension that they would find living conditions unbearable and gladly join with the Americans to bring about the end of the war.³⁹ Outside the towns, American units sought to make continued guerrilla operations and even the existence of guerrilla forces impossible. The pressure, however, was primarily psychological and economic. Terror, brutality, and wanton destruction did not have any role in Bell's pacification program, and he continually worked to insure that his men would carry out their work "dispassionately."⁴⁰

General Bell's operations in southern Luzon were a complete success. The isolation of the guerrilla was completed when, after January 1, 1902, the Americans instituted a pass system that effectively controlled the movement of population in Batangas and Laguna. Eventually, well over 300,000 people gathered in the American zones of protection.⁴¹ In Cavite, Philippine Constabulary units cooperated with American troops to prevent the guerrillas that were hard pressed in Batangas and Laguna from flooding into that province. The civil authorities in Tayabas were less cooperative, and when General Bell sent troops there he provoked a reaction from the civil governor, Cornelius Gardener, that later provided American anti-imperialists with more material for their campaign against the administration in the United States.⁴² In general, however, Bell had accomplished his goal of pacification with little of the friction and brutality that had accompanied General Smith's Samar campaign.

The Batangas revolutionaries were completely "dis-

organized and demoralized" by the American campaign.[43]
General Bell estimated that in its final stages "several
thousand Batangas natives" joined with the Americans in their
search for the guerrillas.[44] The reconcentration policy and the
application of General Order 100 had successfully ended the
effectiveness of guerrilla threats and terror. The educated and
wealthy elite found war too unprofitable to continue their support of the guerrillas, and the guerrillas found themselves
isolated, continually harassed, and unsupported. General Bell
effected the complete breakdown of the complex covert
organization supporting the guerrilla war. Malvar, exhausted,
surrendered on April 16, 1902, after finding himself "without a
single gun or a clerk," separated from his escort by a sudden
American attack, and with all of his staff already in the hands
of the enemy.[45] His surrender marked the end of the war in
Batangas.

In accomplishing his feat, General Bell never had more
than 10,000 men under his command. The active revolutionary
force numbered at least 4,000. The Americans captured over
1,000 guerrillas, and another 3,700 surrendered. Over 4,000
firearms were captured or surrendered during the course of the
campaign. Assuming that the armed Filipinos were aided by
both bolomen in the field and a corps of active supporters in
the towns, the total number of revolutionaries in the Batangas
region was at least as large as the American force. General Bell
estimated that over 8,000 persons who had been engaged in
one capacity or another in the guerrilla war were detected, captured, or forced to surrender. In contrast, General Smith never
faced such large opposition on Samar. Although no comparable
statistics were compiled, probably because Smith's intelligence
system was not as efficient as that of Bell, the revolutionary
force there could not have been as large or as formidable as
that in Batangas. On Samar the guerrillas had far fewer
firearms, certainly less than 1,000, while General Smith had
approximately 7,000 troops at his disposal.[46] The difference
between the two campaigns could be found in the approach
used by the commanders involved.

The Batangas campaign took two months less than that of
General Smith on Samar. It entailed less friction with the civil

government in the adjacent provinces and much less brutality. General Bell's campaign was neither hastily planned nor undertaken in an emotional state that precluded a rational approach to the problems of pacification. His work was firmly based on his previous experience in the Philippines. He maintained control over his subordinates and refrained from unthinking statements or orders that could have led to widespread brutality or atrocity charges at a later date. His reconcentration policy achieved the complete isolation of the guerrilla in a minimal time, and he was effective in enlisting the aid of natives in the latter stages of the campaign. Within the reconcentration zones, American benevolence worked to win popular support for the army. The contrast between the campaigns of Generals Bell and Smith was striking in almost every important element. Bell's operation, unlike Smith's, was a credit to the American army in the Philippines and a masterpiece of counter-guerrilla warfare.

Only after three years of almost continuous warfare had the American army defeated the Philippine revolutionaries, but by the middle of May 1902 the last two strongholds of rebellion were both pacified. At that point the civil and military authorities in the islands began to think in terms of amnesty and reconstruction. Acting governor Wright wrote to Taft at the beginning of May suggesting that the time was right to issue a final peace proclamation, and Secretary Root, following up Wright's dispatch to Taft, asked that the acting governor confer with General Chaffee and send their ideas concerning an amnesty to Washington. By June, after an exchange of correspondence between Root and Wright, plans had been formulated for the issuance of a proclamation. It was officially published in the islands on July 4, 1902.[47]

The amnesty proclamation gave full pardon to all Filipinos who had participated in the revolt. The only exception was for those who had committed crimes subsequent to May 1, 1902 or had been convicted at a prior time for crimes of murder, rape, arson, or robbery. Provision was made, however, for special pardon by the insular authorities of revolutionaries already under sentence. Accompanying the amnesty was an order from the War Department ending the office of military governor and restating the doctrine giving the civil authority supremacy over the military in the islands.[48] Ironically, at the time when the army in the islands had earned itself a well-deserved rest from combat, reports from the Moro regions on the island of Mindanao gave warning of a new menace to the peace not yet firmly established in the Philippines.

Excepting the activity in the Moro provinces, the army's role in the Philippines greatly diminished with the transfer of Batangas Province to the civil government on July 4, 1902. Guerrillas and the threat of continued revolt were no longer a major problem. Banditry became the primary concern of the civil authorities. Some of the bandits had participated in the revolt, but only by the widest stretch of the imagination could they be called revolutionary forces after the middle of 1902. In fact, the revolutionary leadership had been swiftly integrated into the civil government of the provinces, and it often led in the fight against the bandit element. The Americans had appointed Pablo Tecson, an ex-guerrilla, governor of the province of Bulacan, and he organized a volunteer force that succeeded in chasing the ladrones into the hills. Other revolutionaries given similar positions included Juan Cailles in Laguna, Juan Villamor in Abra, and Mariano Trías in Cavite. The revolutionaries had not only accepted American sovereignty, but they were actively participating in the colonial government.[49]

The achievements of the American army during its first three and one-half years in the Philippines had been great. It had ended an organized revolt, established the basis for a benevolent colonial government, and achieved a state of peace sufficient to turn the entire job of maintaining law and order over to Filipinos working only under the supervision of the insular government. President Theodore Roosevelt expressed his pride in the accomplishments of the military in a message of thanks issued to the army on the day the amnesty was proclaimed. He praised its members for their success against both the regular Filipino army and the guerrilla bands. The President commended the way in which commanders scattered throughout the archipelago had effectively dealt with the many difficulties facing them. He lauded the army for its rapid and complete victory, noting the "unvarying courage and resolution" manifested throughout more than three years of war. President Roosevelt also praised the "self-control, patience, and magnanimity" of the soldiers during the campaign, stating that "with surprisingly few individual exceptions its course has been characterized by humanity and kindness to the prisoner and the non-combatant" alike. American soldiers had brought "individual liberty, protection of personal rights, civil order, public instruction, and religious freedom" to the islands, assuring the populace "the blessings of peace and prosperity."[50] In the President's eyes the army had performed its mission with great success.

NOTES

1. *Annual Reports of the War Department for the Fiscal Year Ended June 30, 1902*, HD 2, 57th Cong., 2d sess., XII, 606-609, 625-31. See also, for coverage of both the massacre and American operations on Samar following it, Joseph L. Schott, *The Ordeal of Samar* (Indianapolis, 1964).
2. Hughes to Taft, Aug. 24, 1901, Taft Papers.
3. Lukban to Compatriots of Leyte, Oct. 27, 1901, Philippine Insurgent Records (PIR) 1074.4.
4. Testimony of William J. Gibbs, *Affairs in the Philippine Islands, Hearings before the Committee on the Philippines of the United States Senate*, SD 331, 57th Cong., 1st sess., pt. 3, 2284-85.
5. *War Department, 1902*, HD 2, 57th Cong., 2d sess., XII, 633.
6. See Taylor's note accompanying the original document in Philippine Insurgent Records (PIR) 1074.1.
7. General Orders No. 294, Sept. 28, 1901, Headquarters Division of the Philippines, *General Orders, U. S. Army, Philippine Islands, 1901*.
8. *Affairs in the Philippine Islands*, SD 331, 57th Cong., 1st sess., pt. 2, 1591-92.
9. Chaffee to Corbin, Sept. 30, 1901, Corbin Papers. Taft to Root, Oct. 14, 1901, Root Papers. See also Chaffee to Corbin, Oct. 25, 1901.
10. Taft to Root, Sept. 30, Oct. 14, 1901, Root Papers; Taft to John M. Harlan, Oct. 21, 1901, Taft Papers; report of James Ross, Governor of Ambos Camarines, *Affairs in the Philippine Islands*, SD 331, 57th Cong., 1st sess., pt. 1, 476-77; J. H. Grant to A. W. Fergusson, Oct. 26, 1901, pt. 3, 2336-38.
11. U.S., Congress, Senate, *Federal Party Message to Congress*, SD 187, 57th Cong., 1st sess., 1902, 6.

12. *Annual Reports of the War Department for the Fiscal Year Ended June 30, 1901*, HD 2, 57th Cong., 1st sess., IX, 9.
13. Taft to Archbishop John Ireland, Oct. 15, 1901, Taft Papers.
14. See all of the material collected in PIR 1313.2, in particular the undated report labeled "For the Information of the Division Commander."
15. *Affairs in the Philippine Islands*, SD 331, 57th Cong., 2d sess., pt. 1, 216.
16. Bourns to "My Dear General" [Wright of the commission], Aug. 28, 1901, Taft Papers; *War Department, 1902*, HD 2, 57th Cong., 2d sess., XII, 186-87; *War Department, 1901*, HD 2, 57th Cong., 1st sess., II, 157-60, VIII, 8-11.
17. *War Department, 1901*, HD 2, 57th Cong., 1st sess., VIII, 389.
18. Buencamino to Taft, Jan. 8, 1902, Taft Papers.
19. Testimony of Hughes, *Affairs in the Philippine Islands*, SD 331, 57th Cong., 1st sess., pt. 1, 551-55; *War Department, 1902*, HD 2, 57th Cong., 2d sess., XII, 594.
20. Jacob H. Smith to AG, Division of the Philippines, Oct. 29, 1901, *Affairs in the Philippine Islands*, SD 331, 57th Cong., 1st sess., pt. 3, 2171-72. The sale of hemp to foreign firms is covered in John R. M. Taylor, *Report on the Organization for the Administration of Civil Government Instituted by Emilio Aguinaldo and His Followers in the Philippine Archipelago*, 16-17, 56-68, 85-101.
21. File cover to PIR 928, "Lucban, Vicente"; unsigned comment on PIR 928.3; *War Department, 1902*, HD 2, 57th Cong., 2d sess., XII, 292.
22. *War Department, 1902*, HD 2, 57th Cong., 2d sess., XII, 188.
23. Wright to Taft, Jan. 13, Apr. 19, 1902; Taft to Wright, May 6, 1902, Taft Papers.
24. U.S., Congress, Senate, *Trials or Courts-martial in the Philippine Islands in Consequence of Certain Instructions*, SD 213, 57th Cong., 2d sess., 1903, 2-3.
25. Jacob H. Smith, "Campaign in Samar and Leyte from 10th of October to 31st of December, 1901," *The Manila Critic*, Feb. 1, 1901, in Corbin Papers; Smith, proclamation, Nov. 1, 1901, PIR 1143.9; *War Department, 1902*, HD 2, 57th Cong., 2d sess., XII, 206-10.
26. *War Department, 1902*, HD 2, 57th Cong., 2d sess., XII, 441; *Trials*, SD 213, 57th Cong., 2d sess., 16.

27. *War Department, 1902*, HD 2, 57th Cong., 2d sess., XII, 206-208, 216-23; *Affairs in the Philippine Islands*, SD 331, 57th Cong., 1st sess., pt. 3, 2163-69.

28. Allen to Taft, Mar. 9, 1902, Allen Papers; Wright to Taft, Jan. 13, 1902, Taft Papers; Chaffee to Corbin, Jan. 13, Mar. 17, 1902, Corbin Papers.

29. *War Department, 1902*, HD 2, 57th Cong., 2d sess., XII, 212-13; *Affairs in the Philippine Islands*, SD 331, 57th Cong., 1st sess., pt. 2, 1607-10.

30. *War Department, 1902*, HD 2, 57th Cong., 2d sess., XII, 229, 263-69, 285-88; *War Department, 1901*, HD 2, 57th Cong., 1st sess., VIII, 390.

31. *War Department, 1902*, HD 2, 57th Cong., 2d sess., XII, 190-91.

32. Daniel R. Williams, *The Odyssey of the Philippine Commission*, 296; H. Phelps Whitmarsh to Taft, Mar. 2, 1901, Taft Papers.

33. Bell, address, Dec. 1, 1901, *Telegraphic Circulars and General Orders, Regulating Campaign Against Insurgents and Proclamations and Circular Letters, Relating to Reconstruction after Close of War in the Provinces of Batangas, Laguna, and Mindoro, P.I. Issued by Brigadier General J. Franklin Bell, U. S. Army, Commanding Brigade, from December 1st, 1901 to December 1st, 1902*, comp. M. F. Davis (Batangas, Dec. 1, 1902), AGO 415839.

34. Ibid.

35. *Affairs in the Philippine Islands*, SD 331, 57th Cong., 1st sess., pt. 2, 1606-1607.

36. Ibid., pt. 2, 1614-15, 1620-21, 1631-35 contains orders issued for the administration of the camps. See also *War Department, 1902*, HD 2, 57th Cong., 2d sess., XII, 270-72, XIII, 202; C. D. Rhodes, "Report on Concentration, Military Sub-District of Binan, Laguna Province," Charles Dudley Rhodes Papers; Herbert A. White, "Pacification of Batangas," *International Quarterly* 7 (1903): 431-44; R. D. Blanchard, June 30, 1902, 5th endorsement of Florencio R. Caedo to Civil Governor, Dec. 18, 1901, Records of the Adjutant General's Office (AGO) 453824, incl. A filed with AGO 514839; U.S., Congress, Senate, *Issuance of Certain Military Orders in the Philippines*, SD 347, 57th Cong., 1st sess., 1902, 22-24.

37. *Affairs in the Philippine Islands*, SD 331, 57th Cong., 1st sess., pt. 2, 1607-11, 1622-23, 1625-26; *War Department, 1902*, HD 2, 57th Cong., 2d sess., XII, 192.

38. *War Department, 1902*, HD 2, 57th Cong., 2d sess., XII, 271.

39. *Affairs in the Philippine Islands*, SD 331, 57th Cong., 1st sess., pt. 2, 1628. For evidence that the Filipino elite understood the American policy see Juliana Lopez to Clemencia Lopez, Dec. 21, 1901 in Canning Eyot, *The Story of the Lopez Family* (Boston, 1904), 54-55.

40. *Affairs in the Philippine Islands*, SD 331, 57th Cong., 1st sess., pt. 2, 1628.

41. *War Department, 1902*, HD 2, 57th Cong., 2d sess., XII, 270.

42. Gardener made a report to the insular civil authorities that was highly critical of the army's pacification efforts in his province and contained allegations of brutality. See *Affairs in the Philippine Islands*, SD 331, 57th Cong., 2d sess., pt. 2, 881-85.

43. Testimony of Noberto Mayo [a revolutionary], "Proceedings of Board of Officers to Inquire into Allegations Made by Gardener, 13th U. S. Infantry in His Report December 16, 1901," AGO 421607, incl. 2, 127.

44. *War Department, 1902*, HD 2, 57th Cong., 2d sess., XII, 272.

45. See testimony of revolutionary officers in "Proceedings," AGO 421607, incl. 2, *passim*; Malvar, "The Reasons for My Change of Attitude," Taylor, "Compilation," 89 GV.

46. *War Department, 1902*, HD 2, 57th Cong., 2d sess., XII, 272, 276, 418-19.

47. Root to Wright, May 15, 1901, Wright to Root, May 23, 1901, Root to Wright, June 7, 1901, Taft Papers. Wright to Root, June 20, 1901, Root to Wright, June 27, 1901, Root Papers.

48. *War Department, 1902*, HD 2, 57th Cong., 2d sess., IV, 137-38; Corbin to Chaffee, July 2, 1902, *Correspondence Relating to the War with Spain, April 15, 1898-July 30, 1902*, II, 1350-51.

49. *War Department, 1902*, HD 2, 57th Cong., 2d sess., XIII, 33; "Memorandum on the Honorary Board of Filipino Commissioners to the St. Louis Exposition: A Board Nominated by the Governor of the Philippines and Approved by the Commission," PIR 1310.

50. General Orders No. 66, Headquarters of the Army, July 4, 1902, *Correspondence*, II, 1352-53.

10

CONCLUSIONS

By 1903, less than a year after the official end of the war, only 15,000 American soldiers were needed to garrison the islands. The majority of Filipinos, if not completely satisfied with American rule, were at least willing to accept it temporarily and to work politically for independence. As a result of the army's campaign of pacification, the revolutionary nationalists had abandoned armed resistance, and little threat of continued, large-scale uprisings existed throughout the duration of the United States colonial rule in the islands. Filipinos cooperated actively with the Americans in the development and administration of the colonial government.

No single event or technique of pacification was responsible for the great achievement of the American army in its Philippine campaign. The Americans had found no panacea for victory. Instead, they had won with what could be termed a comprehensive approach that utilized every possible means at their disposal to bring an end to the guerrilla war.

Filipinos supported the Americans for a variety of reasons, and the appeals used by the Americans to obtain support were equally varied. Filipinos were given both positive and negative incentives to accept American sovereignty and end their resistance. Benevolence, astute propaganda, the payment of money for weapons, and the promise of true civil government all represented positive incentives. American efforts in organizing municipal government, schools, public health programs, and public works projects helped convince the Filipinos of the sincerity of the American claims to have come to the islands to help the inhabitants. At the same time, deportation, internment, imprisonment, or death awaited those who refused to end their resistance to the United States. In 1901, Filipinos found that working for the revolution was as much of a risk as the revolutionaries had made working for the Americans. Fear and fear alone could no longer insure that public support would go to the revolutionaries. The Americans succeeded in making themselves feared while, at the same time, giving the people good positive reasons for supporting American sovereignty.

After 1900 the American stress on the isolation of the guerrilla and the protection of townspeople from terrorism and intimidation was an important element in the success of pacification operations. The deployment of American troops in strategic garrisons; wide dispersion of American units; increased surveillance of municipalities to detect insurgent agents, terrorists, and supporters; and, when necessary, population reconcentration enabled Filipinos to show their support for the Americans without fear of harm. At the same time, continuous action by American patrols kept the guerrillas on the run. Off balance, short of supplies, and in continuous flight, the guerrillas were unable to threaten either the American columns or the towns. Sickness, hunger, decreasing popular support, and harassment by the Americans made life in the mountains miserable and provided strong incentives to surrender.

The Americans began using Filipinos to fight the revolutionaries in the first year of the war. As American power increased and as popular support turned to the Americans, they made much greater use of the indigenous population in the pacification effort. Through municipal police organizations and, at a later date, the Philippine Constabulary, Filipinos became actively involved in their own self-defense. This development further increased municipal security and enabled Filipinos to be even more certain of safety while supporting the Americans and withdrawing support from the revolutionaries. As protection for the towns increased, accompanied by evidence of growing popular support for the American occupation, more and more Filipinos were willing to aid the Americans as guides, scouts, agents, and spies.

The Federal party represented a further utilization of Filipinos in the fight against the guerrillas. Through the party, the Americans successfully involved members of the Filipino political and economic elite in the pacification process, and the party became a rallying point for Filipinos seeking to help the Americans pacify the islands. The development of municipal governments and, later, the organization of extended civil government under the Taft Commission also helped to involve Filipinos in the American pacification effort.

Specific events combined to make the American work of pacification a success. McKinley's defeat of Bryan in the election of 1900 and Aguinaldo's mistake in making the certainty of a Bryan victory a chief element in his propaganda campaign seriously lowered revolutionary morale. General MacArthur's new approach to pacification, timed to begin at this opportune moment, helped to convince many Filipinos of the futility of further resistance. Had the Americans not embarked upon their vigorous pacification campaign, the revolutionaries might have been able to recover from the psychological blow of the election results. The need for over six months of hard campaigning by the Americans in 1901 to break the back of the revolution was strong evidence that more than the defeat of Bryan was necessary to make many Filipinos accept American sovereignty.

The capture of Aguinaldo contributed to the revolution's defeat, but should not be overemphasized. Popular and important officers such as Mariano Trías had surrendered before Aguinaldo's capture, and revolutionaries such as Malvar continued to resist the Americans for more than a year after that event. It, like the election of 1900, was only one of the important events contributing to the American victory.

The development of civil government under the auspices of the Taft Commission, like the capture of Aguinaldo, was important but easily overemphasized. The work of the civil authorities did help bring about conciliation between the Americans and the Filipinos, and the lure of civil government was a powerful incentive to islanders who wanted to be free of the restriction of martial rule. The benevolent programs undertaken by the civil government, however, were almost invariably only a continuation of efforts begun by the army.

The war weariness of the Philippine people was another factor contributing to the success of the American campaign. In some areas warfare had been almost continuous since the end of 1896. Popular desire for peace, however, could not be equated with pacification, and although the mass of people might have been anxious for peace the control of the war was not in their hands. They could only show their desire to end it by either withdrawing their support from the belligerents or throwing their support overwhelmingly in favor of one to bring a swift defeat of the other. Up to November 1900 revolutionary terror and the possibility that the Americans might leave the islands if Bryan was elected president prevented Filipinos from aiding the Americans in either way. Only in 1901, after the beginning of the new American approach to pacification, were conditions present that allowed the people to manifest their disposition for peace.

In part, the collapse of the revolutionary movement was caused by friction within the movement itself. Aguinaldo achieved leadership over the Tagalog revolutionaries in 1897 only after a severe division in the ranks of the Katipunan that ended in the death of Andres Bonifacio, the founder of the society and Aguinaldo's foremost rival for the leadership of the revolt. The execution of Bonifacio by followers of Aguinaldo alienated many Filipinos who favored revolution but could not bring themselves to support Aguinaldo after such an act. After the beginning of the war with the Americans, the assassination of General Luna, an Ilocano, had much the same effect on Filipinos participating in the resistance against the United States. Luna represented a rival to Aguinaldo's power, and his death, under highly suspicious circumstances, to say the least, caused some revolutionaries to doubt the motives of their leader.[1] Aguinaldo appeared more as a dictator than a president, and the American colonial government seemed no less democratic than the Philippine Republic.

The outbreak of war in 1899 split the Filipino ranks between those who sought to resist the United States by force and those who, seeing the futility of revolt against such a powerful nation, wanted to reach some form of accord with the Americans. At first this growing movement for peace alienated the leaders of the war group within the Philippine government. At a later date, when the war party had insured that negotiations with the Americans would end in failure, the conservative peace party left the revolution. After this defection, some important and respected Filipino leaders supported the Americans and helped them construct their colonial government.

Class divisions among the population of the Philippine archipelago further weakened the revolutionary movement, and many of its supporters lacked a real commitment to the war. Personal and local interests were often placed above ideals of patriotism and nationalism that the revolutionaries had hoped to instill in the population. Some Filipinos supported the Americans because of opportunism rather than a commitment either to the new colonial power or against the revolutionaries. According to the Philippine historian Teodoro Agoncillo, the Filipino elite, men like those who led in the formation of the Federal party, placed their own prestige and interests above the revolution.[2] These wealthy and educated Filipinos, being men of property and political influence, favored stability over a revolution that, if successful, might diminish their power. They feared the anarchy and factional conflict that could result from a Filipino victory. This group looked to the Americans for the protection of their lives, property, and wealth from the revolution's rank and file. They were ready to support the United States once they were convinced that through such action they could achieve the power and prestige that they had held in Aguinaldo's government in the early stages of its development.

Members of the elite suffered little from the war, and since they might also benefit from a Filipino victory, many of them cooperated with Americans and revolutionaries alike. By arrangements made with the guerrillas, they continued cultivating their estates in the countryside while, at the same time, obtaining further profits from the war through commericial interests in the towns garrisoned by the Americans. Captain John R. M. Taylor, in his detailed study of the Philippine campaign, was also convinced that much Spanish property had passed into the hands of this elite group as the spoils of war.[3] When, in 1901, General MacArthur's new pacification policy made it unprofitable to continue support of the revolution, members of the elite who had failed to respond previously were completely willing to give support to the Americans. The confiscation of the property of those who supported the guerrillas and the threat that the Americans might turn to some other segment of the Philippine population to exercise political power in the developing civil government acted to force the elite to work for the end of the war and the acceptance of American sovereignty.

Opportunism acted against the continuance of the war in other ways. Many Filipino soldiers succumbed to the American offer of money for the surrender of weapons. Others joined the Federal party in hopes of securing appointment to civil office or political power. The relatively high wage paid by the Americans to civil servants, scouts, and constabulary was a further temptation to Filipinos to stop supporting the revolution and cast their lot with the Americans.[4] These incentives probably appealed most to the petty bureaucrats and lower ranking officers who had gained in status by their adherence to the revolutionary cause. This group, the real base of the movement after the defection of the old elite groups, saw a chance to make their increased status permanent by transferring their support to the Americans.

Filipinos were fragmented in another way that was usually not apparent either to the participants in the revolution or to the Americans opposing them. Revolutionary leaders and their supporters among the Filipino elite saw themselves engaged in a forward-looking movement having as its goals such "modern" objectives as economic development, increased world commerce, and the establishment of numerous Western political forms. At the same time, many of the peasants who followed these leaders into the field sought a far different kind of world, a world rooted in a mythical but seemingly utopian past where life was less complex and free from the tensions and insecurities of commercial agriculture. On occasion, the violent response of the peasants was completely divorced from the revolution and manifested itself instead in localized millennial movements of a type that have occurred at other times and in other places when peasants, under stress, were finally pushed to action. These *jacqueries* took place side by side with the revolutionary guerrilla war against the Americans, and agrarian uprisings of a similar sort would take place in the Philippines long after the revolutionary leaders of 1896 and 1898 had joined with the Americans in the administration of the colonial government.[5]

Cultural differences between Filipino ethnic groups prevented the achievement of a really united front against the Americans. Often the Tagalogs, who constituted the largest single group in the revolutionary leadership, were as feared as the invaders. In areas such as Negros, where Visayan leaders tried to link themselves with the Americans from the beginning of the occupation, the revolt never really took shape. The revolution was strongest in the Tagalog areas surrounding Manila. Leadership elements in the other widely dispersed centers of revolt were often only tenuously connected with Aguinaldo's government.

Part of the effectiveness of the American pacification effort and the split within the revolutionary movement can be traced to the great similarity between the original desires of the Philippine revolutionaries and the reforms undertaken by the American military and civil authorities in the islands. The Filipinos wanted the extension of individual liberty, religious freedom, protection of personal property, an honest and competent administration, tax reform, the equality of all races before the law, the end of trade barriers and restrictions, improved transportation, the suppression of the abusive Civil Guard, public secular education for both men and women, immigration laws excluding the Chinese, and the end of political and economic domination of the parishes by the religious orders. All of these things were given them by the American colonial administration working first through the military government and later through a civil government in which Filipinos actively participated. The democratic process was established as the basis for the local, provincial, and, in time, the colonial government. Only the questions of independence and the outright expropriation of the estates of the friars were not dealt with in a manner acceptable to the Filipinos. The Americans, however, had actually implemented more reforms than were desired by either the members of the propaganda movement or the other Philippine revolutionaries in the period prior to 1896. The Americans gave the Filipinos so much that many of them saw little reason for continued resistance.

The American policy of benevolence and the many humanitarian acts of the army throughout the war played a much more important role in the success of the pacification campaign than fear did. Acts of terrorism, brutality, and atrocity committed by members of the army were greatly exaggerated by American anti-imperialists, and as a result the more positive efforts of the army in such fields as education, public health, municipal government, and fiscal and legal reform were minimized. Widespread publicity given to the work of Taft and the civil government also worked to mask the achievements of the army in similar areas. After the seizure of Manila in 1898, the army worked constantly to improve living conditions in the Philippines and win the support of the people for the American government.

Although the humanitarian work of the army did not have a military significance when it started in 1898, American officers recognized the relationship between civil affairs work and pacification when the fighting began in 1899. Both General Otis and General MacArthur thought that school organization, the development of municipal government, and other progressive projects could convince the Filipinos of the sincerity of American pronouncements on Philippine policy and bring an end to the war. The evidence of popular support given the victorious Americans in late 1899 and early 1900 showed that they were correct in their assessment. One Filipino author reminiscing about the revolution in Misamis Province went so far as to declare that the revolutionary forces in that area were conquered "not by the American guns but by American schools." In his words, "the boxes of books were the real peace makers."[6] Revolutionary terror tactics and the inability of the Americans to protect municipal inhabitants, however, more than offset the gains made by the policy of benevolent pacification throughout most of 1900.

Benevolence could change the attitudes of Filipinos toward Americans, but the change was of little significance or value until techniques of pacification were initiated to stem terrorism and give protection to townspeople. This combination was evident in 1901. Before that year, American benevolence had succeeded in winning but not maintaining popular support. With the development of a new approach to the problems of pacification at the end of 1900, Filipinos were finally given a chance to show evidence of their support for the Americans without having to pay the previously inevitable consequence of being victimized by revolutionary terrorists. Aggressive military action against the guerrillas in the field, increased deployment of American troops in municipal garrisons, and swift action by military commissions under the provisions of General Order 100 all combined to furnish the towns security. The arrest and conviction of the revolution's supporters, agents, and terrorists gave evidence to the townspeople that the Americans were capable of protecting them, and circumstances soon showed that when the people cooperated with the Americans protection was even better. Beginning as early as 1899, propertied Filipinos had recognized that peace under United States sovereignty was a reasonable alternative to continued war and the uncertain goal of independence. The protection given them by the Americans in 1901 made it possible for them to actively express those ideas.

An analysis of those elements that made for American success in the Philippines can not end without commenting upon the high level of personnel at work within the army that were responsible for formulating and implementing the program of pacification. General Otis, for all his faults as a troop commander, recognized that the problem facing the Americans in the Philippines was, in reality, a political one. His stress on education, legal reform, honesty in government, and other aspects of the beneficent American colonial policy were all in recognition of that fact. General MacArthur, his successor, was also aware of the continuing need for emphasis on developing an administration and programs that would provide the basis for peaceful American rule. Through this focus, they insured that pacification, when achieved, would be long lasting because the government established would be an acceptable one. Officers such as Enoch H. Crowder and James F. Smith provided the skill in fields such as law needed to develop the structure of a colonial administration within the framework of the military government. Men like Bell, Kobbé, and Allen carried the American policy to the people in the provinces, combining excellence as military commanders with interest and ability as civil administrators. Others such as General Wheaton, because they were good officers, put their energy behind directives that were often personally distasteful to them.

The approach to pacification that the Americans developed and used in the Philippines between 1892 and 1902 was very similar to that favored by officers in the French army who had considerably more colonial experience than their American counterparts. Louis Lyautey, a French lieutenant colonel, published an article in February 1900 on the colonial role of the army in which he spoke of colonial conquest in terms that mirrored, in some cases almost exactly, actions taken by the Americans in the Philippines.[7]

Lyautey emphasized that the best means for achieving pacification in a new colony was the combined application of force and politics. He advised the use of destruction as a last resort and then only as a preliminary to a better reconstruction. Since the territory was destined to receive future colonial enterprises and its inhabitants would be the main agents and collaborators of the colonial power in the development of those enterprises, both, according to Lyautey, should always be treated with consideration. Political action was far more important than military action, and on the role of benevolence in pacification Lyautey quoted from instructions issued by his superior, General Joseph Galliéni. "Every time that an incident of war forces one of our colonial officers to take action against a village or a center of population, his first concern, once the submission of the inhabitants has been achieved, will be the reconstruction of the village, the creation of a market, and the establishment of a school."[8]

Recognizing that "a country is not conquered and pacified when a military operation has decimated and terrorized its population," Lyautey observed that as pacification gained

ground the soldiers' military role diminished while administrative functions became increasingly important. Reconstruction and continued expert administration were necessary, and
Lyautey favored the unification of military and administrative
authority in colonies. He also saw the advantages of a highly
specialized corps of colonial troops to provide the continuity
needed for colonial service.[9]

In an excellent work on French concepts of colonial warfare, the geographer Jean Gottmann stated that "at the dawn of
the twentieth century, Lyautey's article on the 'Colonial Role
of the Army' summed up in a few pages the long experience of
the French in military warfare, practice, and thought."[10] The
Americans, having been in the Philippines less than three years
at that time, were arriving at substantially the same conclusions
outlined by Lyautey. The effectiveness of those ideas for both
the French and the Americans was sufficient evidence of their
validity at least for the colonial wars of the late nineteenth and
early twentieth centuries.

Because of the numerous factors that contributed to
American success in the Philippines, summarizing the campaign in capsule form or deriving lessons from it that might
have application to similar problems of a more contemporary
nature is difficult. The American dilemma in 1899 was how to
end the opposition to the United States and substitute
American forms of control for those of the Philippine revolutionary government. This goal was achieved, in general, by the
application of a threefold approach to pacification. First, continuing efforts were made to win the popular support of the
Filipinos by presenting a positive image of the prospects of
American rule. American colonial policy and the military
government in the Philippines promised and gave the Filipinos
those things they had wanted but failed to obtain from Spain.
When positive incentives were combined with the more
negative ones placed in effect by General MacArthur's new
pacification program in December 1900, the people realized
that little if anything could be gained by continued support of
the revolution and resistance to the Americans. Second, the
Americans worked to separate the population and the guerrillas, thereby ending the influence of the guerrillas in the towns

and destroying the system through which they obtained sanctuary, supplies, and information. Once the army had convinced the Filipinos of the advantages of American rule and shown them that they would be protected from the revolutionaries, it could use the native population as a weapon in the guerrilla war. The third element in the general American program of pacification was the use of military force to defeat the guerrilla in the field. An important part of the overall campaign, in the long run it was probably the least important component of the threefold approach. Without popular support or the protection of the inhabitants that made such support possible the military operations in the field accomplished little.

Despite the obvious success of the army between 1898 and 1902, many problems passed unsolved from the military to the civil authorities. For example, Philippine society, as it had evolved during the Spanish regime, was ill suited to the immediate introduction of American concepts of government. The mass of townspeople were unaccustomed to taking part in the government of their municipalities, and they were easily controlled by the wealthy and educated members of the community. Most Filipinos, elite and commoners alike, had a poorly developed sense of public responsibility and individual rights. If unsupervised, police, constabulary, and scouts continued the petty abuses and tyranny that had been perpetrated by the civil guards of the Spanish regime. Municipal presidents often ruled dictatorially; and graft, corruption, and nepotism seemed part of the normal routine of government left in Filipino hands. Filipinos and Americans had difficulties communicating, and the Americans recognized early that language study and a greater command of Filipino languages would be necessary to administer the Philippines effectively. Cultural differences and the difficulties of communication, however, were really problems of colonial rule rather than pacification. Time, education, direction, and supervision over the long term were needed to solve such problems, and they were transferred to the civil government at the end of the war.

Among the Americans in the Philippines, friction between civil and military authorities remained an unsolved problem of the pacification campaign as long as control of the insular government was divided between them. General Otis had had trouble with the first Philippine commission, and the relations between Taft and MacArthur were strained throughout the latter's tenure as commanding general in the islands. Even when the executive control of the insular government was placed entirely in the hands of the civil authority, friction continued until the end of the pacification campaign. General Chaffee's relationship with Governor Taft was little better than that between Taft and MacArthur, possibly worse because Chaffee was less committed to benevolence and civil government as an important element in the pacification process. The friction between Chaffee and Taft finally provoked the direct intervention of the President, and when Theodore Roosevelt succeeded to that office upon the assassination of McKinley in September 1901, he made known that he would not tolerate a continuance of the dissension evident between civil and military authorities in the Philippines.[11]

Although President Roosevelt could force an end to jurisdictional disputes between civilians and the military, he could not and did not achieve any marked change in their attitudes toward each other. Friction existed and remained an unsolved problem as long as the army was responsible for the pacification of the islands. Part of the problem was caused, no doubt, by the lack of a clear definition of the functions of the civil and military authorities in areas not under the complete jurisdiction of the civil government. Also, as Governor Taft observed, military officers in provinces pacified but still garrisoned had little work of a military character to perform. As a consequence, some "naturally interested themselves in the civil government," and, concluded Taft, "sometimes they asserted authority that they did not have."[12] Friction seemed the inevitable consequence of the transition from military to civil government. The military, constantly in contact with people and provinces in a state of war, had a different assessment of the situation in the islands than civil authorities primarily in contact with Filipinos who were at peace and interested in the establishment of civil government.[13] Considering the campaign as a whole, that friction was kept under control and to a minimum was probably more significant than that it existed at all.

The greatest unresolved problem of the American army was that of officers who failed to see the importance of civil affairs work and the value of benevolence. Although the revolutionaries recognized the effectiveness of the American "policy of attraction" at an early date and instituted a reign of terror to combat it, some American commanders refused to follow the official policy and devoted little time or effort to beneficent civil affairs work. As Governor Taft observed, the implementation of the benevolent policy was "largely a matter of the personal equation of the commanding officer." Men like Otis, MacArthur, Bell, Hughes, Kobbé, and Allen were committed to the policy and used it with great success.[14] Others, like General Young or General Bates, had little use for a humanitarian approach to the problem of continued guerrilla warfare.

A great difference in opinion existed among military commanders on the question of benevolence. The overwhelming frustration of the guerrilla situation accounted for the rejection of the humane policy by some Americans during and after 1900. The Balangiga massacre had the same effect at the end of 1901. In particular, these events accounted for the change in opinion of Americans originally well disposed toward a policy of benevolence who later advocated the use of more severe measures.

Some commanders no doubt found the administration of military government and civil affairs programs a frustrating experience. They could often see no immediate results in their efforts to improve living conditions in the Philippines and to entice people to support the American cause. The army had been given the mission of forcing Filipino nationalists to accept the government of the United States, and the lack of apparent success in its efforts at benevolent pacification before 1901 was a source of pressure on officers. For many, pacification in a short time by any means seemed preferable to any long-term campaign. Some officers thought that a "lesson" of the American Civil War had been that war was always hell and that short wars, no matter how severe, were more humanitarian than long ones no matter how benevolently waged. Even General Bell, a proven advocate of benevolence, had expressed this thought during his Batangas campaign.

Brigadier General J. F. Wade, commanding in southern Luzon at the end of 1901, observed that part of the problem was caused by the conditions facing officers given the task of pacification. The dispersion of the American army was so great that the consequent shortage of officers usually allowed only one for each garrison. This officer, in some cases only a young lieutenant, was called upon to perform all the staff duties, collect customs and internal revenues, act as provost judge, supervise the municipal government and local police, and see that the towns were kept in proper sanitary condition. He also had to prevent townspeople from giving supplies and information to the guerrillas. The garrison commander had to be constantly alert to repel night attacks by guerrillas or mount field operations against them. A large number of the American troops in the islands at any one time were recruits or volunteers with little instruction and no military experience.[15] With all of these problems it was a marvel that the army had time to give any attention to civil affairs.

Conditions in the Philippines not only placed great responsibility on individual commanders, but effectively prevented extensive management of any large portion of the pacification campaign by headquarters in Manila. Poor communications, widely dispersed garrisons, a shortage of officers, and the numerous duties given men of little experience all worked to prevent adequate supervision. Benevolence could be made the official policy, but the commanding general in Manila could do little to insure that the policy would be implemented at the lower levels of command. In such a situation the individual was all important. If he was cruel, callous, unthinking, or just too busy to concern himself with beneficent work in the municipalities, he could hinder the pacification effort. However, humane officers with a real concern for the Filipinos acted in a way that fostered pacification even when they were unsupervised or uninformed about the exact nature of official policy. The individual was the key. As one American officer observed in 1901, what the army needed most was men of "character, learning, experience, and integrity" capable of "justice and patience."[16] In the final analysis, the personal equation could not be avoided.

The long duration of the Philippine campaign had both a positive and a negative effect on the pacification effort. Continued lack of success caused many Americans to lose faith in what were really excellent techniques. At the same time, through continued study, the Americans finally evolved a winning approach to the problem in the form of General MacArthur's new pacification program begun at the end of 1900. What had been needed to fight the guerrilla, as well as develop a colonial government, was patience, dedication, and a willingness to remain on the job for an extremely long time. By the end of the campaign, if nothing else had been learned, Americans knew that many of the problems facing them in the Philippines could not be solved overnight.[17] Much of the final American victory can be credited to those soldiers who refused to abandon their efforts to win over the Philippine populace to the American side. Those men never repudiated the policy of benevolence to which President McKinley had committed them.

The army was lucky in that a number of problems that could have seriously impaired its effectiveness in the Philippines did not appear. For example, because the Philippines had been a long-established colony of Spain, there was no great rush of concession hunters and speculators. Those who did come to the islands were in small enough number to be easily controlled by the military government, and they did not have enough political power in Washington to create serious pressure on the army from that quarter. Within the army and the American government there was no group of "experts" with preconceived ideas on how to run a colonial government, and the very absence of this group made possible the successful pragmatic approach that the Americans did use.

Had the United States been embroiled in any other long-term military venture after the outbreak of hostilities in the Philippines, it would have certainly found it impossible to carry out such large scale commitments in the face of growing political opposition at home. The expedition sent to China in 1900 to help quell the Boxer Rebellion had been a serious strain on military resources in the Philippines. Fortunately that intervention was short lived. Other equally fortunate circumstances helped make the Philippine campaign possible. Puerto Rico submitted peacefully to American rule. The Cuban occupation was of short duration and involved no pacification efforts. There was no need for American intervention elsewhere in the Caribbean during the duration of the Philippine war. Instead, the United States solved its foreign problems sequentially, although certainly by accident rather than design. Construction on the Panama Canal, in which the army was a major participant, did not begin until after the Philippine war had ended. The intervention in Cuba did not come until 1906. Had the United States become involved in these two strategic areas between 1899 and 1902, it would have certainly sacrificed gains in the Philippines to operate in these important regions closer to home.

Although outside of the general subject matter of this work, speculation on the impact of the Philippine campaign on both the islands and the United States Army might prove interesting. Almost every combat unit of the army saw service in the Philippines at one time or another between 1898 and 1902, and almost all of the officer corps participated in the pacification campaign. Because of this unique aspect of the Philippine war, the campaign was bound to be one of the principal learning experiences of the army in the period prior to World War I. The war against the Filipino revolutionaries and the operations undertaken after 1902 against the Moros were the training ground for numerous field commanders who fought with the American expeditionary force in France more than a decade later. Henry T. Allen, Robert L. Bullard, John J. Pershing, and Peyton C. March were a few of the officers who commanded in the Philippines and later held positions of higher authority during World War I.

The Army's experience in developing a successful approach to pacification provided the basis for the American interventions in the Caribbean during the succeeding decade. During the Cuban intervention of 1906, the army made reference to its Philippine experience, and the conduct of similar operations by American military forces in the Caribbean also bore resemblance to the army's operations in the Philippines.[18] In all cases the occupying force gave special attention to civil affairs work and the development within the countries occupied of local police and military units similar to those organized in the Philippines.

When the American government was contemplating intervention in Mexico, following the outbreak of the revolution there in 1910, reference was again made to the Philippine experience. Captain John R. M. Taylor, who had prepared a detailed compilation of Filipino documents and a two volume history of the Philippine campaign, thought that the section of his work on guerrilla warfare would be of value to troops called upon to intervene in Mexico. He wanted it published as a guide for forces in the field should that country be occupied.[19] A special memorandum relating to intervention plans used the experience of the United States Army in the Philippines and that of the British in South Africa to arrive at an estimate of the troops that would be needed in Mexico. The period of military operations was estimated at three months. Pacification, however, was thought to be a process taking "not less than three years."[20] While the military operations would call for approximately 380,000 men, pacification would need over 550,000.

When American intervention did take place in the form of the occupation of Vera Cruz by forces under General Funston, the work of the Americans in that Mexican city was almost an exact duplicate of the work undertaken earlier in the administration of Manila. The army began efforts to clean the city, eradicate malaria, repair public buildings and streets, reform the prison system, and administer justice.[21] The striking similarity between the American military governments of Manila and Vera Cruz could surely be traced directly to the army's Philippine experience.

As a result of the Philippine campaign, some Americans had given much thought to the problems of pacification. Captain Taylor commented extensively on the nature of guerrilla warfare and also upon some of the elements of a successful pacification campaign. He noted the advantages of a benevolent policy capable of winning the support of the inhabitants. Military triumph over the guerrilla bands was not sufficient for victory, but, according to Taylor, one had to "conquer

the support of the country itself." Commenting on the Spanish
campaign of 1896-1897, he remarked that

> it is not sufficient to kill and to destroy; a desert is
> not necessarily at peace. A people who have risen in
> arms submit only of their own will, and only when
> the majority has been induced to believe that their
> property and their lives are safer in the hands of the
> leaders of the conquering army than in the hands of
> the leaders who have called them to the field.[22]

Taylor's observation pinpointed perhaps the greatest lesson of
the war.

Both civil and military officials in the Philippines
recognized that Bell's campaign in Batangas represented
pacification in its most perfected form. In response to a large
demand by officers for copies of Bell's telegraphic circulars, the
orders were compiled into a pamphlet to serve as an example of
his approach to pacification.[23] The issue of atrocities and
criticism of American operations in the Philippines prevented
the distribution of this work, just as similar political considerations prevented the publication of Taylor's compilation. In the
Philippines, however, the commission recognized the success of
the army's approach to pacification, and it passed a reconcentration act in 1903, patterned on General Bell's techniques, for
use in areas plagued by recurrent banditry or peasant uprisings.
Pershing's campaign against the Moros on Mindanao after
1908 greatly resembled the army's successful campaign of
1901.[24]

A final achievement of the army in the Philippines was the
role it undoubtedly played in the transfer of American ideas
and institutions to the islands. The military government was
responsible for developing the basis for the insular educational
system, the code of municipal government, the tax structure,
and the revised legal system. Its work in areas such as public
health and public works was extensive. The first contact most
Filipinos had with Americans was their contact with representatives of the army, and soldiers were responsible, at least in
part, for any transfer of American institutions or ideas to the

islands during the early colonial administration. The army, as President Roosevelt rightly observed, had brought the Filipinos "individual liberty, protection of personal rights, civil order, public instruction, and religious freedom."[25] It had done these things between 1898 and 1902 in its capacity as the major and in many areas the only representative of the United States in the Philippines.

When viewed in the historical perspective of the past several decades, the American occupation of the Philippines seems to take on greater significance than just an example of a successful pacification campaign or one facet of the spread of American ideas overseas. The Philippine revolt represented one of the first vestiges of the rising Asian nationalism so evident in the period since World War II. The fact that it was not successful was relatively unimportant when one considers the greater phenomena that it represented. Its failure was significant evidence of the early date at which certain Filipinos began to conceive of themselves as a national group. Success for the Filipinos as well as their neighbors would come only after the destruction of Western power in Asia by the Japanese.

From the American and world viewpoint, the Philippine venture of the United States marked an increase in American world power and Asian involvement. The seizure of the Philippines placed the United States in eventual conflict with Japan and helped to develop in the American people a Pacific and Asian orientation that remained an important part of their diplomacy in the mid-twentieth century. In that respect the events between 1898 and 1902 had a far greater significance for world history than was apparent to most Americans or any other people at the time.

In the final analysis, ironically perhaps, the greatest significance of the American army's Philippine experience might still be as an example of a successful pacification campaign. Since 1898 many nations have had problems similar to those faced by the United States in the Philippines. Throughout the world, people have been forced to seek ways to end disastrous guerrilla wars, to win popular support from culturally diverse populations threatened by revolutionary movements, and to carry out the formation of a government in the face of armed opposition. The American experience in the Philippines could conceivably offer some insight into how problems of this sort might be solved. The fact that the campaign against the HUK movement in the Philippines following World War II greatly resembled the American campaign of almost fifty years earlier was no coincidence. The American approach to the problem of pacification had been a studied one, and many aspects of it would naturally resemble methods used in subsequent situations.

The American pacification campaign in the Philippines was important. An example of the successful evolution of a counter-guerrilla operation leading to the effective occupation of a vast and hostile territory, it was developed empirically with no pre-existing doctrine from which to draw. The army's approach to the problem was notable for its diversity, including widespread civil affairs efforts, excellent propaganda, well-planned and -executed military operations, effective isolation of the guerrilla, protection of the population, and the involvement of the inhabitants in programs designed for their own protection and the eventual establishment of peace. The army accomplished its major mission in the islands through these well-directed efforts. Sufficient order was restored to allow the development of a purely civil government in which Filipinos actively participated. The threat of the revolutionaries to American rule was eliminated, and the army achieved a condition of long-term stability and security in the islands. Tangentially it worked to transmit American institutions and values to the newly won colonial possession, and its efforts between 1898 and 1902 provided a firm basis for the implementation of President McKinley's policy of benevolent colonial rule.

NOTES

1. Juan Villamor, *Unpublished Chronicle of the Filipino-American War in Northern Luzon, 1899-1901*, I, 20-27.
2. Teodoro A. Agoncillo, "Malolos: The Crisis of the Republic," *Philippine Social Sciences and Humanities Review* 25 (1960): 636-53.
3. Taylor, "Compilation," 54HS.
4. Romeo V. Cruz, "Filipino Collaboration with the Americans, 1899-1902," 194-95. On wage scales, see U.S., Bureau of the Census, *Census of the Philippine Islands, 1903*, IV, 434-36.
5. For a specific example, see David R. Sturtevant, "Guardia de Honor: Revitalization Within the Revolution." The millennial dimension of agrarian unrest in the Philippines will be well covered in Professor Sturtevant's forthcoming book on that subject.
6. Filomeno M. Bautista, "The Bautista Manuscript on the Philippine Revolution in Misamis Province, 1900-1901" (mimeographed and ed. Francis C. Madigan, SJ, Xavier University, Cagayan de Oro City, 1968), 42.
7. Louis Lyautey, "Du rôle colonial de l'Armée," *Revue des Deux Mondes* 157 (1900): 308-28.
8. Ibid., 316. Galliéni issued the orders on Madagascar, May 22, 1898.
9. Ibid., 246, 317.
10. Gottman, "Bugeaud, Galliéni, Lyautey: The Development of French Colonial Warfare," in Edward Mead Earle, ed., *Makers of Modern Strategy: Military Thought from Machiavelli to Hitler*, 245.
11. Roosevelt to Chaffee, Oct. 8, 1901, *Correspondence Relating to the War with Spain, April 15, 1898-July 30, 1902*, II, 1297.

12. Testimony of Taft, *Affairs in the Philippine Islands, Hearings before the Committee on the Philippines of the United States Senate*, SD 331, 57th Cong., 1st sess., pt. 1, 86.

13. Ibid., 88-89.

14. Taft to Root, Feb. 23, 1901, Taft Papers; Taft to Root, Feb. 8, Mar. 17, Apr. 27, 1901, Root Papers; Taft to Root, Oct. 21, 1901, Taft Papers.

15. *Annual Reports of the War Department for the Fiscal Year Ended June 30, 1901*, HD 2, 57th Cong., 1st sess., VIII, 388.

16. E. J. McClernand, "Our Philippine Problem," *Journal of the Military Service Institution of the United States* 29 (1901): 328-29.

17. For a recognition of the importance of time in the solution of both the problems of pacification and colonial government see Root, *War Department, 1901*, HD 2, 57th Cong., 1st sess., II, 85.

18. For an excellent work on the army's use of its Philippine experience in later campaigns see Allan Reed Millett, *The Politics of Intervention: The Military Occupation of Cuba, 1906-1909*.

19. Taylor to Secretary, War College Division, Aug. 24, 1914, Records of the War Department, General Staff, 8699, incl. 3.

20. Entry to M. W. Rowell, "The Military Strength for Armed Intervention in Mexico," Mar. 4, 1916 on record card for "Mexican War Plans," Records of the War Department General Staff, 6474.

21. Robert E. Quirk, *An Affair of Honor: Woodrow Wilson and the Occupation of Vera Cruz* (Lexington, Ky., 1962), 121-55.

22. Taylor, "Compilation," 33FZ.

23. *Telegraphic Circulars and General Orders* [Bell], AGO 415839.

24. See Samuel K. Tan, "Sulu under American Military Rule, 1899-1913" (M.A. thesis, University of the Philippines, 1966).

25. *Annual Reports of the War Department for the Fiscal Year Ended June 30, 1902*, HD 2, 57th Cong., 2d sess., IV, 16.

BIBLIOGRAPHY of WORKS CITED

MANUSCRIPT COLLECTIONS

Aguinaldo Collection. Minnesota State Historical Society Library. St. Paul, Minnesota. Fifteen items, limited value.

Henry T. Allen Papers. Library of Congress. Washington, D.C. Excellent for coverage of pacification operations of the 43rd Infantry on Leyte, 1900-1901. In 1901 Allen left the army to head the Philippine Constabulary. Approximately four file boxes deal directly with Allen's Philippine experience.

Willis Grandy Briggs Papers. University of North Carolina Library. Chapel Hill, North Carolina. Limited value. Contains letters from Briggs's cousin, Major Luther B. Grandy, who served in the Philippines with the 35th Infantry.

William Carey Brown, diary (copy). U.S. Military History Research Collection, Carlisle, Pennsylvania. The diary covers Brown's service in the Philippines from January 1900 to September 1901.

Robert Lee Bullard Papers. Library of Congress. Washington, D.C. Bullard served as a colonel in the 39th Infantry throughout 1900 and most of 1901. The most valuable item in the collection was his MS diary.

Robert Dexter Carter Papers. Rutherford B. Hayes Memorial

Library, Fremont, Ohio. Carter was General Lawton's personal civilian quartermaster clerk. The collection contains 23 letters covering the period May-September 1899. Although they were of limited value in this study, they did contain several critical references to General Otis.

Henry C. Corbin Papers. Library of Congress. Washington, D.C. Of limited value considering Corbin's important position as the Adjutant General, the collection does contain interesting letters to Generals Chaffee and Schwan.

Cushman Kellogg Davis Papers. Minnesota State Historical Society Library. St. Paul, Minnesota. Another source of soldier's letters of limited value.

William Eggenberger, letters. U.S. Military History Research Collection, Carlisle, Pennsylvania. Covering the first three years of the Philippine campaign, these letters give a good view of an enlisted man's reaction to the war.

William George Haan Papers. Wisconsin State Historical Society Library. Madison, Wisconsin. Haan's diary for June 1898 to March 1899, during which time he served in the Philippines, was of some but limited use.

John L. Jordan Papers. Tennessee State Library and Archives. Nashville, Tennessee. The most valuable of the several collections of soldier's letters consulted. Jordan wrote extensively to his mother, and his letters covered the period from the end of 1899 to mid-1901.

Lyman Walter Vere Kennon Papers. Duke University Library. Durham, North Carolina. Contains valuable material on conditions in the Philippines in 1899 and 1900. Kennon was committed to the concept of benevolent pacification. A small collection.

William A. Kobbé Papers. U.S. Military History Research Collection, Carlisle, Pennsylvania. This is a small but excellent collection that includes Kobbé's "Diary of Field Service in the Philippines, 1898 to 1901" and some good material on the development of the military government's plan for municipal government in 1899.

Henry W. Lawton Papers. Library of Congress. Washington, D.C. Nothing of value written by General Lawton, but collection has a few letters written by Commissioner Worcester to Mrs. Lawton.

Arthur MacArthur. "Letterbook." Manila, 1900. Duke University Library. Durham, North Carolina. Correspondence relating to civil affairs in the latter half of 1900.

William McKinley Papers. Library of Congress. Washington, D.C. Although an extensive collection, it was of limited value. The numerous telegrams between the Philippines and Washington have been published, as have many of the reports from military officers. The correspondence from members of the Schurman Commission is duplicated in records in the United States National Archives.

Eugenius Aristides Nisbet Papers. Duke University Library. Durham, North Carolina. Soldier's letters; limited value.

Charles Dudley Rhodes Papers. United States' Military Academy Library. West Point, New York. Valuable for a short report on reconcentration in Batangas.

James Alexander Robertson Papers. Duke University Library. Durham, North Carolina. The most valuable items were correspondence between James A. LeRoy and John R. M. Taylor.

Elihu Root Papers. Library of Congress. Washington, D.C. Much good material, in particular a long series of letters from Taft.

Spanish-American War, Philippine Insurrection, and Boxer Rebellion Veterans Research Project. U.S. Military History Research Collection, Carlisle, Pennsylvania. This project has led to the accumulation of several questionnaires completed by veterans who served in the Philippines. Many of the veterans contacted also contributed memoirs, reminiscences, diaries, letters, photographs, and other memorabilia to the collection being developed in Carlisle. The results of the project, only in progress a very short time, are very impressive, and one can expect that the U.S. Military History Research Collection will become an important center for research into this period of military history.

William Howard Taft Papers. Library of Congress. Washington, D.C. Taft wrote frequently to many of his friends and acquaintances in the United States. These letters contain a great deal of information on developments in the Philippines and the pacification campaign.

John R. Thomas, Jr. "Collection Relating to the Insurrectionist Government of the Philippines, 1898-1899." Library of Congress. Washington, D.C. Small collection; limited value.

MATERIALS IN THE UNITED STATES NATIONAL ARCHIVES

Noble, Robert H., comp. "A Compilation of Insurgent Documents consisting chiefly of letters and orders issued by insurgent officials during the Insurrection in the Philippine Islands from 1898 to 1902 pertaining chiefly to the Visayan group, comprising the islands of Panay, Negros, Cebu, Bohol, Leyte, and Samar." 34 vols. 1902. Microfilm. Consists of Spanish translations and copies of insurgent records captured in the Visayas. Some of the documents duplicate material available in other parts of the Philippine Insurgent Records. Noble's compilation is indexed and contained on rolls 637-643 of the PIR.

Philippine Insurgent Records, 1896-1901 with Associated Records of the U. S. War Department, 1900-1906. Microfilm. Rolls 1-82 consist of those records specially selected as being important by PIR translator and compilor John R. M. Taylor. The records include finding aids, translations, and abstracts prepared by Taylor and his staff. In the military section of the archives there is a photocopy of William C. Gaines, Jr., "General Subject Index to the Philippine Insurgent Records," prepared at Florida Atlantic University, 1965. It was easier, however, to use the finding aids prepared by Captain Taylor and contained in the PIR.

Records of the Adjutant General's Office. Record Group 94. A difficult set of materials to use, these records have a name and subject index, but there is no system whereby materials pertaining to the Philippines are filed together. Location of material is time consuming and often unrewarding. The best single file was the collection of "Diary of Events" for the period May 6, 1900 to Aug. 31,

1902, all filed together under AGO 338335. The "Diary of Events" contained both a summary of the events in the islands, usually covering about a two-week period, and excerpts from the reports sent to Manila by departmental and unit commanders. This was fortunate, because the records of the Philippine command were not organized for research purposes.

Records of the Bureau of Insular Affairs. Record Group 350. Contains material on the army's civil affairs operations in the Philippines. Not as valuable as one would hope, however, because much of the material is only routine correspondence. An excellent finding aid to these records is United States National Archives, *Records of the Bureau of Insular Affairs Relating to the Philippine Islands, 1898-1935: A List of Selected Files*, comp. Kenneth Munden (Washington, 1942).

Records of the Office of the Chief Signal Officer. Record Group 111. Numerous excellent photographs, in particular File 93, "Red Book Collection"; File 96, Signal Corps "Historical File."

Records of the U. S. Commission to the Philippine Islands. General Records of the Department of State. Record Group 59. Valuable for correspondence of the Schurman Commission.

Records of the War Department General Staff. Record Group 165. Some material on the army's use of Philippine experience in the period 1902-1914.

Taylor, John R. M. "The Philippine Insurrection Against the United States—A Compilation of Documents with Notes and Introduction," 5 vols. 1906. Microfilm. See Chapter I, note 19.

U. S. GOVERNMENT DOCUMENTS

Bureau of the Census. *Census of the Philippine Islands, 1903*. 4 vols. Washington, 1905.

Congressional Record. 57th Cong., 1st sess., XXXV (1902), 6143-44.

Correspondence Relating to the War with Spain, April 15, 1898-July 30, 1902. 2 vols. Washington, 1902.

Department of the Interior. *Report of the Commissioner of Education for the Year 1900-1901*. 2 vols. Washington, 1902.

General Orders and Circulars Issued from Department of the Pacific and 8th Army Corps and Office of Military Governor in Philippine Islands, 1899. Manila, 1899.

General Orders and Circulars, Philippine Islands Expeditionary Forces, 1898.

General Orders Issued from Department of the Pacific and 8th Army Corps and Division of the Philippines, 1900.

General Orders, U. S. Army, Philippine Islands, 1901.

Congress. House. *Annual Reports of the Navy Department for the Year 1898: Appendix to the Report of the Chief of The Bureau of Navigation*. HD 3, 55th Cong., 3d sess.

———. *Annual Reports of the War Department for the Fiscal Year Ended June 30, 1898*. HD 2, 55th Cong., 3d sess.

———. *Annual Reports of the War Department for the Fiscal Year Ended June 30, 1899*. HD 2, 56th Cong., 1st sess.

———. *Annual Reports of the War Department for the Fiscal Year Ended June 30, 1900*. HD 2, 56th Cong., 2d sess.

———. *Annual Reports of the War Department for the Fiscal Year Ended June 30, 1901*. HD 2, 57th Cong., 1st sess.

———. *Annual Reports of the War Department for the Fiscal Year Ended June 30, 1902*. HD 2, 57th Cong., 2d sess.

———. *Annual Reports of the War Department for the Fiscal Year Ended June 30, 1903*. HD 2, 58th Cong., 2d sess.

Congress. Senate. *Affairs in the Philippine Islands. Hearings before the Committee on the Philippines of the United States Senate*. SD 331, 57th Cong., 1st sess. 3 pts.

———. *Charges of Cruelty, Etc., to the Natives of the Philippines*. SD 205, 57th Cong., 1st sess.

———. *Civil Government in the Philippine Islands*. SD 119, 56th Cong., 2d sess.

———. *Communications between the Executive Departments of the Government and Aguinaldo*. SD 208, 56th Cong., 1st sess.

———. *Deportation of A. Mabini and Others*. SD 135, 56th Cong., 2d sess.

————. *Education in the Philippine Islands.* SD 129, 56th Cong., 2d sess.

————. *Federal Party Message to Congress.* SD 187, 57th Cong., 2d sess.

————. *Issuance of Certain Military Orders in the Philippines.* SD 347, 57th Cong., 1st sess.

————. *Lands Held for Ecclesiastical or Religious Uses in the Philippine Islands.* SD 190, 56th Cong., 2d sess.

————. *Number of Deaths of Soldiers in the Philippines, Etc.* SD 426, 56th Cong., 1st sess.

————. *Papers Relating to the Treaty with Spain.* SD 148, 56th Cong., 2d sess.

————. *Petitions of Natives of the Philippine Islands.* SD 323, 57th Cong., 1st sess.

————. *The Philippine Situation.* SD 422, 57th Cong., 1st sess.

————. *Political Affairs in the Philippine Islands.* SD 259, 57th Cong., 1st sess.

————. *Protests Against American Civil Government in the Island of Cebu, Philippine Islands.* SD 234, 56th Cong., 2d sess.

————. *Report of the Philippine Commission to the President, January 31, 1900.* SD 138, 56th Cong., 1st sess.

————. *Report of the United States Philippine Commission.* SD 112, 56th Cong., 2d sess.

————. *A Treaty of Peace between the United States and Spain.* SD 62, 55th Cong., 3d sess.

————. *Trials or Courts-Martial in the Philippine Islands in Consequence of Certain Instructions.* SD 213, 57th Cong., 2d sess.

————. *Trip through the Island of Luzon.* SD 196, 56th Cong., 1st sess.

Philippine Islands Military Governor: General Orders and Circulars, 1900.

Philippine Islands Military Governor: General Orders and Circulars, 1901.

Taylor, John R. M. *Report on the Organization for the Administration of Civil Government Instituted by Emilio Aguinaldo and His Followers in the Philippine Archipelago.* Washington, 1903.

COLLECTED LETTERS AND DOCUMENTS

Bacon, Robert and James Brown Scott, eds. *The Military and Colonial Policy of the United States: Addresses and Reports by Elihu Root.* Cambridge, Mass., 1916.

Lodge, Henry Cabot. *Selections from the Correspondence of Theodore Roosevelt and Henry Cabot Lodge, 1884-1918.* 2 vols. New York, 1925.

Mabini, Apolinario. *La Revolución Filipina (con otros documentos de la época).* Comp. Teodoro M. Kalaw. Manila, 1931.

Mariano Ponce: Cartas sobre la revolución, 1897-1900. Comp. Teodoro M. Kalaw. Manila, 1932.

Morison, Elting E. *The Letters of Theodore Roosevelt.* 8 vols. Cambridge, Mass., 1951.

Richardson, James D. *A Compilation of the Messages and Papers of the Presidents.* 20 vols. New York, 1917.

Speeches and Addresses of William McKinley from March 1, 1897 to May 30, 1900. New York, 1900.

REMINISCENCES, AUTOBIOGRAPHIES, AND DIARIES

Aguinaldo, Emilio. "True Review of the Philippine Revolution." *Congressional Record: Appendix,* 57th Cong., 1st sess., XXXV (1902), 439-50.

Alejandrino, José. *The Price of Freedom.* Manila, 1949.

Altamirano, Enrique. *Filipinas, Relato histórico de actos y hechos realizados en los últimos dias de nuestra dominación.* Madrid, 1902.

Bautista, Filomeno M. "The Bautista Manuscript on the Philippine Revolution in Misamis Province, 1900-1901." Mimeographed and ed. by Francis C. Madigan, S. J. Xavier University, Cagayan de Oro City, 1968.

Bellairs, Edgar G. [Charles Ballentine]. *As It Is in the Philippines.* New York, 1902.

Brown, John Clifford. *Diary of a Soldier in the Philippines.* Portland, Maine, 1901.

Buck, Beaumont B. *Memories of Peace and War.* San Antonio, 1935.

Crane, Charles J. *The Experiences of a Colonel of Infantry.* New York, 1923.

Fiske, Bradley A. *War Time in Manila.* Boston, 1913.

Funston, Frederick. *Memories of Two Wars: Cuban and Philippine Experiences.* New York, 1914.

Ganzhorn, John W. *I've Killed Men: An Epic of Early Arizona.* New York, 1959.

Lininger, Clarence. *The Best War at the Time.* New York, 1964.

Palma, Rafael. *My Autobiography.* Manila, 1953.

Palmer, Frederick. *With My Own Eyes.* Indianapolis, 1932.

Parker, James *The Old Army.* Philadelphia, 1929.

Quezon, Manuel Luis. *The Good Fight.* New York, 1946.

Rio, Antonio del. *Sitio y rendición de Santa Cruz de la Laguna: suerte de la colonia.* Manila, 1899.

Rivera, Fernando Primo de. *Memoria dirigida al senado por el capitán general D. Fernando Primo de Rivera y Sobremonte acerca de su gestión en filipinas. Agosto de 1898.* Madrid, 1898.

Robinson, Albert G. *The Philippines: The War and the People, A Record of Personal Observations and Experiences.* New York, 1901.

Sawyer, Frederick L. *Sons of Gunboats.* Annapolis, 1946.

Schofield, John M. *Forty-Six Years in the Army.* New York, 1897.

Sheridan, Richard Brinsley. *The Filipino Martyrs: a Story of the Crime of February 4, 1899.* London, 1900.

Slavens, T. H. *Scouting in Northern Luzon, P. I., 1899-1900.* N.p., 1947.

Taft, William Howard, and Theodore Roosevelt. *The Philippines.* New York, 1902.

Villamor, Juan. *Unpublished Chronicle of the Filipino-American War in Northern Luzon, 1899-1901.* 3 vols. Manila, 1924.

White, John R. *Bullets and Bolos.* New York, 1928.

Williams, Daniel R. *The Odyssey of the Philippine Commission.* Chicago, 1913.
Younghusband, G. J. *The Philippines and Round About.* New York, 1899.

NEWSPAPERS AND PERIODICALS

New York Tribune, 1898-1903.
Philippine Information Society. *Facts about the Filipinos.* 1901.
The United States Army and Navy Journal, 1898-1902.

ARTICLES

Agoncillo, Teodoro A. "Malolos: The Crisis of the Republic." *Philippine Social Sciences and Humanities Review* 25 (1960).
Anderson, T. M. "Our Rule in the Philippines." *North American Review* 170 (1900): 272-83.
Barrett, John. "Some Phases of the Philippine Situation." *Review of Reviews* 20 (1899): 65-74.
Berthoff, Rowland Tappan. "Taft and MacArthur, 1900: A Study in Civil-Military Relations." *World Politics* 5 (1953): 196-213.
Boughton, D. H. "How Soldiers Have Ruled in the Philippines." *International Quarterly* 6 (1902): 215-28.
Carmony, Donald F. et al. "Three Years in the Orient: The Diary of William R. Johnson, 1898-1902." *Indiana Magazine of History* 63 (1967): 262-98.
Coletta, Paolo E. "McKinley, the Peace Negotiations, and the Acquisition of the Philippines." *Pacific Historical Review* 30 (1961): 341-50.
Conant, C. A. "American Work in the Philippines." *International Monthly* 5 (1902): 358-70.
Corpus, Enrique J. "Japan and the Philippine Revolution." *The Philippine Social Science Review* 6 (1934): 249-98.
Corpus, Onofre. "Western Colonization and the Filipino

Response." *Journal of Southeast Asian History* 3 (1962): 1-22.

Cox, John and LaWanda. "General O. O. Howard and the 'Misrepresented Bureau.'" *Journal of Southern History* 19 (1953): 427-56.

Crook, George. "The Apache Problem." *Journal of the Military Service Institution of the United States* 7 (1886): 257-69.

Eyre, James K., Jr. "Japan and the American Annexation of the Philippines." *Pacific Historical Review* 11 (1942): 55-71.

──────. "Early Japanese Imperialism and the Philippines." *United States Naval Institute Proceedings* 75 (1949): 1267-75.

──────. "Japanese Imperialism and the Aguinaido Insurrection." *United States Naval Institute Proceedings* 75 (1949): 901-907.

Fall, Bernard B. "Insurgency Indicators." *Military Review* 46 (April, 1966): 3-11.

Farrell, John Thomas. "An Abandoned Approach to Philippine History: John R. M. Taylor and the Philippine Insurrection Records." *Catholic Historical Review* 39 (1954): 385-407.

Fite, Gilbert C. "The United States Army and Relief to Pioneer Settlers, 1874-1875." *Journal of the West* 6 (1967): 99-107.

Fonacier, Tomas S. "The Chinese Exclusion Policy in the Philippines." *Philippine Social Sciences and Humanities Review* 14 (1949): 3-28.

Greenleaf, Charles R. "A Brief Statement of the Sanitary Work so far Accomplished in the Philippine Islands, and of the Present Shape of the Sanitary Administration." *Reports and Papers of the American Public Health Association, 1901* 27 (1902): 157-65.

Harrington, Fred H. "The Anti-Imperialist Movement in the United States, 1898-1900." *Mississippi Valley Historical Review* 22 (1935): 211-30.

Hendrickson, Kenneth E., Jr. "Reluctant Expansionist—Jacob Gould Schurman and the Philippine Question." *Pacific Historical Review* 36 (1967): 405-21.

King, James T. "George Crook, Indian Fighter and

Humanitarian." *Arizona and the West* 10 (1968): 333-48.

LaCuesta, Manuel G. "Foundations of an American Education System in the Philippines." *Philippine Social Sciences and Humanities Review* 28 (1958): 115-40.

Lanzar, Maria C. "The Anti-Imperialist League." *Philippine Social Science Review* 3-5 (1930-33).

LeRoy, James A. "Mabini on the Failure of the Filipino Revolution." *American Historical Review* 11 (1906): 843-61.

———. "The Philippines Health Problem." *Outlook* 71 (1902): 777-82.

Leuchtenburg, William E. "Progressivism and Imperialism: The Progressive Movement and American Foreign Policy, 1898-1917." *Mississippi Valley Historical Review* 39 (1952): 483-504.

Levine, Daniel. "The Social Philosophy of Albert J. Beveridge." *Indiana Magazine of History* 58 (1962): 101-16.

Link, Arthur S. "The Progressive Movement in the South, 1870-1914." *North Carolina Historical Review* 23 (1946): 172-95.

Lyautey, Louis. "Du rôle colonial de l'Armée." *Revue des Deux Mondes* 157 (1900): 308-28.

McClernand, E. J. "Our Philippine Problem." *Journal of the Military Service Institution of the United States* 29 (1901): 327-32.

Majul, Cesar Adib. "The Political and Constitutional Ideas of the Philippine Revolution." *Philippine Social Sciences and Humanities Review* 21 (1956).

Martin, Harold. "The Manila Censorship." *Forum* 31 (1901): 462-71.

Munro, J. N. "The Philippine Native Scouts." *Journal of the U. S. Infantry Association* 2 (1905): 178-90.

Packard, R. L. "Political Organization of the Filipinos." *Scientific American Supplement* 49 (1900): 20459-60.

Palmer, Frederick. "White Man and Brown in the Philippines." *Scribner's Magazine* 27 (1900): 74-86.

Parker, James. "Some Random Notes on the Fighting in the

Philippines." *Journal of the Military Service Institution of the United States* 27 (1900): 317-40.

Plehn, C. C. "Municipal Government in the Philippine Islands." *Municipal Affairs* 5 (1901): 793-801.

———. "Taxation in the Philippines." *Political Science Quarterly* 16, 17 (1901, 1902): 680-711, 125-48.

Rakestraw, Lawrence. "George Patrick Ahern and the Philippine Bureau of Forestry, 1900-1914." *Pacific Northwest Quarterly* 58 (1967): 142-50.

Rhodes, Charles D. "The Utilization of Native Troops in Our Foreign Possessions." *Journal of the Military Service Institution of the United States* 30 (1902): 1-22.

Rowland, H. C. "Fighting Life in the Philippines." *McClure's Magazine* 19 (1902): 241-47.

Seaman, Louis Livingston. "Native Troops for Our Colonial Possessions." *North American Review* 171 (1900): 847-60.

Sibert, W. L. "Military Occupation of Northern Luzon." *Journal of the Military Service Institution of the United States* 30 (1902): 404-408.

Sturtevant, David R. "Guardia de Honor: Revitalization within the Revolution." *Asian Studies* 4 (1966): 342-52.

"The Soldier Teacher in the Philippines." *Harper's Weekly*, Jan. 18, 1902, 74.

Tompkins, E. Berkeley. "Scylla and Charybdis: The Anti-Imperialist Dilemma in the Election of 1900." *Pacific Historical Review* 36 (1967): 143-61.

———. "The Old Guard: A Study of the Anti-Imperialist Leadership." *Historian* 30 (1968): 366-88.

Ward, John W. "The Use of Native Troops in Our New Possessions." *Journal of the Military Service Institution of the United States* 31 (1902): 793-805.

Welch, Richard E., Jr. "Motives and Policy Objectives of Anti-Imperialists, 1898." *Mid-America* 51 (1969): 119-29.

Wheeler, Joseph. "Tranquilizing the Philippines." *Independent* 52 (1900): 3043-44.

White, Herbert A. "Pacification of Batangas." *International Quarterly* 7 (1903): 431-44.

Whitmarsh, Phelps. "Conditions in Manila." *The Outlook* 63 (1899): 917-23.
Whittaker, William George, "Samuel Gompers, Anti-Imperialist." *Pacific Historical Review* 38 (1969): 429-45.
Wickberg, Edgar. "The Chinese Mestizo in Philippine History." *Journal of Southeast Asian History* 5 (1964): 62-100.
Williams, Henry Porter. "Iowa's First Overseas Expedition." *Annals of Iowa* 32 (1955): 561-75.
Worcester, Dean C. "General Lawton's Work in the Philippines." *McClure's Magazine* 15 (1900): 19-31.

BOOKS

Agoncillo, Teodoro A. *The Revolt of the Masses: The Story of Bonifacio and the Katipunan.* Quezon City, 1956.
Beisner, Robert L. *Twelve Against Empire: The Anti-Imperialists, 1898-1900.* New York, 1968.
Bigelow, John. *The Principles of Strategy.* Rev. ed. Philadelphia, 1894.
Birkhimer, William E. *Military Government and Martial Law.* Washington, 1892.
Brown, Fred R. *History of the Ninth U. S. Infantry, 1799-1909.* Chicago, 1909.
Bumpus, E. C. *In Memoriam: Everett Chauncey Bumpus.* Norwood, Mass., 1902.
Clark, Edward B. *William L. Sibert: The Army Engineer.* Philadelphia, 1930.
Coffman, Edward M. *The Hilt of the Sword: The Career of Peyton C. March.* Madison, 1966.
Cosmas, Graham A. *An Army for Empire: The United States Army in the Spanish American War.* Columbia, Mo., 1971.
Croly, Herbert. *The Promise of American Life.* New York, 1909.
Davis, Allen F. *Spearheads for Reform: The Social Settlements*

and the Progressive Movement, 1890-1914. New York, 1967.

Dictionary of American Biography. 22 vols. New York, 1928-1944.

Dulles, Foster Rhea. *The Imperial Years*. New York, 1956.

Elarth, Harold H. *The Story of the Philippine Constabulary, 1901-1948*. Los Angeles, 1949.

Eyot, Canning. *The Story of the Lopez Family*. Boston, 1904.

Faust, Karl Irving. *Campaigning in the Philippines*. San Francisco, 1899.

Fernandez, Leonardo H. *The Philippine Republic*. New York, 1926.

Foreman, John. *The Philippine Islands*. 2d ed. New York, 1899.

Forbes, William Cameron. *The Philippine Islands*. 2 vols. Boston, 1928.

Gabriel, Ralph Henry. *The Course of American Democratic Thought: An Intellectual History since 1815*. New York, 1940.

Gatewood, Willard B., Jr. *"Smoked Yankees" and the Struggle for Empire: Letters from Negro Soldiers, 1898-1902*. Urbana, 1971.

Goldman, Eric F. *Rendezvous with Destiny*. Rev. ed. New York, 1956.

Gottmann, Jean. "Bugeaud, Galliéni, Lyautey: The Development of French Colonial Warfare." In Edward Mead Earle, ed. *Makers of Modern Strategy: Military Thought from Machiavelli to Hitler*. Princeton, 1941. 234-59.

Grunder, Garel A. and William E. Livezey. *The Philippines and the United States*. Norman, 1951.

Haber, Samuel. *Efficiency and Uplift: Scientific Management in the Progressive Era, 1890-1920*. Chicago, 1964.

Hays, Samuel P. *Conservation and the Gospel of Efficiency: The Progressive Conservation Movement, 1890-1920*. Cambridge, Mass., 1959.

Herman, Frederick J. *The Forty-Second Foot: A History of the 42d Regiment of Infantry, United States Volunteers, Organized for Service in the Philippine Insurrection*. Kansas City, Mo., 1942.

Historical Sketch of the Twentieth United States Infantry. N.p., n.d.

Hofstadter, Richard. *The Age of Reform: From Bryan to F. D. R.* New York, 1955.

Hurley, Vic. *Jungle Patrol.* New York, 1938.

Huntington, Samuel P. *The Soldier and the State.* Cambridge, Mass., 1957.

Janowitz, Morris. *The Professional Soldier.* Glencoe, 1960.

Jansen, Marius B. *The Japanese and Sun Yat-sen.* Cambridge, Mass., 1954.

Jessup, Philip C. *Elihu Root.* 2 vols. New York, 1938.

LeRoy, James A. *The Americans in the Philippines.* 2 vols. Boston, 1914.

——. *Philippine Life in Town and Country.* New York, 1905.

Lockmiller, David A. *Enoch H. Crowder: Soldier, Lawyer, and Statesman.* Columbia, 1955.

McAlexander, Ulysses G. *History of the 13th Regiment United States Infantry.* N.p., 1905.

McDevitt, V. Edmund. *The First California's Chaplain.* Fresno, Calif., 1956.

Majul, Cesar Adib. *Apolinario Mabini, Revolutionary.* Manila, 1964.

Markey, Joseph I. *From Iowa to the Philippines: A History of Company M. Fifty-First Iowa Infantry Volunteers.* Red Oak, Iowa, 1900.

May, Ernest R. *Imperial Democracy: The Emergence of America as a Great Power.* New York, 1961.

Millett, Allan Reed. *The Politics of Intervention: The Military Occupation of Cuba, 1906-1909.* Columbus, 1968.

Morgan, H. Wayne. *William McKinley and His America.* Syracuse, 1963.

Mowry, George E. *The Era of Theodore Roosevelt and the Birth of Modern America, 1900-1912.* New York, 1958.

Noyes, Theodore W. *Oriental America and Its Problems.* Washington, 1903.

Oregon, State of. *The Official Records of the Oregon Volunteers in the Spanish War and Philippine Insurrection.* 2d ed. Salem, 1903.

Pratt, Julius W. *Expansionists of 1898*. Baltimore, 1936.

Pratt, Richard Henry. *Battlefield and Classroom: Four Decades with the American Indian, 1867-1904*. New Haven, 1964.

Quirk, Robert E. *An Affair of Honor: Woodrow Wilson and the Occupation of Vera Cruz*. Lexington, 1962.

Salamanca, Bonifacio. *The Filipino Reaction to American Rule, 1901-1913*. N.p., 1968.

Sastrón, Manuel. *La insurrección en Filipinas y guerra hispano-americana en el archipiélago*. Madrid, 1901.

Schott, Joseph L. *The Ordeal of Samar*. Indianapolis, 1964.

Sefton, James E. *The United States Army and Reconstruction, 1865-1877*. Baton Rouge, 1967.

Sexton, William Thaddeus. *Soldiers in the Sun*. Harrisburg, 1939.

Spear, Percival, ed. *The Oxford History of India*. 3d ed. Oxford, 1964.

Thomas, David Yancey. *A History of Military Government in Newly Acquired Territory of the United States*. New York, 1904.

Tompkins, E. Berkeley. *Anti-Imperialism in the United States: The Great Debate, 1890-1920*. Philadelphia, 1970.

Weigley, Russell F. *Towards an American Army: Military Thought from Washington to Marshall*. New York, 1962.

Wickberg, Edgar. *The Chinese in Philippine Life, 1850-1898*. New Haven, 1965.

Wiebe, Robert H. *The Search for Order, 1877-1920*. New York, 1967.

Worcester, Dean C. *The Philippines, Past and Present*. 2 vols. New York, 1914.

UNPUBLISHED MANUSCRIPTS, THESES, AND DISSERTATIONS

Brown, Richard C. "Social Attitudes of American Generals, 1898-1940." Ph.D. dissertation, University of Wisconsin, 1951.

Coats, George Yarrington. "The Philippine Constabulary: 1901-1917." Ph.D. dissertation, The Ohio State University, 1968.

Cruz, Romeo V. "Filipino Collaboration with the Americans, 1899-1902." M.A. thesis, University of the Philippines, 1956.

Humber, Robert C. "Military Government in the Philippines." MS study, U.S. Army War College, Washington, D.C., 1943.

Lynn, Harry Richmond. "The Genesis of America's Philippine Policy." Ph.D. dissertation, University of Kentucky, 1936.

Minger, Ralph Eldin. "William Howard Taft: The Development of His Conceptions of American Foreign Policy, 1900-1908." Ph.D. dissertation, University of Southern California, 1958.

Swendiman, Dorothy Della. "The Development of Education in the Philippine Islands since 1898." M.A. thesis, Duke University, 1942.

Tan, Samuel K. "Sulu under American Military Rule, 1899-1913." M.A. thesis, University of the Philippines, 1966.

Index

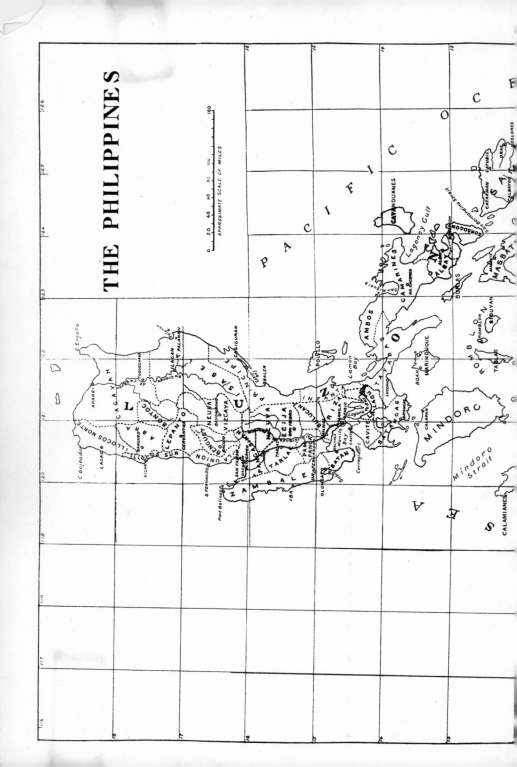

THE PHILIPPINES

APPROXIMATE SCALE OF MILES

0   20   40   60   80   100   160